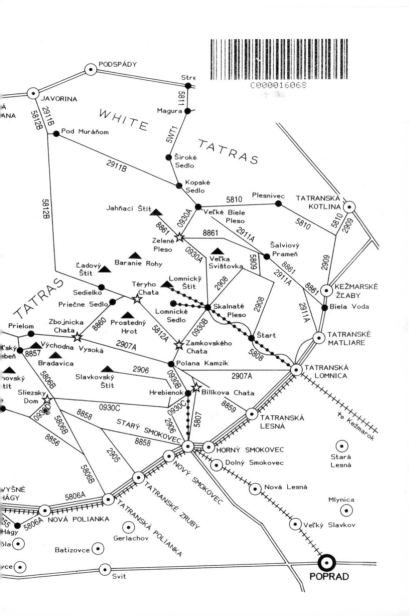

WALKING IN THE HIGH TATRAS
(SLOVAKIA & POLAND)

Sunbathing by one of the Five Spiš Tarns

WALKING IN THE HIGH TATRAS
(SLOVAKIA & POLAND)

Including the
Western Tatras in Poland and the White
Tatras in Slovakia

by
Colin Saunders & Renáta Nárožná

CICERONE PRESS
MILNTHORPE, CUMBRIA

© Colin Saunders and Renáta Nárožná 1994
ISBN 1 85284 150 8
A catalogue record for this book is available from the British Library.

ACKNOWLEDGEMENTS

With special thanks to Janusz Arnold, one of the leading mountain guides in Zakopane, for his invaluable help with and advice on the section on the Polish Tatras.

Thanks also to Ian Mitchell, Peter Šperka, Michal Labus, Julian Tippett; members of the Anglian Fell and Rock Club and the Vanguards Rambling Club; and the staff of T-Ski Travel Agency in Starý Smokovec, Trip Travel in Zakopane, and Waymark Holidays in England, all of whom have provided help and encouragement.

The authors are indebted to the following publications for corroboration of certain facts and figures:

Vysoké Tatry Turistický Sprievodca, by Július Andráši, published by Šport Slovenské Telovýchovné Vydavatelstvo, Bratislava.

Tatry Polskie, by Józef Nyka, published by Sport i Turystyka, Warsaw.

Everyman's Guide to the High Tatras 1992/93 (Limba Publishing House).

Maps are drawn by Barry Saunders.

All photographs are by the author, except where indicated.

Advice to Readers

Readers are advised that whilst every effort is taken by the author to ensure the accuracy of this guidebook, changes can occur which may affect the contents. It is advisable to check locally on transport, accommodation, shops etc but even rights-of-way can be altered and, more especially overseas, paths can be eradicated by landslip, forest fires or changes of ownership.

The publisher would welcome notes of any such changes

Front Cover: On Giewont

CONTENTS

PREFACE

In August 1988 I had the very good fortune to be sent, all expenses paid, by my then employers, a tour operator specialising in walking holidays, to undertake a feasibility study into the High Tatras as a new centre. I was most impressed, not only by the beauty of the area but by the enthusiasm of the local people for their mountains, none more so than that of my guide, Renáta Nárožná. She was then working for the Czechoslovak state travel agency, without whose say-so no progress could be made - at that time.

Two years later I read somewhere that there was no English language guide to the High Tatras, and suggested to Renáta that we give it a try. By this time both of us had set up our own businesses, and we believed that, with me doing the writing and her providing the local knowledge, we had a reasonable chance of producing the goods.

This book is the result. Much has happened since Renáta and I first met. The "velvet revolution" of 1989, which overthrew the communist regime, was followed by the "velvet divorce" of 1993, which saw Czechoslovakia split into its two constituent parts. Now the Tatras find themselves shared by the Republics of Poland and Slovakia.

Equally profound changes were taking place simultaneously in Poland, and Cicerone Press felt that it would make good sense to include the Polish part of the Tatras in the same book. We were fortunate to enlist the help of a Polish mountain guide, Janusz Arnold, whose extensive knowledge of the walking north of the border has proved invaluable.

Since my first visit in 1988, I have visited the Tatras four times, exploring new territory on each occasion. Even so, I still have much ground to cover: this gives you an idea of the scope for walkers in this comparatively small area. Renáta, Janusz and I hope that you will be encouraged by this book to visit the Tatras, that it will provide a great deal of help in finding your way around, and play some part in the enjoyment of your stay.

Recent history has shown how quickly the political situation can change, especially in the former "iron curtain" countries, to an extent that would have been inconceivable only a few years ago. When I first visited what was then Czechoslovakia, a visa was necessary and it took 90 minutes to pass through three separate passport and visa checks at Prague Airport. These days visas are no longer necessary for most English-speaking visitors to the Czech Republic, Slovakia or Poland, and border formalities are quick. One hopes that the political situation will continue settled, allowing tourism to flourish in the beautiful Tatras.

If you find any inconsistencies or changes, please write to Colin Saunders via the publisher, then the information can be updated in future editions. We will in any case welcome your comments.

A typical rustic signpost in the Slovak Tatras (see page 44)

An Introduction to the Tatras

Approaching from the plain of the Poprad river in Slovakia, the sight of the craggy peaks of the High Tatras mountains is unforgettable, beautiful and dramatic. Soaring abruptly skywards, they are like a phalanx of gigantic sentries barring the way to and from the north. With a dusting of snow and a swirl of mist, they assume the ghostly appearance of a phantom army.

On the Polish side, your first sight of the High Tatras comes, if approaching from Kraków, as you pass the town of Nowy Targ. Here they are preceded by several hill ranges, so the impact is not quite so impressive as in Slovakia, yet even here these awesome mountains stamp their authority as a force to be reckoned with.

From either side, the mountain faces are forbidding and steep; the ridges are narrow and turreted. Yet as you close in, reaching small towns and villages that line the slopes at around 1,000 metres above sea level, you discern the valleys that separate the peaks, and realise that there are ways of overcoming and surmounting these resolute watchmen.

This is easier than may at first seem possible, because a network of well engineered, waymarked paths links the resorts with peaks, lakes and mountain chalets. On some paths a good head for heights is needed, as there is scrambling, exposure and the use of fixed wires - if these terms are strange to you, all will be revealed in the chapter on Paths and Waymarking. Other routes lead gently through meadows and forests, yet still within sight of the fearsome summits above.

To find the High Tatras on a physical map of Europe, first imagine the Alps in the form of an antique pistol. Its butt lies near the Mediterranean Sea; the handle curves through France into Switzerland; and the barrel stretches on into Austria. The pistol is fired at Vienna, point blank; the bullet leaves the gun and passes over the city and across the Danube, but after travelling just half the barrel's length, it strikes a range of mountains beyond. They are the High Tatras, straddling the border between Slovakia and Poland.

These mountains are very well known to Central and Eastern Europeans. Until the early twentieth century they were much visited by royalty and nobility from Austria-Hungary and other nearby states. During the communist era, this was the most accessible region of alpine mountains for those who lived "behind the iron curtain". Then in 1991 Count Otto von Hapsburg, the senior surviving member of the famous Austro-Hungarian ruling dynasty, and his family revived the earlier tradition with a visit to the Tatras, as recorded in the visitor's book at the National Park Museum in Tatranská Lomnica.

People in the "western world" have only recently been introduced to this mountain delicacy. Now that they can visit the countries of the Tatras with a minimum of fuss, we hope that this book will encourage them to acquire the taste fully. To visit either Poland or Slovakia, most English-speaking visitors no longer require a visa - though at the time of writing those from Australia, New Zealand and South Africa still do.

A word of warning though. You need to be of a fairly gregarious disposition to enjoy the walking covered by this book. Though there are some quiet and little visited areas, you are likely to find a jolly crowd of people at most of the summits when you arrive. This is not an area for those who like to be on their own at the top.

The High Tatras are the highest and most northerly part of the Carpathian Mountains, a sickle-shaped range, 1,200 kilometres long, which starts near Vienna, then passes through the Czech Republic, Slovakia, Poland, Hungary, Ukraine and on into Romania, to finish at the Kazan gorge on the Danube. In general, the Carpathians are not very high as mountains go - over half the peaks fail to reach 1,000 metres. But the High Tatras are a notable exception: nearly 100 of its more than 500 rocky summits surpass 2,000 metres; ten come very close to or exceed 2,500 metres; and the highest reaches 2,655 metres. With so many walking routes surrounding the summits, you can view most of them from many different angles - even set yourself "name that peak" competitions.

A miscellany of delights is provided by this compact microcosm of alpine scenery, now a World Heritage Region. The High Tatras was one of the few parts of the Carpathians to be glaciated during the last Ice Age, and in an area just 27 by 10 kilometres, you can find much evidence of this. Small glaciers formed dozens of valleys containing more than a hundred lakes and tarns; they left moraines, and moulded corries, ravines and basins.

The erosion of many different types of rock - granite, gneiss, sandstone, limestone and schists - has resulted in a wide variety of beautiful scenery; it recalls, in such a small area, that of many parts of the Alps. In just one day you may see needlepoint summits, toothy ridges, steep walls, deep valleys with lakes, tinkling streams and splashing waterfalls. Other areas recall English landscapes on a grand scale: graceful, grey, rounded domes with grass-covered shoulders, shallow valleys and dry stream beds.

An immense diversity of wildlife is protected by the existence of neighbouring national parks in Slovakia and Poland, that together cover all of the High Tatras, as well as the adjoining White Tatras and most of the Western Tatras.

Though most of the villages are purpose-built mountain resorts, some date from the late eighteenth century and many of the alpine-style buildings are full of character, with much use of wood. Blending well with the surrounding pine trees, the colours chosen to decorate walls, beams, balconies and window-frames offer a soothing mixture of mustard, custard, chocolate and cream, while rust-red dominates the roofs.

Every upside must have its downside though, and to appreciate the picturesque you will sometimes have to tolerate the grotesque - the architecture of recent decades has done no favours for the Tatras. Now, because of the fragile ecology, and in realisation of the mistakes of the past, there is a ban on major new developments in the national park areas.

For the urban-dwelling visitor, the air of the High Tatras seems incredibly pure, enhanced by the altitude, the scent of the surrounding pine forests, and the low level of traffic, which is banned from the mountain valleys, even where there are roads. This is an ideal location for a mountain holiday, and especially for the adventurous walker. It is an area that offers enough variety to fill a fortnight, yet small enough to provide the satisfaction of being able to explore it reasonably thoroughly in the same period.

At one time it was possible to cross the mountain border between Slovakia and Poland with little if any formality. But the rise of Poland's Solidarity movement in the early 1980s scared the then Czechoslovak authorities, and they clamped down on free transit in the mountains. At the time of writing it has still not been restored, though you can cross at Lysá Poľana, the one and only official border post in the Tatras.

Actually, the walking in the area covered by this book falls fairly distinctly into the Slovak and Polish sectors, so it is convenient to place the route descriptions in a separate section for each country. In Slovakia, since the Slovak Western Tatras is quite difficult to reach from the main resort, nearly all the walking covered by this book is in the High Tatras, plus a small amount in the White Tatras. In Poland, much of the Western Tatras is easily accessible from the main resort of Zakopane, so these as well as the Polish High Tatras are included. We start, though, with an inspection of general topics common to both countries.

A GENERAL DESCRIPTION

The name "Tatra" and its variants ("Tatry" is the plural form) applies to several mountain ranges, in total 78 kilometres long and on average 10 kilometres wide, that lie on the border between Slovakia and Poland. There is also the completely separate Low Tatras range to the south, wholly within Slovakia. To sort out the various parts of these ranges, it will help if you can refer to one of the walking maps of the area at 1:50,000 scale (see below).

Written across and around the mountainous areas are a number of titles of large and medium size, both with and without the word "Tatry". One of the two largest is simply "POLSKO" (Poland). The other is "TATRY" (Tatras), which applies to the whole region, both in Slovakia and Poland. It stretches from the town of Zuberec in the west to the valley of the Biela river in the east, and between the line of valleys to the north (in one of which lies the Polish town of

Zakopane) and the Sub-Tatras Basin (the broad valleys of the rivers Poprad and Vah) to the south.

Next in size come two or three titles (depending on which map you have): "ZÁPADNÉ TATRY" (Western Tatras), "VÝCHODNÉ TATRY" (Eastern Tatras), and "PODTATRANSKÁ KOTLINA" (Sub-Tatras Basin). The latter does not concern us much, except that you will frequently be overlooking it from the mountains. Western and Eastern Tatras are self-explanatory. "Eastern Tatras" is a term which you may hear in Poland, but hardly ever in Slovakia, since most people use the names by which its two constituent areas - High and White - are known.

In a slightly smaller typesize comes "VYSOKÉ TATRY" (High Tatras). It extends for 27 kilometres in the form of a shallow, upside-down arch from Ľaliové Sedlo eastwards to another saddle, Kopské Sedlo (due north of Starý Smokovec). With six peaks exceeding 2,600 metres (culminating in Gerlachovský Štít at 2,655 metres), this range lays claim to several "highest" titles: in the Tatras, in Slovakia and in the whole Carpathian chain.

The **High Tatras** consist mostly of granite and gneiss rock. There are many short lateral spurs, most of which descend northward into Poland. A much longer spur extends south-westward for 7 kilometres from near the bottom of the huge crook in the border with Poland to the valley of Kôprová Dolina; another of 9 kilometres reaches north to Lysá Poľana, the only border crossing between Slovakia and Poland in this area.

Becoming progressively smaller, the names in block capitals now refer to sectors or outliers of the main ranges named above. Liptovské Tatry refers to the highest part of the Western Tatras (Liptov being the lowland region that lies to the south), while Osobitá, Roh**áč**e, Sivý Vrch (Grey Hill), Červené Vrchy (Red Hills) and Liptovské Kopy are groups of minor peaks in the same range.

The official dividing point between the High and Western Tatras is one of the two neighbouring saddles on the Slovak-Polish border to the north-west of Štrbské Pleso, depending on which authority you follow. For Slovakia, it is Ľaliové Sedlo (Liliowe in Polish); for Poland, Sucha Przełęcz (Suché Sedlo in Slovak). This dichotomy results in the intervening summit, Beskid or Beskyd, not knowing whether it belongs to the High or Western Tatras. (Note: the valley called Tichá Dolina, which runs south-westwards from Ľaliové Sedlo, is generally considered to be in the High Tatras, though on the maps it appears to lie in the Western Tatras.)

The **Western Tatras** form the second highest mountain range in Slovakia and the Carpathians, with some twenty summits above 2,000 metres; the highest is Bystrá (2,248 metres). Actually the Western Tatras stretch for a little further westwards than the limit of the most extensive map used for walking, and outside the National Park boundary.

Whilst the slate peaks of the Western Tatras are generally lower and less spectacular than those of the High Tatras, its ridge walks are longer, more

The White Tatras from Lomnický Štít. (photo Jeston Price)
(The saddle near the left edge of the picture is Široke Sedlo, with Ždiarska Vidla to the left and Hlúpy to the right.)

numerous and more accessible to walkers without a guide.

Two particularly worthwhile waymarked ridge walks follow separate sections of the border between Slovakia and Poland - the westernmost is accessible from Slovakia only, the easternmost from Poland only. With a guide (see below), the whole length of the main ridge can be walked, though it requires at least two days. There is not enough space in this book to describe the Western Tatras in Slovakia, which in any case are not easy to reach from the High Tatras resorts, though you may see them from some vantage points. From Zakopane in Poland, however, some fine routes in the Western Tatras are easily accessible, and so are included in this book.

Belianske Tatry **(White Tatras)** is a distinctive, 13-kilometre long range of pale grey, limestone peaks rising from grassy slopes. They adjoin the High Tatras transversely, like a hammerhead, at Kopské Sedlo. The highest summit is Havran (The Raven, 2,152 metres).

In 1978, the whole of the White Tatras, then part of the Tatras National Park, was closed to tourists, apart from two short low-level walking routes. This was because the routes to the summits and along the ridge had become badly eroded, and the delicate ecology was under threat. In 1993, the whole range was handed over to the Urbariat (Association of Historical Landowners) of the village of Ždiar. At the time this book was being written, they had decided to reopen one route across the range to link up with the High Tatras network (this is described at the end of the section on green routes in the Slovak Path Descriptions chapter), and planned to reopen some of the paths to the summits.

The number of visitors to the White Tatras is still strictly limited, however, and there is an entry fee. If you do not manage to get into the range itself, you can still admire its graceful beauty from several points in the eastern High Tatras, such as Jahňací Štít and Kopské Sedlo, or from the top of the cable-car at Lomnický Štít, or even from the main road at Ždiar to the east.

Adjoining the Tatras and just creeping on to the maps are the lesser ranges of **Skorušinské Vrchy** to the west and **Spišská Magura** to the east. They are not parts of the main Tatras range, so are not covered in this book. Neither is the completely separate Nízke Tatry (**Low Tatras**) range, south of the Sub-Tatras Basin and off our maps; it is nevertheless a very attractive area for walkers. Good walking maps of these three ranges are available.

EARLY HISTORY

"Tatras" is the anglicised version of Tatry, the Slovak name, or Tatrzy (pronounced "tat-zhee"), the Polish - these are the plural versions of Tatra. Though the origin is not certain, it seems likely that the name comes from the Old Slavonic word "trtri", which means high cliffs - and there are certainly plenty of them in these rugged mountains. The first record of the name so far discovered is dated 1086, as "Tritri", in the archives of the archbishopric of Prague. The first instance of the present spelling, Tatry, was used in a handwritten document dated 1255, and in print in 1545.

Much of the rock that forms the Tatras was created 300 million years ago, by sediment deposited in a huge ocean. 100 million years ago, over a period of several thousand years, the immense force of a collision between the once separate tectonic plates that carried what is now Italy and the rest of Eurasia created what is now the Alps and, behind them, the Tatras. So great was this force, that some of the land that lay to the south was pushed up and over what is now the High Tatras, to form the hills now lying on the north side.

During various Ice Ages, the Tatras region was one of the few parts of the Carpathians to be covered by glaciers, and successive glacial periods shaped the peaks, gouged the valleys, and left the moraines that dammed the tarns.

Evidence of Late Stone Age human activities (about 5,000 years ago) has been unearthed at several locations in the Tatras foothills - this includes a cast of the skull of "Ganovce Man", now lying in state in the National Museum in Prague. In the early Bronze Age (about 3,000 years ago), the area to the south was densely settled by Turkic people, engaged mainly in sheep-farming and other agricultural activities, who appear to have been much influenced by the

Mycenean culture of the Eastern Mediterranean. Many of their settlements were sited to afford a view of the High Tatra peaks, and it has been suggested that this may have some connection with the religious customs of the time - or they may have just wanted to enjoy the view!

The land to the north of the Tatras was uninhabited at this time.

Subsequent history is related in the separate sections for Slovakia and Poland.

VEGETATION AND WILDLIFE

Please remember that **picking flowers and taking cuttings is strictly forbidden** in the Tatras National Park areas.

It is unlikely that English-speaking tourists will bring their pets with them to the Tatras, but if you do you should note that **dogs are not allowed in the national park areas**, to protect the environment and wild animals.

It has been established that some 1,300 plant species can be found in the ranges that make up the Western, High and White Tatras, including at every level the most primitive plants - lichens and mosses - clinging to rocks and deadwood.

Those interested in further study of these plants may find useful a small book, on sale in bookshops in the Slovak Tatras, called *Kvety Tatier* (Flowers of the Tatras) by R.Šoltés, A.Šoltésová and I.Mihál. It is nearly all in Slovak, unfortunately, but contains excellent colour photographs of 244 Tatras species, together with their Latin names. A similar book in Polish, called *Kwiaty Tatr*, is available in Zakopane.

In autumn, frost burns the leaves of many of the shrubs and trees to a whole variety of rich hues from orange and gold to purple and dark brown, enhanced by early morning frost and perhaps a dusting of snow.

There is animal life in abundance in the Tatras, but most species are extremely shy and keep well away from the waymarked walking routes. If you wish to see the more unusual varieties, the best time is early in the morning, when the nocturnal ones are returning to their homes, and before most walkers have arrived. Keep very quiet, and wear dark clothes. Take binoculars if you have them. They will help to identify the many species of birds, as well as animals on distant rocks.

Vegetation and wildlife in mountainous regions are strongly affected by the altitude and prevailing weather. The mountains can be divided into a number of biological zones, described below. The altitudes are given as a general guide, but there will be many variations in particular areas, influenced by prevailing weather and rock type.

Sub-Tatras Basins (below 700 metres)

Approaching the High Tatras from the Podtatranská Kotlina (Sub-Tatras Basin) in Slovakia, or the Podhale (Below the Mountain Meadows) valley in Poland, you are surrounded by rather poor quality agricultural land which mainly produces such crops as potatoes and oats, and to a lesser extent rye and millet. Farming communities at altitudes of between 700 and 900 metres mark the edge of the agricultural plains. In Slovakia, these include Tatranská Štrba, Mengušovce, Batizovce, Gerlachov, Nová Lesná, Stará Lesná and Stráne pod Tatrami. In Poland, the town of Zakopane, now a major tourist resort, dominates the Podhale, but the surrounding villages are still mainly farming communities.

In and around these villages, as well as the common birds seen in most parts of Europe, and of course cattle and sheep, you may see white storks nesting in the spring, and perhaps some black grouse. In Zakopane, sheep roam free in the unfenced town parks, and if you are driving you should watch out for them on nearby streets!

Forest Zone (700 to 1,600 metres)

From the northern edge of Slovakia's Sub-Tatras Basin, at just below 1,000 metres, and from the southern fringes of Zakopane and nearby villages, coniferous forest, predominantly spruce, rises steadily. In Slovakia it hides another string of villages that line the southern slopes of the Tatras giants. These villages take advantage of the clean air and shelter provided by the trees to pronounce themselves mountain resorts or spas: Štrbské Pleso, Vyšné Hágy, Nová Polianka, Tatranská Polianka, Smokovce (the Smokovec villages), Tatranská Lesná, Tatranská Lomnica and Tatranské Matliare. Occasionally, among the spruce, you will find a specimen or clump of interlopers such as larch, pine, birch, mountain ash and willow. In Poland there is no equivalent line of villages in the forest, just the tourist station of Kuźnice and some collections of shepherd huts.

A few shrubs can be found in the undergrowth of the spruce forest: bilberry, cranberry, mountain strawberries and raspberries, the poisonous daphne and the alpine clematis. But the best floral displays occur in the spring and summer, taking over the clearings and meadows in the forest. At various times, crocus, cowslip, daisies, buttercups, foxglove and golden lily are in abundance, while in certain areas rarer species such as orchids (including lady's slipper) may be spotted. A wide variety of fungi can be seen.

During the daytime, roe-deer, red deer and foxes may run across the meadows, or browse among the trees within sight of the paths. Early risers may see a badger, otter, weasel or stoat. On autumn evenings, the baying and bellowing of the deer can be heard for miles. In the parks and woods of the mountain resorts, brown squirrels run riot, and on the Slovak side red ones may also be spotted in more remote areas.

Less likely to be seen, in areas rarely visited by (and in some cases barred to) walkers are wildcats, martens, lynxes, wolves, wild boar and even bears. These are mostly on the eastern, western and northern fringes of the High Tatras. Bears tend to hibernate in Poland, since the snow lies longer there. Remember that these potentially dangerous animals are very rarely seen by tourists, and are even more unlikely to attack unless provoked. If you are nervous about meeting such creatures, and if you visit the less crowded areas, do not go alone but with a number of companions.

Something that may surprise you, if you have visited other mountainous parts of Europe such as the Alps or Pyrenees, is the almost total lack of cattle and sheep on the mountain pastures. They were banned in the 1950s because they were considered to have caused too much soil erosion, and a law was passed forbidding farming in the national parks except in a few places. In the Tatras, at the time of writing, they were only to be seen at a few meadows in Poland, such as Polana Chochołowska and Hala Kalatówki in the Western Tatras; Hala Kopieniec and Rusinowa Polana in the High Tatras; not at all on the Slovak side. However this law may be relaxed in the near future, so the tinkling of cowbells may yet return more generally to the Tatras.

Among the birds, wood-grouse, woodcock and partridge abound, and you may hear the distinctive song of a thrush, or the mocking call of a cuckoo. Fluttering over and around the many turbulent streams, you will surely spot the dipper, or a yellow wagtail. And in the streams themselves swim several varieties of trout.

Sub-Alpine (Dwarf Pine) Zone (1,600 to 1,850 metres)

At around 1,600 metres, the lofty conifers run out of soil deep enough for their sprawling roots. Here, densely huddled for protection against the fierce winter wind and cold, dwarf pines with their shorter roots take over for another 250m or so, before the ground becomes too rocky even for the grip of these tenacious little trees. Here the edelweiss, gentian and other hardy species thrive.

Alpine Zone (1,850 to 2,300 metres)

From 1,850 metres upwards, the surface is predominantly bare rock which seems to have no capacity to harbour life. Yet life can be found in the cracks - usually tufts of grass or a stunted dwarf pine. There are some grassy alpine meadows, too, where flowers will bloom briefly in July and August. At this altitude, only the hardiest plants manage to exist.

You will see an occasional lone giant, or a small clump of them, among the dwarves, and sometimes even higher. Usually they are oval-crowned limba-fir (*sembra*), defiantly thrusting roots through cracks in the rock to find soil. The outermost limbas in a clump will be branchless on their northern sides, where they are battered by the prevailing winter winds - they are called flag-trees. Sometimes a birch, mountain ash or willow may occur in the dwarf-pine belt. The fruit of the limba was once collected by shepherds to provide an aromatic additive to oil used in spa treatments, but this activity is now banned in the national parks.

You should watch out particularly for the black moss that covers some granite boulders high up above the tree-line: it is very slippery when wet, and rough enough to cut your skin.

You are likely to see on distant rocks a single marmot, or a whole family basking in the sun. This large brown rodent is closely related to the squirrel, but in size and shape is comparable to the badger. You will probably hear its gull-like yelp, even if you fail to see one. Also above the tree-line you may see a group of chamois, the symbol of the TANAP national park in Slovakia, and of the mountain guides in Poland, springing nimbly from ledge to precarious ledge. Binoculars would certainly be an advantage at this level.

High above, you may see a rock eagle hovering, then perhaps swooping down on its unsuspecting prey.

Sub-Nival Zone (about 2,300 metres)

The very highest part of the High Tatras is called the sub-nival ("below the snowline") zone: that is, below the level where snow always exists. Of course, in this area, that only occurs close to the highest summits. Even at this altitude, a wide variety of very tough flowering species can be found if you look carefully, such as mosses, lichens and in summer the glacier gentian. Among the fauna, birds of prey are predominant, especially eagles, yet even among the rocks such creatures as ermine, snow-vole and species of mountain mice may be hiding. Some lower areas in the Polish High Tatras, where snow always exists, are in effect "sub-nival" - these include an area to the south of Morskie Oko, the big tarn in the south-east corner.

WEATHER

As in all mountain ranges, one thing you can be sure of in the Tatras is that the weather will be changeable. The High Tatras are even more exposed to climatic changes than most other ranges, because of their comparatively small area and great elevation at the heart of Europe, and the weather in the mountains may be completely different from that in the surrounding plains.

Summer is a short season in the mountains: from the beginning of July to the end of August. The Tatras experience high precipitation, which may fall as snow on higher ground. July and August are generally the warmest months, but as usual in mountains the hotter the weather the greater the likelihood of thunderstorms - the areas in Poland around Morskie Oko (south-east of Zakopane) and Czerwone Wierchy (south-west of Zakopane) are particularly prone to thunderstorms between noon and 2pm.

The average daytime temperature in the mountain resorts in summer is 20-

22 degrees Celsius, but it may be much cooler first thing in the morning and in the late evening. Flowers should be at their best in early July.

It is often the case in summer that there are blue skies in the morning, a gathering of clouds during the late morning and early afternoon, followed by a heavy downpour and perhaps a thunderstorm, then the blue skies return in the evening. The wise walker does not let this weather pattern detract from enjoyment of a day's excursion, but allows for it in the plan. Be ready to set off early on a fine morning, so that you can either be back in the village when the storm breaks, or enjoy an extended lunch in a hospitable chalet.

Autumn is the best season for many walkers: from the end of August to mid October, when it is more settled, warmer than in the spring, the air is clear and brisk, and the walking is delightful - though sometimes restricted by early snow. The average daytime temperature in the resorts is 10-12 degrees Celsius (warmer at the end of August and beginning of September).

Winter walking (November to March) can be invigorating and charming, providing you take wise precautions - see the chapter on winter walking below.

Spring is not a good time for walking in the mountains. In late March and April, there is a high risk of avalanches. In May and June, the lower routes are awash from melting snow, and the higher ones are closed to protect the baby wild animals then being reared.

There are as yet no **weather forecasts** in English by radio or telephone. You should get information about the weather in English from your hotel reception or a travel agency. Mountain rescue stations (see Appendix 6) will have weather forecasts, though the staff may not be able to communicate in English.

Please read the chapter on safety in the mountains regarding the wind chill and altitude factors.

NATIONAL PARKS

The whole of the High and White Tatras ranges, as well as most of the Western Tatras, are included in the Tatranský Národný Park (TANAP) in Slovakia, or the Tatrzański Park Narodowy (TPN) in Poland. Both mean Tatras National Park. Established in 1949 (Slovakia) and 1954 (Poland), the two organisations on either side of the border work closely together to protect the natural environment and provide facilities for rest and enjoyment. Together they cover approximately 730 square kilometres (280 square miles), of which 70% lies in Slovakia, 30% in Poland.

Most facilities you will use while walking in the Tatras are provided by the national park authorities: path building and maintenance, waymarking, nature trails, guides, wardening and mountain rescue.

As in all national parks, there are strict prohibitions to protect the environment. These are really just common sense, and would be followed as a matter of normal practice by all readers of this guide, but for the record you are forbidden to: walk away from the waymarked routes, or take short cuts on bends; pick flowers, mushrooms or fruits of the forest; break off branches; set up tents anywhere except in designated campsites; light fires; swim or use boats anywhere except places specified for these activities; leave litter; damage or remove any notices or waymarks. Failure to observe these very sensible rules may result in a heavy fine.

National park rangers in both Slovakia and Poland wear a green uniform, and a badge which, in Slovakia, bears the words "Strážca Tanapu" (TANAP Ranger), and in Poland an edelweiss emblem. Mountain rescue personnel and guides wear red sweaters - in Poland plus blue-and-white armband; in Slovakia a "Horská Služba" (Mountain Rescue) badge.

The administrative headquarters of the Slovak TANAP is in Tatranská Lomnica (telephone 967951), in a modern building 500 metres east of the railway station. It also contains a research institute and an interesting museum, which displays various aspects of life in the park. A guide leaflet to the museum in English is available at the entrance, and there is an audio-visual display in the morning and afternoon.

There are also TANAP offices in Starý Smokovec (Horská Služba = Mountain Rescue Centre), Podbanské (by the main road junction), in Tatranská Kotlina (near the start of routes 2909/5810), and in Javorina (on the main road by the bus stop); and in summer only at Popradské Pleso and Skalnaté Pleso. Note: these offices are intended to give out information about the national parks only, not general tourist information.

In Poland, the headquarters of the National Park and Mountain Rescue Service is in Ulica Józefa Piłsudskiego in Zakopane (telephone 3444).

LANGUAGES

Since the High Tatras together with its outliers straddles Slovakia and Poland, you will of course encounter the languages of both these nations in the appropriate parts. Both are descended from the Old Slavonic which was almost universally spoken by Slav peoples until the Middle Ages, and there are still many similarities between the two languages. Slovak is also very similar to Czech, but there are some subtle and some substantial differences. Little English is spoken in the High Tatras, except at some higher category hotels, and usually in tourist offices or travel agencies. German is widely understood and spoken in tourist resorts in the Slovak Tatras, but not so much on the Polish side.

The pronunciation of Slav languages can be very difficult for English speakers. Some words appear impossible to pronounce, with far too few vowels, or even none at all, in relation to the number of consonants! Actually,

Skupniów Upłaz, above Zakopane (Poland). It helps if you are gregarious!

in both Slovak and Polish, most letters are pronounced as in English - remember that G is always hard as in "goat". The stress nearly always goes on the first syllable. The differences are described later in this book, in the language chapter for each country, to the best of our ability, though some sounds are almost impossible to explain in writing.

In both Polish and Slovak, there are no articles, definite or indefinite. All nouns have gender, ie. masculine, feminine or neuter, and this together with grammatical cases affects the endings of many words in a way that is far too complicated to describe here - there are literally dozens of different ways of ending each noun or adjective in all the Slav languages!

In this book we use where possible the unaffected versions of all the words for simplicity, but on maps, signposts etc. you may find the endings altered. For example, the word for Tatra can also be seen in Slovak as Tatry, Tatier, Tatram, Tatrach and Tatrami; in Polish as Tatry, Tatr, Tatrami and Tatrach.

We use the Slovak or Polish place names, as appropriate, and translate them where possible, either in the main text or in the gazetteers, to add interest and help with identification. Appendix 1 contains a glossary of words that you are likely to encounter on the Tatras maps, or in the mountains and villages, as well as some useful words or phrases, for example to help you order a drink or a meal.

For further help, you can buy inexpensive pocket dictionaries in bookshops in the Tatras resorts (see the "Shopping and services" chapter for each country).

As you will see on Slovak maps, it is the tradition for names applied to geographical features that the initial letter of the feature itself is usually written in lower case, whether this comes first or second, eg. Skalnaté pleso, Suchy žľab, Lomnický štít, Kopské sedlo, Kôprová dolina, hrebeň Svišťových veží, pleso Nad Skokom. This looks wrong to English speakers, so in this book we have given capital letters to all the words, to make clear that they are all part of the place name. An exception to this rule in Slovak is made when the name is applied to towns or villages, then both words have capital letters, eg. Štrbské Pleso, Kežmarské Zľaby.

On Polish maps, the names of features are written as in English, ie. both words always have capital letters.

Preparing for the Walking

WHEN TO GO

Try to avoid the peak period from mid July to late August if possible. Not only is it then more difficult to find accommodation, but the more popular walking routes can get very crowded.

If you have to go at this time, book your accommodation as far ahead as possible. For your walks, leave as early as possible in the morning - take a packed breakfast and stop to eat it on the way up, or buy breakfast at a mountain hotel, refuge or chalet.

For settled weather and to avoid crowds, the best time to go is the end of August to early October. See also the section on weather.

ACCOMMODATION

As you would expect in a holiday area that has been established for over 200 years, there is plenty of accommodation in the High Tatras. On the Slovak side, there are over 10,000 beds in hotels, pensions etc., making it the most important tourist area in the country.

However, until recently, the choice for visitors from "western" countries was very limited, because until the early 1990s virtually all the accommodation was owned either by government agencies, which limited their opportunities for commercial enterprise, or by trade unions for the exclusive use of their members. Since the 1989 revolution, the situation is slowly changing, with many of the former government-owned hotels sold to private owners (in some cases handed back to their original owners), or trade union holiday centres made available to non-members. Some of the latter are now part hotel, part trade union holiday centre.

Accommodation is available for foreign visitors in hotels, guest houses, trade union holiday centres, mountain chalets, youth hostels, private houses and camp-sites, and is inexpensive by comparison with most other European countries.

During the communist era, it was not possible to book direct with hotels - you had to go through one of the state-owned agencies. Nowadays you are free to book direct, though it can still be more practical to contact one of the travel agencies located in the High Tatras (see Appendix 3), which are better placed to find out which hotels have space available, and are more likely to have

English-speaking staff.

A small number of tour operators (some are listed in Appendix 3) specialise in package holidays to Central and Eastern Europe, including the High Tatras - for details consult your local travel agents.

Hotel accommodation is graded by a star system - most come in the two-star (tourist class) or three-star (first class) categories. Appendix 2 shows the establishments available to tourists as at Summer 1993.

Inexpensive **private house** accommodation is available in most resorts, though usually breakfast and other meals are not provided - you have to eat at nearby hotels or restaurants. If you wish to book these in advance, you have to go through the local agencies.

There is just one **youth hostel** in the High Tatras: at Horny Smokovec in Slovakia (Juniorhotel).

It is well worth considering spending several nights at a **mountain hotel, refuge or chalet,** or touring from one to another. Apart from saving the effort of ascending several hundred metres each day, there is a special atmosphere and camaraderie among the guests that cannot be experienced at the resort hotels. Chalet accommodation is very inexpensive, but is in great demand during the summer months and you should book ahead if possible. For further information about these places see the chapter on refreshments.

It is always advisable to book accommodation in advance if possible, but some local agencies will do their best to find accommodation for tourists who arrive without a booking (see Useful Addresses in Appendix 3).

Camping within the National Park areas is only permitted at the sites shown in Appendix 2. Some in Slovakia are permanent car-camping sites, where tents are provided, as well as facilities such as kitchens, catering, showers and entertainment.

You may not under any circumstances camp outside these sites within the national park areas, unless by advance agreement in writing with the park authorities (see above); if you do and are caught, you will be heavily fined. You must also observe the following rules: register with the camp-warden, pay the appropriate fee, pitch your tent only at an allocated space, light fires only at the permitted places, do not break branches off trees for firewood.

Camp cooking may prove difficult. You cannot take fuel on an aircraft, and gas canisters are difficult to buy in the Tatras. Meths and petrol can be bought in shops or garages. Most camp-sites have restaurant facilities.

FITNESS

To get the most from any walking holiday, the fitter you are when you start, the better. Prepare yourself by doing some hard walking at home, preferably in mountain or hill country. At the very least, tone up your muscles and flex your joints with stretching exercises. Remember, too, that you will probably be spending all or most of your time at a higher altitude than you are used to, and it may take a few days to adjust to this. There is less oxygen at high altitudes, and you may find yourself getting out of breath more quickly than you expected.

Plan your first few walks along the easier routes, leaving the tougher ones till later. Since the latter are usually scenically more spectacular, this should also provide the added benefit of building up to a climax. If you should find that you are having difficulty on the easier routes, you would be well advised not to tackle the harder ones.

If there are children in your party, unless they have walked in high mountains before, you should plan to keep to the easier routes, to see how they adapt, before you consider tackling any harder ones.

CLOTHING AND EQUIPMENT

What you wear in the evening is best left to your own judgement, though formal clothes are rarely seen in the High Tatras. Some guidance on your walking apparel may be helpful, however. To enjoy your holiday to the full, it is wise to take clothing that is both hard-wearing and comfortable.

Modern clothing specially designed for outdoor activities can provide considerable advantages. For example, "breathable" materials allow perspiration to escape while keeping rain out, though garments made from them can be expensive. Cheaper alternatives may suffice if you are lucky with the weather, but you must decide whether it is worth spending the extra money for added protection. Study advertisements and articles in one of the walkers' magazines that are readily available in most newsagents, and ask for advice at outdoor equipment shops.

Since your feet, naturally, are going to be the most important parts of your body on this holiday, let us start with **footwear** and work up. The section on mountain safety lays out the reasons for taking walking boots, rather than trainers or walking shoes, though on some low level walks the latter may be adequate. Modern lightweight walking boots may be suitable for most walking in the Tatras, but you should seek advice at an equipment shop. Whichever kind of footwear you have, make sure that it fits well and is well worn in, because nothing is more certain to spoil your holiday than new boots that have raised blisters by the end of the first day.

The composition of your **socks** will be a matter of trial and error. Some walkers manage with one thick pair in boots; others find two pairs (a thick pair on top of a thin one) necessary for comfort. Wool is generally most suitable for a thick pair, though thin cotton or silk ones underneath are often worn.

Whether you should cover your **legs** (with trousers or breeches) or bare them (with shorts or skirt) is again up to your own inclination, but if you opt for the latter, be prepared to don waterproof trousers, or change into breeches, if it turns cold or windy, especially when stopping for an extended open-air break.

For your **upper half**, if possible wear something underneath your shirt that will "wick" (carry away) the perspiration from your body, helping to keep your back dry under a rucksack. Whatever the weather down in the valley, always carry at least one warm pullover, and/or a fleece-lined jacket. When you stop, perspiring, for lunch on a high mountain pass, wind whistling across your shoulders, you will need the extra layer. For the same reason, **hat and gloves** will be appreciated. When you are wet (from rain or perspiration), a spare tee-shirt or shirt will be welcome when you stop for lunch. A sweatband for your head or wrist may be useful.

Never tackle a mountain without **waterproof clothing,** carried in your rucksack. There is often some reluctance to don waterproofs, as condensation can make you as wet or wetter than rain. However, as many modern waterproofs are breathable, this should not be a problem. In the mountains you should carry a full set of waterproofs, that is, trousers and a jacket with hood, or a hat. You may also find **gaiters** invaluable as they help to keep water and snow out of your boots.

The most efficient way of carrying all your spare items is in a **rucksack**, since it leaves both hands free in situations when you need to hold on to something. A small "day sack" will be adequate for most excursions into the mountains. The capacity of rucksacks is usually measured in litres - that is, the amount of water that can be poured inside - and those suitable for day trips are in the 20 to 35 litre range, with smaller ones available for children. Always put both straps over your shoulders - you never know when you may need the full support of both hands and arms in an emergency.

Your choice of rucksack will depend on what you intend to put in it. The very least would include the items mentioned in the section on Mountain Safety and Equipment, ie. spare clothing, waterproofs, water bottle, first aid kit, map, compass, whistle and emergency food. Unless you are sure of eating at a mountain chalet, you may also carry your lunch food, and perhaps a camera.

If you are planning to stay overnight in a mountain chalet, a larger rucksack may be needed, since you need toilet accessories and a sheet sleeping bag, and possibly more spare clothing.

On the waymarked routes, no special **climbing gear** is needed. However, if you go off these routes with a mountain guide, you may need some form of harness, to be clipped on to some of the ironware encountered. This can be hired locally if necessary - your guide will advise. An **ice-axe** may be useful if you are visiting the Tatras in September or October, since early snow may then be encountered, especially at the high saddles.

A **torch** will be needed for a couple of the waymarked routes in Poland, which descend into or through caves. In any case, it is a good idea to carry a small torch (with spare battery and bulb) in case you get benighted on tricky mountain paths - this is more likely in the late season (September/October) or in winter.

MAPS

No walker should venture into the mountains without a good walking map of the area. Even though "tourist routes" in the Tatras are usually very well waymarked, it is possible to get lost or disorientated, and a map is essential. Always keep in contact with your map - in other words, whenever you reach a path junction, a chalet or other identifiable feature, identify your location on the map. Then if you do get lost you should have some idea of where you are.

There are some excellent walking maps covering the High Tatras in Slovakia and Poland at a scale of 1:50,000 (2 centimetres = 1 kilometre, or approximately 1.25 inches = 1 mile), and one showing the Polish Tatras only at 1:30,000 (3.3 centimetres = 1 kilometre, or approximately 2.1 inches = 1 mile). These maps are described in more detail below. There are no maps of the Tatras available to the public at the 1:25,000 scale.

Try to buy your maps before you go if possible, as planning your excursions in advance, in conjunction with this book, should bring much enjoyment! Most of the following can be bought at specialist map shops in other countries, otherwise there are many places in the Tatras where you can buy them, including bookshops in Horný Smokovec, Tatranská Lomnica and Zakopane, as well as some hotels and travel agencies.

Some of these maps have information on the reverse that would be useful, were it not all in Polish, Slovak or German! However all the maps have a key to symbols which includes an English translation.

Some of the map text is tiny - you may find a magnifying glass helpful (some compasses include one).

Sheet 21 Vysoke Tatry (High Tatras, scale 1:50,000, published by Slovenská Kartografia of Bratislava). Covers all of the High Tatras, including the Polish part (but with names in Slovak), and a small part of the Western Tatras, as well as the contours of the mountains, the lakes, streams and forested areas, it shows waymarked routes in their respective colours, and mountain chalets. The reverse has information in Slovak about villages, chalets and peaks. The official Slovak national park path numbers are shown, so this map goes well with this book.

A Polish version of the same map, called *Tatry Polskie i Słowackie*, is available in Zakopane, and published jointly by Slovenská Kartografia of Bratislava and Wydawnictwo Karpaty of Kraków.

Sheet WK CS 1 Hohe Tatras und Westliche Tatra (High and Western Tatras, scale 1:50,000, published by Freytag & Berndt of Vienna). Covers the whole of the Tatras National Park areas, ie. the High Tatras, White Tatras and most of the Western Tatras in both Slovakia and Poland. It is based on the Slovenska Kartografia map (Sheet 21 above), and therefore the names on the Polish side are the Slovak equivalents, but the mountain chalets stand out more clearly. The reverse contains much useful information in German. The official Slovak national park path numbers are not shown on this map.

Tatrański Park Narodowy (Polish Tatras National Park, scale 1:30,000, published by Polskie Przedsiębiorstwo Wydawnictw Kartograficznych of Warsaw). Includes all of the Polish Tatras National Park area, including parts of the High and Western Tatras. Waymarked routes, mountain chalets, forested areas and lakes are clearly shown. The reverse shows useful information about the area in Polish.

Tatry i Podhale (Tatras and Podhale valley, scale 1:75,000, published by Polskie Przedsiębiorstwo Wydawnictw Kartograficznych of Warsaw). Includes all of the High and White Tatras and most of the Western Tatras. Not much use for walking, but gives a good overall picture of the area from Nowy Targ in the north to Štrbské Pleso in the south.

Euromap sheet 11290 - Czechoslovakia East (scale 1:300,000, published by GeoCenter International). Covers the whole of what is now Slovakia (the next edition may have a more up-to-date title) and part of southern Poland. Useful for an overview, and has street plans of Bratislava and other Slovakian cities.

The following are very useful, but probably obtainable only at outlets in the Tatras:

Tatry Polskie i Słowackie - Mapa Grzbietowa (Polish & Slovak Tatras - ridge map, published by Wydawnictwo Schola-Tur of Gliwice, obtainable in Zakopane bookshops). A diagrammatic map showing the ridge-lines of the whole of the Western, High and White Tatras. Also clearly shows the waymarked walking routes in their respective colours. The reverse shows walking times and other information in Polish.

Tatranské Strediská (Tatras Resorts, varying scales at around 1:7,500 to 1:10,000, published by Slovenská Kartografia, obtainable in Slovak bookshops). Street plans for most of the villages in the Slovak part of the High Tatras, showing hotels, shops, post offices, bookshops, bus-stops, railway stations and other facilities clearly marked.

Zakopane (scale 1:15,000, published by Polskie Przedsiębiorstwo Wydawnictw Kartograficznych of Warsaw). Street map of Zakopane and outlying areas, including Kuźnice. Shows walking routes within that area - note that routes coloured yellow on the Tatransky Park Narodowy map are shown in brown on this map. The reverse gives details of tourist services in Polish.

Poprad. A street map can be obtained at the tourist information centre.

Negotiating a fixed chain (Giewont, Poland)

The view north from Lomnický Štít (Photo: Jeston Price)
Lto R the neighbouring peaks are: Pyšny Štít, Čierny Štít, Kolovy Štít, Zmrzlá Veža
and Jahňací Štít. The western peaks of the High Tatra are in the background.)

Ascending Slavkovsky Stít (Photo: Ian Mitchell)

PATHS AND WAYMARKING

The Tatras National Park areas in both Slovakia and Poland are blessed with a dense network of well maintained and waymarked walking routes - some 600 kilometres (375 miles) altogether. This is more than may appear likely from a glance at the map, but you should remember that, in the mountains, paths twist and turn, rise and fall, much more than in flatter terrain. At high levels, they frequently zigzag for quite long distances. The combined effect can in some cases double the apparent length of a path.

You must keep to the waymarked routes, unless you are accompanied by a qualified local mountain guide. You are also forbidden to take short cuts. If you are caught "off-route" by a national park ranger, you are likely to be fined. This may annoy some walkers, but there are sound reasons. Partly to protect wildlife in the more sensitive areas; also to prevent erosion, or give badly eroded areas a chance to recover - the Tatras, being the most accessible alpine mountains for a considerable section of the populations of Central and Eastern Europe, have suffered much overuse and erosion.

For many walkers, the waymarked routes will provide enough scope for their visit, and will take them to some of the highest summits. More experienced mountain walkers can extend their range by engaging a guide - see below.

Unfortunately, at the time of writing, **you are not permitted to cross from Slovakia to Poland or vice versa in the mountains**, though you can take buses or drive round via the frontier post at Lysá Poľana. People do try to cross from one country to another, but there are border guards at strategic locations in the mountains, and if you are caught you will be taken to a border guard station for questioning, possibly fined, then taken back. The matter is taken very seriously because of the current refugee situation in Central and Eastern Europe.

Visitors to the national parks in both Slovakia and Poland are charged a nominal **entry fee**. The fee is charged daily, there is not as yet a season ticket. In Poland the charge is compulsory - you will encounter fee collectors at the foot of each path into the mountains, and they expect you to pay. In Slovakia the system is voluntary at the time of writing, with tickets on sale at offices of TANAP (the national park authority), though it is intended to make it compulsory in the near future.

Some visitors, especially those from Britain, may find this system irksome and contrary to their tradition of free entry to national parks. However, it is an accepted practice in other countries, the charge is very small, and the amounts collected are used to maintain and improve the paths and facilities. Please do not try to evade payment in Poland, and it will be greatly appreciated if you offer to pay in Slovakia.

In both Slovakia and Poland, you will frequently encounter on the waymarked routes a variety of **green signs**, bearing text in either yellow (Slovakia) or white (Poland), always in the appropriate language but usually with a translation into German, Russian or Hungarian - rarely if ever English! These are invariably exhortations of a common sense nature, for the sake of walkers' safety or protection of the environment. They include, for example, "Keep to the waymarked routes", "do not pick flowers or fruit", "no camping or fires", "no bathing in the tarns".

The higher paths are closed during the winter and spring, from 1 November to 30 June inclusive, though also at other times when there is snow and ice, or danger from avalanches. Some paths may be closed outside this period when similar dangers threaten, and you may see signs saying either (in Slovakia) *otvorená* (open) or *zatvorená* (closed); (in Poland) *przejście uzbronione* (no entry) or *uwaga lawiny* (beware avalanches). Even when these paths are closed, a considerable number remain open, and it is possible to enjoy a walking holiday in the snow - see the chapter on winter walking.

There is no general significance for walkers in the four-digit **reference number** shown on some maps beside each waymarked route in Slovakia - this is for administrative purposes and does not appear on the waymarks themselves. However, for ease of reference, we use these numbers in the route descriptions in the Slovakia section of this book. Such numbers do not appear on Polish maps, so we have devised our own numbering system (with three digits) for the routes in Poland.

On the suggested routes appearing later in the book, the average **walking time** is shown, but you should allow plenty of extra time, in case of unexpected delays. As a rough guide, for every 300 metres (1,000 feet) of altitude, you can expect to take around one hour for the ascent, and 30-45 minutes for the descent, though on some routes descending is as tricky or strenuous as ascending. Whilst paths are well constructed, the terrain is often steep and rocky. You will need strong knees and ankles, to stand up to the pounding you will give them on the descents.

Some short stretches of routes described in this book as **"airy"** or **"exposed"** (steep ground with a long drop below) are protected, usually by **fixed chains**, or sometimes wires of about 2 centimetres in diameter. They are firmly attached to the rock, and you use them to haul yourself up - or lower yourself down, which is more difficult, as it is not so easy to see where to put your feet. If there is a choice, you are advised to walk in the direction which will allow you to ascend, rather than descend, such sections. In either direction, you must always face the mountain, as this provides greater stability. Some busy routes with chains or wires have a one-way system, so that there is no conflict of interest between walkers travelling in opposite directions, and to reduce the risk of being hit by a rock dislodged by another walker.

Apart from the chains and wires, on some routes there are short, steep stretches which involve **scrambling** - using hands as well as feet to get yourself up or down. Stretches involving fixed chains, wires or scrambling are clearly marked in this book. So, if you do not like the sound of such activity, it can be avoided.

On routes needing a qualified mountain guide, you may encounter **ironware** of a more exotic nature, such as fixed ladders and pegs, which you use to negotiate trickier sections in exposed situations. For walkers with a sense of adventure, confidence, a cool head and no great fear of heights, such routes represent the pinnacle of their experience. Provided that you take care, and do not rush it, there is rarely cause for alarm.

For more detailed information about the **waymarking** system in Slovakia and Poland, see the introductory chapters in Sections 3 and 4.

Finally, a word of warning to those who prefer to be on their own in the mountains. Some routes in the Tatras are very popular, and you can expect to be in a long line of gregarious walkers, school parties and the like. This applies particularly to the routes to the main summits and the more accessible chalets and refuges.

REFRESHMENTS

It is safe to drink **water** from taps in the Tatras villages, and from the mountain chalets. You can refill your water-bottles from springs (the water from some of these contain iron); also from the higher tarns and streams in the mountains, provided that they are above the level of the mountain chalets. It is not recommended to drink water from below this level, because there is a danger that it will have been contaminated by sewage from the huts.

You can buy **food for picnic lunches** in the supermarkets and food shops in the villages - look for the sign *potraviny* (food) in Slovakia, or *sklep spożywczy* (grocer's shop) in Poland. In the supermarkets, note that you are expected to carry a wire basket, and it is common at busy times to see a queue for the baskets.

Most of the resorts also have **cafes and restaurants** (often in hotels) where meals and refreshments can be obtained. In Slovakia you will often find places called *denný bar* (day bar) - this means that they close earlier than bars in hotels etc., but some stay open till quite late. They sell drinks hot and cold, alcoholic and non-alcoholic, but usually a limited range of food. In Poland, Zakopane has a very wide range of refreshment facilities, while Kuźnice and some of the other outlying villages and hamlets also have buffets, taverns and restaurants: the entries for these places in the Gazetteer sections indicate whether there are any refreshment facilities.

There is also a network of **establishments in the mountains**. In the Slovak High Tatras there are eleven, called *chata* or *chaty* (chalet, singular/plural). On the Polish side there are eight, called *schronisko* or *schroniska* (refuge). Slovaks happily refer in English to chalets; Poles prefer to translate to refuge, since the word "chalet" implies "toilet" to them! Some of these establishments are actually mountain hotels, offering full hotel facilities including overnight accommodation. Most of the chalets or refuges offer accommodation, but usually only in dormitories (see Appendix 2).

The chalets or refuges (sometimes called mountain huts by English speakers) are located in such strategic positions that you are unlikely to undertake a day's walk in the Tatras without passing by or close to one or more of them. They are usually in splendid, often spectacular situations, beside a tarn, in a remote valley or below a towering cliff face. Food and drink are inexpensive, and if it is cold or wet outside, a steaming bowl of goulash soup, or mug of delicious, spiced lemon tea, will soon warm you up.

Some Polish refuges operate a system whereby you must first queue to order and pay for your food and hot drinks at a separate counter, then you are given a ticket which you take to the kitchen hatch. The problem is knowing what you want to order, as the menu is difficult to establish! Under this system, cold drinks are sold at the cash counter.

The chalets also offer toilet facilities, though some of these are rather primitive, and you may wish to carry a small supply of your own toilet paper, as it may have run out.

All the chalets or refuges have a rubber stamp, which many walkers use to record their visit in a notebook. Those in Poland also have a visitors' book for you to sign.

Most of the chalets are owned by the respective national mountaineering associations: in Slovakia by SK (Slovenské Karpaty or Slovak Carpathia); in Poland by PTTK (Polskie Towarzystwo Turystyczno-Krajoznawcze or Polish Touring and Country-lovers Association). In Slovakia the chalets are leased to individual wardens. The mountain hotels are operated by hotel chains.

Since the revolution in 1989, two of the Slovak chalets have reverted to their pre-war names, because new ones were given by the communist authorities against the wishes of local people. The names on your map may be the old ones. The chalets concerned are Zamkovského Chata (formerly Nálepkova Chata or Chata Kapitána Nálepku); and Chata pri Zelenom Plese (formerly Brnčalova Chata).

The former names of the Polish refuges were particularly long and tongue-twisting, usually in honour of some local dignitary - these are shown on the Slovak maps. Very few people used these names, and most have a shorter name by which they are known locally. Unfortunately, the latest Polish TPN map shows neither the former nor the commonly used names, though it does show their position.

The Gazetteer sections give more information about individual chalets and refuges.

See also the chapter on mountain safety regarding emergency rations.

MOUNTAIN GUIDES

In the High Tatras, you will need a qualified mountain guide if you wish to explore excellent recognised routes away from the waymarked network. Furthermore, **in Poland, all groups of ten or more people wishing to walk on the waymarked routes must be accompanied by such a guide.**

Although this book is not aimed at mountain climbers, it is as well to mention here that **members of recognised climbing clubs** can walk off the waymarked routes, provided that they have the appropriate equipment and take the shortest possible route to their climb. In Poland, a permit to do this must be obtained in advance from the national park authority; in Slovakia no permit is needed for the climb (though one is needed if you wish to set up a camp), but if stopped by a ranger you must show that you have the necessary equipment.

Routes needing a guide include the two highest Tatras summits, Gerlachovský Štít (2,655m) and Lomnický Štít (2,632m), and some exciting ridge walks. They are not included on the waymarked network, either because they are too difficult or dangerous to undertake without specialised local knowledge, or to restrict the number of walkers using them where excessive use will cause damage, or a combination of both. For example, only thirty walkers per day are allowed to ascend Gerlachovský Štít.

All these routes are regularly used by permitted groups. If you try to follow them without a guide, you may put yourself at risk of an accident, and it is certain that you will be spotted by a helicopter patrol, or challenged and fined by a national park warden or a mountain guide.

All routes requiring a guide involve a fair amount of scrambling, use of wires and other fixed apparatus in exposed situations, so they are all rated "difficult" by our system.

Another reason for hiring a guide is to enable you to get away from the crowds if you are visiting in the high season (July and August). At this time, you are advised to book your guides at the earliest opportunity (even before you go if possible), as they are in great demand. Of course, even on the waymarked routes you will benefit from having a local guide with you to provide local knowledge, not only of the locations but of flora and fauna.

Unlike in the Alps, where hiring a guide costs a small fortune, guide fees in the High Tatras are quite reasonable, especially if there are several of you to share the cost - though the maximum number of walkers that can be escorted by one guide is five. At 1993 prices, the daily fee per guide is the equivalent of approximately £35-40 sterling or US$50-60, so the cost per person per day could be as little as £7 or US$10.

In Slovakia, the guides are provided by the Mountain Rescue Service (Horská Služba), and you can book your guide at their offices in Štrbské Pleso,

Starý Smokovec and Tatranská Lomnica. In Poland, guides are provided by the Tatras Guides Association, but the booking system is under review at the time of writing and we are unable to give a contact - you should check the latest position at the tourist information centre near the railway station. You can in any case book guides through a local travel agency in either country, or at your hotel reception office.

MOUNTAIN SAFETY AND EMERGENCY SERVICES

Anyone who walks in mountainous areas should be aware of the possible dangers that lurk around the corner, though they are most unlikely in normal circumstances. Thunderstorms, falling stones and falls resulting in injuries to limbs (or worse) are the most usual. It should be stressed that, whilst accidents can happen to anyone at any time, those who are prepared for them and know what to do in the event of an emergency are less likely to suffer serious consequences as a result. Never say "It won't happen to me"!

First and foremost, you must wear **suitable footwear. Waterproofs, spare clothing, hat, gloves, water bottle, small first aid kit, map, compass, whistle and emergency food** complete your minimum preparations for safety and comfort in the mountains. They need not be heavy - modern equipment of this kind is usually compact and light. The section on clothing and equipment describes some of these items more fully. Here are the reasons for wearing or carrying them.

Footwear. In the mountains, both for your own sake and that of other walkers, you must always walk carefully. Good quality walking boots with a deep tread almost force you to do so, since they grip the surface in a way that no ordinary shoes can. Walking boots protect your ankles from damage on rocks and hidden cracks; trainers and walking shoes do not.

Waterproofs and spare clothing. Weather can change quickly in the mountains (see above). Cloudbursts may catch you before you have time to reach shelter. In such conditions, without waterproofs and spare clothing, the danger of suffering from hypothermia is very real indeed. Carry them!

Even though you may become very warm and perspire profusely while climbing, when you reach the top you will stop to rest, admire the view or take refreshment. This is usually in a high position where the wind is at its strongest, so you quickly start to feel cold. An extra pullover or windproof jacket, hat and gloves will then be much appreciated. On the other hand, do not allow yourself to overheat while climbing - take off as many layers as will allow you to continue to walk in comfort and decency!

First aid kit. If you suffer a fall, or cut yourself on rocks, it may take several hours to reach a place where first aid is available. A basic kit should contain a selection of plasters, antiseptic cream and a triangular bandage. Buy one that includes some instructions on what to do in common cases needing treatment. Optional extras may include a blister kit, something for insect bites, insect repellent and sun protection cream. Depending on your susceptibilities, you may also need sunglasses, skin cream and lip salve.

Map and compass. Whilst waymarking on most routes in the High Tatras is very good, when tired or in poor visibility you may become disorientated, or take a wrong turning. Then a map and compass will be of enormous help in deciding which way to go, or how to regain your intended route.

Whistle. For attracting attention in emergency. If you cannot easily reach help, attract attention to your plight by giving the international distress call: six long blasts, repeated every minute. An answering series of three blasts means that your signal has been noticed, and help is on the way. A torch can perform the same function in the dark, using flashes instead of whistle blasts.

Emergency food. If you should suffer an accident, or become lost and dispirited, it will boost both your morale and physical strength to dig out that bar of chocolate, or packet of peanuts or raisins, when the nearest refreshment facilities may be several hours away.

Weather forecast. Each day, before you set out, get the weather forecast from your hotel reception, from an information office, or from the mountain rescue service, and plan a route that takes the weather into account.

Remember the **wind chill factor.** The higher the wind speed, the more it cools the temperature, so that you may not only have to battle against the wind but also wear more clothes to guard against the cold. The more effort you have to put into your walking, the greater the cooling effect. The actual fall in the temperature experienced varies, depending on the wind speed and the amount of effort being expended, but while walking at a steady pace is approximately in the region of 1 to 3 degrees Celsius for every kilometre per hour of wind speed. You are likely to notice the wind speed more as you climb, especially where there is no protection from the trees.

Remember the **altitude factor** (also called the lapse rate). On top of the wind chill effect, the temperature drops as you climb, by about 2 degrees Celsius for every 300 metres.

Thunderstorms. When a thunderstorm threatens, do not go higher but descend straight away, especially if you are on or near a summit or ridge, as lightning tends to strike in such places. Do not take shelter under a tree or prominent rock, as these are also favourite targets of lightning. Get down into a valley, or find a mountain chalet where you can sit out the storm.

Falling stones or rocks. Take care, especially when walking or scrambling on a steep slope with loose rocks, that you do not dislodge one. Watch out for those dislodged by walkers higher up the slope. If you should set loose a rock which threatens to roll some way downhill, yell out a warning: in English one would shout "below!" or "look out!" but this will not mean much in the Tatras! Try a double warning in Slovak ("pozor") or Polish ("uwaga", pronounced oovahga), as appropriate, and German ("Achtung!").

Slippery rocks and paths. In wet weather, some kinds of moss- or lichen-bearing rock, and wooden rain channels, become slippery, and paths can turn into torrents. Some walkers find a walking stick or ski-pole helpful on steep or rough ground, though they can also get in the way when scrambling or using chains and other fixtures.

Leave word of your proposed route with someone, such as the hotel reception, who will realise if you fail to return that something may have happened, and will know where the mountain rescue will need to look. Some hotels keep a walks book for this purpose. Obviously you should then stick to your proposed route, and report in when you return.

Know your limits. If the weather should deteriorate, or you are finding the going too hard, do not be ashamed to turn back.

Walk in company. Try to avoid walking alone on the more remote and less popular routes. If you should fall and twist your ankle, the sooner you get help the better, and an uninjured companion will be able to reach it much more quickly. Ideally there should be at least three in your party, so that one can go for help while the other stays with the injured person.

Help! If an accident should happen, for which help is needed, keep calm. In most parts of the High Tatras, there is usually a mountain chalet or hotel nearby, which is linked by telephone or radio to the Mountain Rescue Service. If you are closer to a village, find a hotel or telephone and contact the Mountain Rescue Service by dialling 2820 or 2855 in Slovakia, 63444 in Poland - try to have someone with you who speaks English as well as the local language. There is normally no charge for being rescued, unless due to wilful negligence on your part such as ignoring professional advice. This information is repeated and expanded in Appendix 6 near the back of this book.

WINTER WALKING

The higher routes in the Tatras are closed in winter and spring (generally 1 November to 30 June), because of the dangers from snow and ice on steep slopes, and from avalanches. Substantial snowfalls may occur from November onwards, more unusually in late October, and the lakes start to freeze over. The average winter temperature in the High Tatras resorts is around minus 5 to minus 6 degrees Celsius.

However, most of the lower routes, up to the mountain chalets or refuges, remain open and well used - as do the chalets and refuges themselves for welcome refreshment. Provided that you are well prepared, walking through the snow in winter can be a delightful experience. You will probably find that others have gone before you, treading out a path in the snow. Most of the mountain chalets are open all year round, so there will be ample opportunity for a hot drink or meal.

The path descriptions in Sections 3 and 4 include an indication as to whether each is open or closed in winter and spring. The walking maps also include a symbol to indicate that certain routes are closed in winter.

You should wear and carry everything that you would in summer, with the addition of **gaiters** which stop snow and water from entering your boots. Remember especially to carry a **hat, gloves and a spare pullover or fibre-pile jacket.**

A phenomenon of autumn and winter weather in mountainous areas is that of **inversion.** On windless days the cold, heavy air streams down from the mountains into the plains, pushing the warmer air up into the mountains, where it may stay for several days. This can make the temperature in the mountains, up to an altitude of around 1,800 metres, warmer than that in the plain by up to 10 degrees Celsius. This also results in a layer of cloud at the level where the cold and warm air mix, so that there is sun in the mountains when it is gloomy in the plain.

MOUNTAIN PHOTOGRAPHY

Neither of the authors is an expert on photography, but we gladly pass on some hints gleaned from friends who are, and hope that this may be helpful.

In the mountains, photographs exaggerate the ultra-violet glare, giving a bluish effect. This can be overcome by fitting (preferably) an ultra-violet filter, otherwise a blue one will do. A filter of any kind will help to protect your lens from getting scratched. In winter, a grey filter absorbs the extra light reflected from snow.

Two to three hours after noon is a period to avoid for photography - at this time, the ultra-violet is at its strongest, and there is no shadow so the picture lacks depth.

To avoid fuzzy or blurred pictures, either carry a lightweight tripod or monopod, or rest the camera on a rock for steadiness.

More general tips: use a wide-angle lens for better panoramas; keep your camera in its case in case you slip; take close-ups of flowers and insects; use a zoom lens for wild animals at a distance; keep notes of what you take - you are sure to forget where you took some of your best shots.

HOW TO USE THIS GUIDE

The two sections that follow respectively describe the details relevant to walking in the Slovak High Tatras and the Polish Tatras. Within each section, first comes an introduction, including some local history, followed by route suggestions, then path descriptions and tables of walking times and summits. After the two country sections, you will find several appendices devoted to various aspects of travel and tourism information.

Some **route suggestions** are circular, others start and finish at different points. All the starting and finishing points are served by the very efficient local public transport system, so you can use any of these routes, wherever you are staying.

Some routes can only be followed in one direction, in order to reduce conflict of interests at difficult sections - in such cases this is indicated in the text. The maps also have arrow symbols where this one-way traffic applies, but you should be careful not to confuse them with other arrows indicating either routes closed in winter and spring, or roads closed to traffic - this is clarified in the map keys.

Detailed **path descriptions** are shown separately, taking advantage of the existing numbering scheme in the Slovak Tatras National Park area. This avoids tedious repetition within the route suggestions, and also allows you to string together your own routes if required. The four-figure path numbers are shown on the 1:50,000 scale map published by Slovenská Kartografia (Sheet 21), but not on other maps. Nor are they shown on signposts along the routes.

There is no equivalent numbering on the Polish side, so we have taken the liberty of providing our own three-figure system there. Diagramatic plans of the route networks appear on the end paper maps: Slovakia at the front, Poland at the back.

On both sides of the border, the first digit of the path number corresponds to the colour. So, as with the numbering followed by the official system in Slovakia, all the red routes start with "O"; blue with "2"; green with "5" and yellow with "8". There are no black routes in Slovakia, but in our system the Polish ones start with "9".

The Slovak path numbering system generally runs from west to east, and we have followed the same principal as far as possible, for both the Slovak and Polish sections. The path descriptions are generally written in the uphill direction, so if you follow them downhill you will need to reverse the instructions. Longer paths have been divided into sections, by adding the letters A-B-C etc. to the path numbers.

Within the path descriptions, rather than interrupt the flow with notes on places of interest passed along the way, some of which occur in more than one section, such places are shown in **bold type**, and can be looked up in the gazetteer at the end of the section.

All the route suggestions and path descriptions give the following information in bold type at the top: grade of walk (see next chapter); approximate distance; average gradient; height gain or loss; average walking time; whether open in winter/spring.

All **distances** are approximate, and are only quoted as a rough guide. Distances are a poor guide in the mountains, because of the effect steepness and roughness of terrain will have on your walking time. You should take more notice of the average walking times quoted.

Distances are given in metres and kilometres. For a rough conversion, to convert metres into yards add ten per cent; for kilometres into miles divide by five then multiply by eight. Altitudes are given in metres; for a rough conversion into feet multiply by three then add ten per cent. Some altitudes are an estimate, calculated from map contours.

Average **gradients** are calculated from the height gain or loss, divided by the estimated distance, so are themselves a correspondingly rough guide to the steepness of each route.

For each route and section, an estimated **walking time** is shown, that generally corresponds to those shown on signposts in the area. These are usually on the generous side, and fit walkers may find that they can cover the distance in a shorter time. In some cases the figures quoted on these signposts are clearly misleading, and we have tried to give a more accurate figure. Walking times make no allowance for refreshment and other stops. It is not a good idea to make strenuous efforts to beat these times; much more enjoyment will result from taking your time and admiring the views and surroundings.

Within the longer path descriptions, an idea of the time taken to cover each section is shown in italics at the end of the paragraph. Where a range of times is quoted, the shorter time is for the descent, the longer time for the ascent.

Every effort has been made to be accurate, but changes can take place either through natural causes (eg. landslides during the winter), or through human activity (eg. forestry, removal or addition of a landmark, human error!).

GRADING OF WALKS

There are walks in the High Tatras to suit walkers of most degrees of capability, so the route suggestions later in this book are graded to help you choose. Inexperienced walkers should start with the easier routes, then if they can cope with those they may wish to try something harder, a grade at a time. Strong experienced walkers should not ignore the easier routes - they may sometimes need an easy day, and sometimes the weather may restrict everyone to lower altitudes.

There is no official grading of waymarked routes in the High Tatras, so ours is necessarily arbitrary, and should be treated as a guide. The path descriptions in Sections 3 and 4 give further information about specific stretches of route, including where you may expect to encounter scrambling or fixed wires.

Our grading is a guide to the terrain you may expect to encounter. You should also take into account the walking times shown for each route suggestion and path description. Do not overestimate your capability.

There are four grades:

Easy Mostly on paths, tracks or forest roads up to an average gradient of about 10%. Can be undertaken in trainers or tough walking shoes.

Moderate Mostly on steeper, rockier paths and tracks up to an average gradient of about 15%. No continuous scrambling or exposed situations, though there may be an occasional short section of this. No fixed chains. Walking boots strongly recommended.

Strenuous Very steep and rocky paths above 15% average gradient, usually including substantial sections of scrambling and exposure, and at least one fixed chain. Walking boots essential. Most of the high summits and passes on the waymarked route network come within this grade.

Difficult These routes can only be undertaken in the company of a qualified local mountain guide. Terrain as for "Strenuous", but with more scrambling, fixed wires and other metal aids in exposed situations. Walking boots essential. The guide will advise if any other climbing equipment is necessary (this can be hired locally).

The Slovak High and White Tatras

LATER HISTORY

Excavations of Žltá Stena (Yellow Wall) near Tatranská Polianka have revealed the existence of a major fortified habitation which was destroyed by fire. It occupies a strategic site commanding extensive views over the Podtatranská Kotlina, the huge basin between the High and Low Tatras. The fort appears to date from the Bronze Age, at about the beginning of the first millennium BC, when the area was populated by Celtic people.

The area was invaded and settled during the ninth and eighth centuries BC by successive waves of Slavonic people who are thought to have originated in what is now eastern Poland and Belarus. One of these waves consisted of the Slovaks and the closely related Slovenes - in Slovak the words for these are respectively Slovensko and Slovinsko - who settled the area between the Tatras and the Adriatic Sea.

During the ninth century AD, this area was part of the Greater Moravian Empire, which extended from what is now the Czech Republic to Rumania. Excavations at Slavkov, on the south-eastern slopes of the High Tatras between Poprad and Starý Smokovec, have revealed the existence during this period of a human settlement, which could have been a resting-place of some importance on the overland trade route linking the Baltic and Mediterranean Seas. At this time, the mountains were generally feared, visited only by an occasional brave hunter.

At the end of the ninth century, the Greater Moravian Empire was destroyed by the Magyars and associated tribes, who originated in the area to the east of the Urals. They established a new homeland in what is now Hungary, driving a wedge between the Slovaks and the Slovenes. Slovakia was devastated, and became part of the Hungarian domain, with Hungarian nobility owning the land which continued to be worked by Slav peasants.

The thirteenth century brought further invasion and terror, this time by the Tatars from Asia. They totally destroyed the Sub-Tatras Basin and surrounding areas in the Spring, with the result that the entire population either died of hunger through lack of crops, or sought refuge elsewhere. Travellers reported that they had walked through the area for days without seeing any sign of human life. To restore civilisation, King Bela IV of Hungary invited people from German-speaking lands, especially Saxony, to settle in the more low-lying areas; this Germanic influence still dominates the Spiš basin to the east and south-east of the High Tatras.

On the walls of the nave of the Roman Catholic parish church in the nearby town of Poprad can be found a painting dating from the late fourteenth or early fifteenth century. It depicts the Tatras as the background of a Bible scene. Another pictorial record, dated 1475, shows Lomnický Štít, the second highest Tatra peak; it forms part of the coat of arms of the Berzevicky family from the village of Velká Lomnica. The oldest plan of the Tatras forms part of a map of Hungary, dated 1556, drawn by a Viennese historian called Vlk Lazius.

During the fifteenth and sixteenth centuries, there was continuous strife caused by religious enmity (especially between the Hussites, followers of the Bohemian Jan Hus, and the Roman Catholic church), by various claimants to the Hungarian crown, and by pressure from refugees from the wars with the Ottoman Turks, especially from Wallachia (Southern Rumania). This forced many Slovaks to take refuge in the mountain valleys, eking out their existence by resorting to poaching and robbery.

These disturbances were subsiding by the seventeenth century, and people all over Europe began to take an interest in nature study, and in exploring mountainous areas. In 1615, the first recorded climb of a Tatras peak was undertaken, by a student called David Frölich from Kežmarok; it is not certain which peak was climbed, though it was probably Kežmarsky Štít which is visible from Kežmarok.

By the early eighteenth century, the Ottoman Turks had been expelled from Central Europe, which became more settled under the domination of the Hapsburg dynasty. Permanent settlements appeared in the foothills of the Tatras. Local people thoroughly explored the valleys and peaks, and established societies devoted to various aspects of their natural resources and culture.

Wealthier and more educated people from all over Europe began to travel around and explore the mountainous areas. The first ascents of Lomnický Štít, Jahňací Štít and Kriváň were made in 1793 by a Scottish physician and geographer, Robert Townson. He may have stayed at the chalet that was built in the same year on the southern slope of Slavkovsky Štít, in a location that later developed into the resort of Starý Smokovec.

More exploration of the Tatras was carried out in 1813 by the Swedish botanist and natural historian, Göran Wahlenberg. His principal objective was the study of the flora, but his records also contain much about other branches of nature study, and served for many years as a valuable reference work for other explorers.

In 1843, the Irishman, John Ball, was the first to ascend Ľadovy Štít; he later became the first president of the London Alpine Club. In those days, it took two days to climb the highest peaks, with much use of horses and mules. The intervening night was spent in a hayloft, in a cave or under an overhanging rock.

Until 1871, the Tatras remained a relative backwater for tourists, since it lay so far from the railways and main roads. In that year, a railway line was completed from Ostrava to Košice, passing through Štrba and Poprad, making possible connections from Vienna, Prague and Berlin, and the Tatras tourist industry began to flourish.

Soon after this were founded the local associations which actively promoted walking and mountaineering in the Tatras. These included the Hungaro-Carpathian Association on the Slovak side and the Towarzystwo Tatrzanskie on the Polish side; their work included building and marking the paths, many of which are still used today, as well as organising the guiding and mountain rescue services, and starting the network of mountain chalets.

Although World War I resulted in Slovakia being declared part of the new Republic of Czechoslovakia, the fighting did not affect the Tatras. It was a very different story during World War II. In 1939, a puppet Slovak state was established under the Nazis, but with strong opposition in the form of local resistance units (partisans). This peaked at the end of 1944 and beginning of 1945, in what is now known as the Slovak National Uprising. There was fierce fighting in and around the Tatras villages, and in the valleys and forests, especially in the area around Podbanské. You may come across memorials at the places where important battles took place, and some of the mountain chalets are named after partisan leaders.

To come right up to date, following the fall in 1989 of the communist regime in Czechoslovakia (the "velvet revolution"), an amicably agreed separation into two independent states - Slovakia and the Czech Republic - took effect on 1st January 1993 (the "velvet divorce").

INTRODUCTION TO THE WALKING

Nearly all the walking in Slovakia covered in this book takes place in the High Tatras (Vysoké Tatry). The Western Tatras (Zapadné Tatry), though providing extensive walking, are too remote and difficult of access to be of interest to people staying in the High Tatras resorts. Tourists are banned altogether from almost all of the White Tatras (Belianske Tatry), as well as from certain smaller areas in parts of the High Tatras not provided with waymarked routes - this is to protect the very fragile ecology, which has suffered from overuse in the past.

Six high summits on the Slovak side lie on the waymarked route network, and are therefore accessible without a guide. They are Kriváň, Kôprovský Štít, Rysy, Východná Vysoká, Slavkovský Štít and Jahňací Štít, all between 2,200 and 2,500 metres. Predné Soliско at 2,093m above Štrbské Pleso, though not particularly high, also provides fine views, and is easily accessible.

High passes on waymarked routes make a rewarding goal for a day's excursion - these include Sedielko (2,372m), Priečne Sedlo (2,352m), Prielom (2,288m) and Poľský Hrebeň (2,200m) while Hladké Sedlo (1,994m) on the border provides a magnificent view into the "Valley of Five Polish Tarns". High tarns and mountain chalets also make satisfying targets, and there are plenty of these between 1,500 and 2,000 metres.

The two highest summits, Gerlachovský Štít (2,655m) and Lomnický Štít (2,632m), and some exciting ridge walks, require a qualified mountain guide. It is easy and not too expensive to hire one for the day - see the chapter on mountain guides.

Waymarks in the Slovak High Tatras consist of three horizontal bands, the upper and lower ones being white, with the middle one either red, green blue or yellow, to correspond with that shown for each route on the maps. There is no significance in the colour, though the predominant red route is the Tatranská Magistrála (Tatras Highway, see below). At route starting points and junctions, the various waymarks (including an indication of walking times to major destinations) are attached to charming, picturesque and colourful rustic posts, made from sawn-off boughs to which a small roof has been fixed. (see p8)

ROUTE SUGGESTIONS

WAYMARKED NETWORK

Sections marked (*) include at least one fixed chain or wire, and/or some scrambling.

1) PODBANSKÉ (940m) - TICHÁ DOLINA - HLADKÉ SEDLO (1,994m) - KÔPROVÁ DOLINA - PODBANSKÉ (940m)

Grade: the walking is moderate though the distance is strenuous
Distance: 31.5km   **Time: 8h 00m**   **Average gradient: 7%**
Height gain: 1,054m   **Height loss: 1,054m**
Refreshments: Podbanské only

From Podbanské bus stop/car park follow sections:
8851 (yellow) 11km N along Tichá Dolina to Rázcestie pod Tomanovou Dolinou;
0931 (red) 7km E to Sedlo Závory and Hladké Sedlo, returning to Sedlo Závory;
5801 (green) 2.5km S to Rázcestie pod Hlinskou Dolinou;
2902 (blue) 6km SW to Rázcestie pod Grúnikom;
5802 (green) 3.5km W to Tichá;
8851 (yellow) 1.5km SW to Podbanské.

Uses easy access routes, with short moderate ascents to Hladké Sedlo on the border, which has a magnificent view of the beautiful Valley of Five Polish Tarns. As a circular route it is best done in the direction described, providing a more direct return to Podbanské. Hladké Sedlo can be reached more easily by going in the opposite direction and returning by the same route, with an optional short diversion to Nižné Temnosmrečinské Pleso.

2) ŠTRBSKÉ PLESO (1,355m) - JAMSKÉ PLESO (1,447m) - CHATA KAPITÁNA RAŠU (1,180m) - TRI STUDNIČKY (1,140m) - PODBANSKÉ (940m)

Grade: easy   **Distance: 13.5km**   **Average gradient: 5%**
Height gain: 185m   **Height loss: 600m**   **Time: 3h 45m**
Refreshments: Chata Kapitána Rasu, Podbanské

From Štrbské Pleso tarn follow sections:
0930F (red) 4.5km NW to Jamské Pleso;
0930F (red) 3.5km W to Chata Kapitána Rašu and Tri Studničky;
0930G (red) 5.5km W to Podbanské (infrequent buses to Štrbské Pleso).
    A gentle introduction, or wet-weather walk, including the delightful Jamské Pleso tarn and fine views over the Sub-Tatras Basin.

3) ŠTRBSKÉ PLESO (1,355m) - KRIVÁŇ (2,494m) - TRI STUDNIČKY (1,194m)

Grade: strenuous   **Distance: 12km**   **Average gradient: 20%**
Height gain: 1,139m   **Height loss: 1,300m**   **Time: 6h 15m**
Refreshments: None on the route (Chata Kapitána Rašu near Tri Studničky)

From Štrbské Pleso station follow sections:
0930F (red) 4.5km NW to Jamské Pleso (turn off shortly before lake);
2903 (blue) (*) 4km NW to Kriváň summit, and return to Rázcestie pod Kriváňom;
5803 (green) 3.5km SW to Tri Studničky (infrequent buses to Štrbské Pleso).
    A well used route with no fixed chain but some scrambling to one of the most popular summits - Kriváň, national symbol of Slovakia.

4) ŠTRBSKÉ PLESO (1,355m) - KÔPROVSKY ŠTÍT (2,367m) - TRI STUDNIČKY (1,194m)

Grade: strenuous   **Distance: 25km**   **Average gradient: 9%**
Height gain: 1,012m   **Height loss: 1,173m**   **Time: 8h 30m**
Refreshments: None on the route (Chata Kapitána Rasu near Tri Studničky)

From Štrbské Pleso station follow sections:
0930E (red) 4.5km N to Popradské Pleso;
2902B (blue) 5km NW to Vyšné Kôprovské Sedlo;
0934 (red) 1km N to Kôprovský Štít and return 1km to Vyšné Kôprovské Sedlo;

2902A (blue) 13.5km SW to Tri Studničky (infrequent buses to Štrbské Pleso).

A less well used route to a comparatively easy summit with no chains or scrambling, providing fine views over lake-filled valleys.

5) ŠTRBSKÉ PLESO (1,355m) - VODOPÁD SKOK (1,700m) - BYSTRÉ SEDLO (2,314m) - VYŠNÉ WAHLENBERGOVO PLESO (2,145m) - ŠTRBSKÉ PLESO (1,355m)

Grade: strenuous   **Distance: 14.5km**   **Average gradient: 15%**
Height gain: 959m   **Height loss: 959m**   **Time: 6h 30m**
Refreshments: Chata pod Soliskom (on optional alternative only)

From Štrbské Pleso station follow sections:
8853 (yellow) 4.5km NW to Vodopád Skok and 2.5km further (*) to Bystré Sedlo;
8853 (yellow) 1km SW to Vyšné Wahlenbergovo Pleso, 2.5km to junction 2836 (blue), 1.5km to junction 0930 (red).
0930F (red) 2.5km SE to Štrbské Pleso.
Optional alternative: Take 2836 (blue) 1km SE to Chata pod Soliskom (some climbing), then either walk 3.5km down 2836 (blue) to Štrbské Pleso or take chair-lift (total 15 or 11.5km).

A popular route, being easily accessible from Štrbské Pleso, mostly above the tree-line, and with excellent views of Skok waterfall, and over lake-filled valleys. The route is easy as far as the waterfall, but there is a fixed chain and some scrambling near the top. You are strongly advised to follow the route anticlockwise, as described, to avoid meeting oncoming walkers on the chain, and because if there is snow near the saddle the route is more difficult to find clockwise.

6) ŠTRBSKÉ PLESO (1,355m) - CHATA POD SOLISKOM (1,830m) - PREDNÉ SOLISKO (2,093m) - CHATA POD SOLISKOM (1,573m) - FURKOTSKÁ DOLINA - ŠTRBSKÉ PLESO

Grade: moderate   **Distance: 11.5km**   **Average gradient: 13%**
Height gain: 738m   **Height loss: 738m**   **Time: 4h 15m**
Refreshments: Chata pod Soliskom

From Štrbské Pleso station follow sections:
2836 (blue) 3.5km NW to Chata pod Soliskom (or take chair-lift);
0935 (red) 1.5km N to Predné Solisko and return to Chata pod Soliskom;

2836 (blue) 1km NW to Furkotská Dolina;
8853 (yellow) 1.5km SE to junction 0930;
0930F (red) 2.5km SE to Štrbské Pleso.

Predné Solisko is a very popular minor summit, because it is just a short walk from the chair-lift, and provides good views over Štrbské Pleso. Optional alternative: From Chata pod Soliskom return on 2836 (blue) to Štrbské Pleso - this has better views than 2836/8853/0930 (total 10km).

7) ŠTRBSKÉ PLESO (1,355m) - POPRADSKÉ PLESO (1,494m) - RYSY (2,499m) and return.

Grade: strenuous   **Distance: 18km**   **Average gradient: 15%**
Height gain: 1,144m   **Height loss: 1,144m**   **Time: 9h 00m**
Refreshments: Popradské Pleso, Chata pod Rysmy

From Štrbské Pleso station follow sections:
0930E (red) 4.5km N to Popradské Pleso;
2902 (blue) 1.5km N to junction 0933;
0933 (red) (*) 3km NE to Chata pod Rysmy and Rysy summit.
Return by same route.

One of the most popular routes, since Rysy is the highest summit on the waymarked route network, with fine views into Poland (remember that you cannot continue into Poland). Avoid the weekends, when there may be long queues for the fixed chains. You can save 15 minutes' walking in each direction by starting instead at Popradské Pleso railway station, using blue route 2902 to and from the tarn.

8) ŠTRBSKÉ PLESO (1,355m) - POPRADSKÉ PLESO (1,494m) - OSTRVA (1,926m) - BATIZOVSKÉ PLESO (1,879m) - SLIEZSKY DOM (1,678m) - STARÝ SMOKOVEC (1,010m)

Grade: moderate   **Distance: 19km**   **Average gradient: 10%**
Height gain: 571m   **Height loss: 916m**   **Time: 7h 00m**
Refreshments: Popradské Pleso, Sliezsky Dom, Starý Smokovec

From Štrbské Pleso follow sections:
0930E (red) 4.5km N to Popradské Pleso;
0930D (red) 1.5km SE to Ostrva; then 3.5km E to junction 8855 (yellow), then 1km NE to Batizovské Pleso and 1.5km SE to junction 8856 (yellow), then 2km NE to Sliezsky Dom;
5806 (green) 0.5km SE to junction 8858 (yellow);

8858 (yellow) 2km SE to junction 2905 (blue) and 2.5km to Starý Smokovec.

A route featuring one of the more dramatic sections of the Tatranská Magistrála, with good views of the Sub Tatras Basin. It can be followed in the reverse direction, but would then involve more climbing unless you take the funicular to Hrebienok. For those wishing to return to Štrbské Pleso or Tatranská Lomnica, green route 5806 from Sliezsky Dom to Tatranská Polianka provides a quicker descent to the bus or train.

9) POPRADSKÉ PLESO RAILWAY STATION (1,250m) - POPRADSKÉ PLESO TARN (1,494m) - ŠTRBSKÉ PLESO (1,355m)

Grade: easy	**Distance: 7.5km**	**Average gradient: 5%**
Height gain: 244m	**Height loss: 139m**	**Time: 2h 15m**
Refreshments: Popradské Pleso, Štrbské Pleso		

From Popradské Pleso station (train, 1km NE of Strbské Pleso) follow sections:
2902 (blue) 3.5km N to Popradské Pleso tarn;
0930E (red) 4km SW to Štrbské Pleso.
Optional alternative:
Diversion on section 8854 (yellow to Symbolický Cintorín (Symbolic Cemetery) adds 0.5km/15 minutes - plus viewing time!

An easy and popular short route to and from a beautiful tarn, plus an opportunity to view the unique Symbolic Cemetery. In winter you will have to use green route 5805, since 0930E is closed because of avalanche danger.

10) VYŠNÉ HÁGY (1,085m) - BATIZOVSKÉ PLESO (1,879m) - SLIEZSKY DOM (1,678m) - TATRANSKÁ POLIANKA (1,010m)

Grade: moderate	**Distance: 13.5km**	**Average gradient: 12%**
Height gain: 794m	**Height loss: 869m**	**Time: 6h 00m**
Refreshments: Sliezsky Dom, Tatranská Polianka		

From Vyšné Hágy railway station follow routes:
8855 (yellow) 4.5km N to junction 0930D (red);
0930D (red) 1km NE to Batizovské Pleso, 1.5km SE to junction 8856 (yellow), then 2km NE to Sliezsky Dom;
5806 (green) 4.5km SE to Tatranská Polianka.

11) TATRANSKÁ POLIANKA (1,010m) - SLIEZSKY DOM (1,678m) - STARÝ SMOKOVEC (1,010m)

Grade: easy	**Distance: 11km**	**Average gradient: 12%**
Height gain: 668m	**Height loss: 668m**	**Time: 4h 00m**
Refreshments: Sliezsky Dom		

From Tatranská Polianka railway station follow routes:
2806 (blue) 5km NW to Sliezsky Dom;
5806 (green) 0.5km SE to junction 8858 (yellow);
8858 (yellow) 2km SE to junction 2905 (blue) and 2.5km to Starý Smokovec.
   Though the walking is generally easy, there are some steep sections. Sliezsky Dom is well situated on the beautiful small tarn of Velické Pleso.

12) LYSÁ POĽANA (970m) - BIELOVODSKÁ DOLINA - POĽSKY HREBEŇ (2,200m) SLIEZSKY DOM (1,663m) - TATRANSKÁ POLIANKA (1,010m)

Grade: moderate	**Distance: 23km**	**Average gradient: 11%**
Height gain: 1,230m	**Height loss: 1,190m**	**Time: 9h 15m**
Refreshments: Sliezsky Dom, Tatranská Polianka		

From Lysá Poľana follow routes:
2907 (blue) 12km S to Litvorová Kotlina, then 2.5km SE to Litvorové Pleso, Zamrznuté Pleso and Poľský Hrebeň;
5806 (green) 3.5km SE to Sliezsky Dom, and 5km SE to Tatranská Polianka.
   Optional alternative: from Zamrznuté Pleso continue E on 2907 (blue) to Prielom (*), 2km E to Zbojnícka Chata, and 5km SE to Kamzík; then on 8859 (yellow) 1.5km SE to Hrebienok (same distance but grade is strenuous - to be avoided if there is much snow; not recommended in the reverse direction).
   Optional extension to Východná Vysoká (2,428m) adds 228m of ascent and 1h 15m.
   This route can be followed in the reverse direction if preferred, providing less climbing, but the suggested direction allows a more gentle ascent, and gets the long bus journey out of the way in the morning.

13) STARÝ SMOKOVEC (1,010m) - HREBIENOK (1,285m) - VODOPÁD STUDENÉHO POTOKA (1,265m) - TATRANSKÁ LESNA (905m)

Grade: easy	**Distance: 7.5km**	**Average gradient: 9%**
Height gain: 275m	**Height loss: 380m**	**Time: 2h 30m**
Refreshments: Hrebienok, Zamkovského Chata		

From Starý Smokovec (funicular railway station) follow sections:
5807 (green) 2.5km NE to Hrebienok, 0.5km N to Bilíkova Chata/junction with 8859 (yellow), and 0.5km to Vodopád Studeného Potoka; return 0.5km to Bilíkova Chata then:
8859 (yellow) 3.5km SE to Tatranská Lesna.
Optional extensions:
a) From Hrebienok, take 0930B (red) 1.5km NW to Kamzík, and 1.5km NE to Zamkovského/Nálepkova Chata, passing Obrovský Vodopád; return to Kamzík, then take 2907 (blue) and 5807 (green) 1km to Bilíkova Chata and 8859 (yellow) 3.5km to Tatranská Lesná (adds 1.5km).
b) From Tatranská Lesná follow footpath beside Cesta Slobody (Freedom Highway) back to Starý Smokovec (adds 3km).
Optional alternative: From Vodopád Studeného Potoka take 2907 (blue) 6km E to Tatranská Lomnica (adds 2km).

A low level walk which is mostly in forest but provides an excellent view of the Studený Potok cascades.

14) HREBIENOK (1,285m) - VELICKÉ PLESO (1,687m) - STARÝ SMOKOVEC (1,010m)

Grade: easy to moderate **Distance: 10.5km** **Average gradient: 10%**
Height gain: 402m **Height loss: 677m** **Time: 4h 00m**
Refreshments: Hrebienok, Sliezsky Dom, Starý Smokovec

Take funicular from Starý Smokovec N to Hrebienok, then follow sections:
0930C (red) 5.5km W to Velické Pleso/Sliezsky Dom;
5806 (green) 0.75km SE to junction with route 8858 (yellow);
8858 (yellow) 4km SE to Starý Smokovec.
Optional extension to Poľský Hrebeň and Východna Vysoká adds 765m of ascent and 5 hours.

A route using the Tatranská Magistrála with good views over the valley and up to the peaks. There is a short section of easy scrambling on route 0930C, without much exposure.

15) HREBIENOK (1,285m) - ZBOJNÍCKA CHATA (1,960m) - PRIELOM (2,288m) - POĽSKÝ HREBEŇ (2,200m) - SLIEZSKY DOM (1,678m) - TATRANSKÁ POLIANKA (1,010m)

Grade: strenuous **Distance: 17.5km** **Average gradient: 15%**
Height gain: 1,003m **Height loss: 1,278m** **Time: 8h 15m**
Refreshments: Zbojnícka Chata, Sliezsky Dom, Tatranská Polianka

Take funicular from Starý Somokovec N to Hrebienok, then follow sections:
0930B (red) 1.5km NW to Kamzík;
2907 (blue) 5km NW to Zbojnícka Chata, and 2km W to Prielom (*);
5806 (green) (*) 0.5km SW to Poľský Hrebeň, and 3.5km SE to Sliezsky Dom, and 5km SE to Tatranská Polianka.
Optional alternatives:
a) From Hrebienok follow 5807 (green) NW to Vodopád Studeného Potoka, then 2907 (blue) as before - this makes little difference to the distance, adds a little climbing, and allows a view of the waterfall.
b) From Sliezsky Dom follow 5806 (green) and 8858 (yellow) to Starý Smokovec (total 17km).

Optional side-trip: From Poľský Hrebeň on 8857 (yellow) E to Východna Vysoká (2,428m) would add 1km, 228m of climbing and 1h 15m.

The crossing of the Prielom saddle is one of the most exciting parts of the waymarked network, with fixed chains and exposed situations. The route is less strenuous in this direction, providing less height gain, but anyone feeling nervous about the descent from Prielom may find the opposite direction more comfortable.

16) HREBIENOK (1,285m) - ZAMKOVSKÉHO/NÁLEPKOVA CHATA (1,475m) - TÉRYHO CHATA (2,013m) - PRIEČNE SEDLO (2,352m) ZBOJNÍCKA CHATA (1,960m) - HREBIENOK (1,285m)

Grade: strenuous   **Distance:** 18km   **Average gradient:** 15%
Height gain: 1,067m   **Height loss:** 1,067m   **Time:** 8h 00m
Refreshments: Zamkovského Chata, Téryho Chata, Zbojnícka Chata, Hrebienok

Take funicular from Starý Smokovec N to Hrebienok, then follow sections:
0930B (red) 1.5km NW to Kamzík, and 1.5km NE to Zamkovského/Nálepkova Chata;
5812 (green) 3.5km NW to Téryho Chata;
8860 (yellow) (*) 1.5km W to Priečne Sedlo, and 3.5km SW (*) to Zbojnícka Chata;
2907 (blue) 5km SE to Kamzík;
0930B (red) 1.5km SE to Hrebienok.

A well used route linking two popular chalets via an exciting saddle. The route must be followed in this direction, since there is one-way traffic on the chain at Priečne Sedlo.

17) HREBIENOK (1,285m) - ZAMKOVSKÉHO/NÁLEPKOVA CHATA (1,475m) - TÉRYHO CHATA (2,013m) - SEDIELKO (2,372m) - JAVOROVÁ DOLINA - JAVORINA (1,018m)

Grade: strenuous   **Distance: 20.5km**   **Average gradient: 12%**
Height gain: 1,087m   **Height loss: 1,354m**   **Time: 7h 45m**
Refreshments: Zamkovského Chata, Téryho Chata, Javorina

Take the funicular from Starý Smokovec N to Hrebienok, then follow sections:
0930B (red) 1.5km NW to Kamzík, and 1.5km NE to Zamkovského/Nálepkova Chata;
5812 (green) 3.5km NW to Téryho Chata, and on 2km to Sedielko;
5812 (green) 12km along Zadná Dolina and Javorová Dolina to Javorina.
    A testing route which is not difficult but includes some very steep sections. It is recommended in this direction to reduce the amount of ascent. Sedielko should be avoided if there is much snow, as it can then be dangerous.

18) TATRANSKÁ LOMNICA - CABLEWAY - SKALNATÉ PLESO (1,761m) - ZAMKOVSKÉHO/NÁLEPKOVA CHATA (1,475m) - HREBIENOK (1,285m) - STARÝ SMOKOVEC (1,010m)

Grade: easy   **Distance: 6.5km**   **Average gradient: 11%**
Height gain: nil   **Height loss: 751m**   **Time: 2h 30m**
Refreshments: Skalnaté Pleso, Zamkovského Chata, Hrebienok, Starý Smokovec

From Tatranská Lomnica take the cable-car (arrive as early as possible) or gondola NW to Encián, then follow sections:
0930B (red) 2.25km SW to Zamkovského/Nálepkova Chata, and a further 2km S to Hrebienok;
5807 (green) 2km S to Starý Smokovec.
    The last section (5807) can be avoided if required by taking the funicular from Hrebienok to Starý Smokovec.
    Downhill nearly all the way, mostly in dwarf pine and forest, but with some fine viewpoints and several refreshment opportunities. This section of the Tatranská Magistrála is an "instructional path" - the information boards are translated in the path description for 0930B.
    With an early start, you can include a side-trip by cable-car from Skalnaté Pleso to the summit of Lomnický Štít, though space is limited and you should be there early to get a good place in the queue. Note that the extension of green route 5808 from Skalnaté Pleso to Lomnické Sedlo, shown on older maps, is no longer accessible on the waymarked system.

19) TATRANSKÁ LOMNICA - CABLEWAY - SKALNATÉ PLESO (1,761m) - VEĽKÁ SVIŠŤOVKA (2,037m) - ZELENÉ PLESO (1,551m) - VELKÉ BIELE PLESO (1,600m) - TATRANSKÁ LOMNICA (860m)

Grade: moderate (but with one short fixed chain)
Distance: 16.5km   Average gradient: 10% Height gain: 276m
Height loss: 1,177m   Time: 6h 30m
Refreshments: Skalnaté Pleso, Zelené Pleso, Tatranské Matliare

From Skalnaté Pleso cable-car station follow sections:
0930A (red) 2.5km N to Veľká Svišťovka, and 2km NW (*) to Zelené Pleso;
0930A (red) 2km NE to Veľké Biele Pleso;
2911 (blue) 4.5km SE to Salviový Prameň, and 2km further to junction with 8861 (yellow);
2911 (blue) 2km S to Tatranské Matliare (Metalurg);
8864 (yellow) 1.5km SW to Tatranská Lomnica
Optional alternatives; From Zelené Pleso take 8861 (yellow) 3.5km E then SE to junction, then 5809 (green) 1km S to junction, then 2908 (blue) 3.5km SW to Štart, then 5808 (green) 3km SE to Grandhotel Praha and 0.5km SW to Tatranská Lomnica (total 16km).
Taking yellow route 8861 from Šalviový Prameň to Biela Voda for the bus saves one hour.
Using a section of the Tatranská Magistrála, this popular route includes the minor summit of Velká Svišťovka with its outstanding views over the valleys and "green lake", and of surrounding summits. The zigzag descent to Zelené Pleso includes a short section of fixed chain, with only minimal exposure.

20) TATRANSKÁ LOMNICA (860m) - ŠTART (1,140m) - ZELENÉ PLESO (1,551m) - VEĽKÉ BIELE PLESO (1,600m) - TATRANSKÁ KOTLINA (765m)

Grade: moderate   Distance: 23.5km   Average gradient: 10%
Height gain: 740m   Height loss: 835m   Time: 7h 00m
Refreshments: Zelené Pleso, Tatranská Kotlina

From Tatranská Lomnica railway station follow sections:
5808 (green) 0.5km NE to Grandhotel Praha, then 3km NW to Štart;
2908 (blue) 3.5km NE to junction with 5809 (green);
5809 (green) 1km N to junction with 8861 (yellow);
8861 (yellow) 3.5km NW to Zelené Pleso;
0930A (red) 2km NE to Veľké Biele Pleso;
5810 (green) 5km E to Plesnivec, and 3km SE to junction with 2909 (blue);
2909 (blue) 2km NE to Tatranská Kotlina.

Optional alternatives: Take the cable-car to the halfway point at Štart, saving nearly 300m of ascent.

Use blue/yellow routes 2911/8861 to Biela Voda for the bus, saving 1h 30m.

Mostly in forest, but with the beautiful Zelené Pleso and the haunting Veľké Biele Pleso as fine targets.

21) BIELA VODA (925m) - ZELENÉ PLESO (1,551m) - TATRANSKÁ LOMNICA (860m)

Grade: easy   **Distance: 16km**   **Average gradient: 8%**
Height gain: 626m   **Height loss: 691m**   **Time: 5h 45m**
Refreshments: Chata pri Zelenom Plese, Tatranské Matliare, Tatranská Lomnica

From Biela Voda (bus, 2.5km NE of Tatranská Lomnica) follow sections:
8861A (yellow) 3km NW to Šalviový Prameň;
8861B (yellow) 4km NW to Zelené Pleso;
8861B (yellow) 4km SE to Šalviový Prameň;
8861A (yellow) 1.5km SE to junction with route 2911 (blue);
2911 (blue) 2km S to Tatranské Matliare (Metalurg);
8864 (yellow) 1.5km SW to Tatranská Lomnica.
The quickest and easiest route to and from one of the most beautiful lakes in the Tatras.

22) BIELA VODA (925m) - ZELENÉ PLESO (1,551m) - KOLOVÉ SEDLO (2,118m) - JAHŇACÍ ŠTÍT (2,229m) and return

Grade: strenuous   **Distance: 19km**   **Average gradient: 15%**
Height gain: 1,304m   **Height loss: 1,304m**   **Time: 9h 15m**
Refreshments: Zelené Pleso

From Biela Voda (bus, 2.5km NE of Tatranská Lomnica) follow sections:
8861A (yellow) 3km NW to Šalviový Prameň; and 4km NW to Zelené Pleso;
8861C (yellow) 2.5km NW to Kolové Sedlo and Jahňací Štít.
Return by same route.
This route is not difficult but provides outstanding views, including the "green lake" and a full panorama of the White Tatras from Jahňací Štít.

23) BIELA VODA (925m) - VEĽKÉ BIELE PLESO (1,600m) - KOPSKÉ SEDLO (1,749m) - JAVORINA (1,018m)

Grade: moderate   **Distance: 17.5km**   **Average gradient: 10%**
Height gain: 824m   **Height loss: 731m**   **Time: 5h 45m**
Refreshments: Javorina (also Zelené Pleso on optional alternative)

From Biela Voda (bus, 2.5km NE of Tatranská Lomnica) follow sections:
8861A (yellow) 3km NW to Šalviový Prameň;
2911 (blue) 4.5km NW to Veľké Biele Pleso, and 1.5km further to Kopské Sedlo;
2911 (blue) 6km NW along Zadné Meďodoly to Pod Muráňom, and 2km further
to Javorina.

Optional alternative: From Šalviový Prameň, continue on 8861A (yellow)
4km NW to Zelené Pleso, then 2km NE on 0930A (red) to Veľké Biele Pleso (adds
1.5km).

This route provides opportunities to cross the range with no difficult
sections, and to use one of the few paths that touch the White Tatras.

**There are many other possibilities and variations, using the waymarked
network. Use the diagram inside the front cover of this book, together
with your walking map, to devise your own routes. All the paths are
described in the Path Descriptions chapter.**

WITH A GUIDE
**The following route suggestions all require the services of a mountain
guide.** They all include substantial sections off the waymarked routes, and
nearly all involve to some extent a degree of exposure (in some cases very
exposed), scrambling and use of chains and other iron fixtures. These routes
should only be attempted by experienced mountain walkers, with a good head
for heights, who know that they can cope with such situations. Usually a very
early start from the resort is necessary (around 5 or even 4 am), to avoid the
crowds on the mountain lifts, and to complete the ascent before the possibility
of thunderstorms. The times shown are for the guided section only; to these,
in most cases, you must add the walks from and to the resort (see Timings
section).

24) SATAN (2,416m)

Grade: strenuous   **Distance: 14km**   **Average gradient: 15%**
Height gain: 1,072m   **Height loss: 1,072m**   **Time: 6h 00m**
Refreshments: Štrbské Pleso, Popradské Pleso
Guide meeting point: Štrbské Pleso

This is one of the easiest guided routes, with no chains or scrambling. From

Štrbské Pleso you follow yellow route 8853 up Mlynická Dolina past Vodopád Skok, then about 1km further divert east to Nižne Kozie Pleso to use a rocky corridor to Satan's north summit. The return is by one of several routes eastward into Mengusovská Dolina, where you can go to either Popradské Pleso or Štrbské Pleso for refreshment.

25) VYSOKÁ (2,560m)

Grade: difficult   **Distance: 16km**   **Average gradient: 14%**
Height gain: 1,100m   **Height loss: 1,100m**   **Time: 7h 00m**
Refreshments: Popradské Pleso, Chata pod Rysmi
Guide meeting point: Popradské Pleso

This is one of the most testing guided routes. Vysoká has two tops - the lower of these at 2,526m is sometimes erroneously shown as the highest altitude. From here you have outstanding views over most of the High and White Tatras. From Popradské Pleso the route goes immediately off the waymarked network north-east up Zlomisková Dolina, then shortly north up a side valley, over Dračie Sedlo (Dragon Pass, beside Zlomisková Veža). At the end of a long gully you come to a 40-metre wall with chains and rungs, after which it is just 100 easy metres to the top. Your descent takes you further north-west along another gully to a natural rock arch and a ledge, which leads to Kohútik (Little Cock). A 50-metre chain takes you down to a path leading to Sedlo Váha on red route 0933, from where you can make an optional diversion to Rysy summit before descending to Chata pod Rysmi.

26) GERLACHOVSKÝ ŠTÍT (2,655m)

Grade: difficult   **Distance: 15km**   **Average gradient: 22%**
Height gain: 1,655m   **Height loss: 1,655m**   **Time: 7h 00m**
Refreshments: Sliezsky Dom
Guide meeting point: Sliezsky Dom

A chance to stand at the highest point in the Carpathians! From Sliezsky Dom you use an unwaymarked path north-west, which traverses beneath Kotlový Štít. You come to a gully with 100 metres of chains and rungs to reach a pass called Sedielko nad Kotlom (2,450m), then traverse with great exposure over several gullies to another pass (Štrbina v Kotlovom, 2,580m), finally ascending another gully to approach the summit from the east, with some scrambling. The descent is to the south, almost immediately using a 25-metre chain below the summit before following one of two gullies. These lead to a 200-metre section of chains and rungs which bring you into Batizovská Dolina, then Batizovské Pleso on red route 0930 (Tatranská Magistrála). From here you can either return to Sliezsky Dom, or continue to Popradské Pleso and Štrbské Pleso, or descend directly to Vyšné Hágy.

27) BRADAVICA (2,476m)

Grade: strenuous	**Distance: 12km**	**Average gradient: 14%**
Height gain: 813m	**Height loss: 813m**	**Time: 6h 00m**
Refreshments: Sliezsky Dom		
Guide meeting point: Sliezsky Dom		

This route has no chains, but on one section you may have to be roped up. Bradavica has four summits, though it is usually the south-easternmost that is ascended. From Sliezsky Dom you ascend Velická Dolina on green route 5806 to Kvetnica. You then climb a gully for 150m to a minor summit called Rohatá Veža, and go through a natural rock arch. A very narrow path leads to a ridge, which is easily followed to the top. There are several descent possibilities, none of them very difficult.

28) ŠIROKÁ VEŽA (2,461m)

Grade: strenuous	**Distance: 14km**	**Average gradient: 17%**
Height gain: 1,198m	**Height loss: 1,198m**	**Time: 7h 00m**
Refreshments: Zamkovského Chata, Téryho Chata, Zbojnícka Chata		
Guide meeting point: Hrebienok or Skalnaté Pleso		

This summit lies only a short distance off yellow route 8860, and would make a comparatively easy introduction to chains and scrambling under the watchful eyes of a guide, for those who feel a little nervous about the idea. From Hrebienok or Skalnaté Pleso, you follow red route 0930 to Zamkovského Chata, then green 5812 to Téryho Chata, and yellow 8860 to Priečne Sedlo, where the chains are encountered. From the saddle you divert up to Široká Veža, with some scrambling. The descent from Priečne Sedlo is on yellow 8860 south-west to Zbojnícka Chata (more chains), then blue 2907 south-east to Hrebienok.

29) PROSTREDNÝ HROT (2,440m)

Grade: difficult	**Distance: 14km**	**Average gradient: 17%**
Height gain: 1,177m	**Height loss: 1,177m**	**Time: 7h 00m**

Refreshments: Hrebienok, Zamkovského Chata, Téryho Chata.
Guide meeting point: Hrebienok or Skalnaté Pleso

Though it has no chains, this route is very steep, and very exposed in places, but you are rewarded with outstanding views. From Hrebienok or Skalnaté Pleso as in route suggestion 28 to Téryho Chata. From there you ascend a steep gully south-west to Sedlo pod Prostredným Hrotom (the saddle below Prostredný Hrot), then follow a very narrow ridge to the summit. You can descend either by the same route, or continue south on an exposed zigzag path, where you may have to be roped up, into Veľká Studená Dolina for blue route 2907 to Hrebienok.

30) ĽADOVÝ ŠTÍT (2,627m)

Grade: difficult   **Distance:** 18km   **Average gradient:** 15%
Height gain: 1,364m   **Height loss:** 1,364m   **Time:** 9h 00m
Refreshments: Hrebienok, Zamkovského Chata, Téryho Chata
Guide meeting point: Hrebienok or Skalnaté Pleso

In some references you may see the altitude of this peak as 2,528m, which is wrong. From Hrebienok or Skalnaté Pleso as in route suggestion 28 to Téryho Chata, then you divert from the waymarked route to pass the tarns at the head of Malá Studená Dolina, to ascend a steep zigzag path to Sedlo Ľadová Priehyba. You follow a very narrow ridge for 20 minutes - not difficult but very exposed in places and you may have to be roped up - to the summit. To descend you continue a little further along the ridge to a section which is in effect a Grade 2 climb, where you are roped up for 100 metres. This leads to a gully which you follow down to Sedielko and green route 5812.

31) BARANIE ROHY (2,526m)

Grade: difficult   **Distance:** 17km   **Average gradient:** 15%
Height gain: 1,263m   **Height loss:** 1,263m   **Time:** 8h 00m
Refreshments: Hrebienok, Zamkovského Chata, Téryho Chata
Guide meeting point: Hrebienok or Skalnaté Pleso

The ascent is not difficult, though exposed in places. From Hrebienok or Skalnaté Pleso as in route suggestion 28 to Téryho Chata, then you go round the second of the Five Spiš Tarns and ascend a zigzag path to Baranie Sedlo (2,393m) - this was once a waymarked route, but it has been withdrawn from the network. You follow a gully to the left, then ascend rock fields to the summit. The descent is by the same route; alternatively another route continues north-east into Veľká Zmrzlá Dolina and Zelené Pleso, but this adds 9km and 2 hours.

32) LOMNICKÝ ŠTÍT (2,632m)

Grade: strenuous   **Distance: 4/12km**   **Average gradient: 11%**
Height gain: 442m   **Time: 2h 30m/7h 00m**
Refreshments: Skalnaté Pleso, Lomnický Štít
Guide meeting point: Tatranská Lomnica (cable-car station) or Skalnaté Pleso

Although Lomnický Štít is accessible by cable-car, you will have the satisfaction of reaching the second highest summit in the Tatras under your own power. You must not attempt to undertake this route without a guide, because the route is difficult to find in places, and you could otherwise land yourself in trouble. From Skalnaté Pleso, you continue by chair-lift to Lomnické Sedlo (2,190m), then walk up the ridge to the summit of Lomnický Štít (1h 30m). It is mostly an easy scramble, but there are also some long fixed chains and a ladder to negotiate. A very challenging route can be taken from Hrebienok via Bachledové Sedlo - this takes 6 hours, and involves a steep gully, an exposed ridge traverse, 200 metres of steep and exposed chains to another ridge which is easily followed to Lomnický Štít. The descent back to Lomnické Sedlo takes an hour, or you can take the cable-car direct to Skalnaté Pleso.

SLOVAK HIGH TATRAS: PATH DESCRIPTIONS

CESTA SLOBODY
Before we start on the paths themselves, a word about **Cesta Slobody** (Liberty Highway), since you may find it useful as a walking route to return to your accommodation, rather than take the train or bus. If you need a change from the mountains, or in bad weather, it could make an interesting easy walk in its own right, passing several places of interest.

The road was so named in 1918, to celebrate the foundation of the then Czechoslovak Republic. It has been modernised from time to time, and you will come across old sections that have been by-passed and left for the use of local traffic, or sometimes just pedestrians.

A hard surfaced footway parallels Cesta Slobody for some 18 kilometres from Vyšné Hágy to Tatranské Matliare, via Nová Polianka, Tatranská Polianka, Tatranské Zruby, the Smokovec community, Tatranská Lesná and Tatranská Lomnica. Whilst it is sometimes beside the traffic, it often meanders away from the road into the trees, or uses the old road before it was straightened.

TATRANSKÁ MAGISTRÁLA

This grand route provides an opportunity to feast your eyes on a whole variety of typical High Tatras scenes. Called in Slovak Tatranská Magistrála (Tatras Highway), it is the only substantial "red route" in the Slovak High Tatras (the others are short routes to summits).

The Magistrála parallels the main High Tatras ridge on its south side. So, when climbing from the resorts, you are bound to cross it, and will recognise it by the white-red-white horizontally banded waymarks. It has the lowest reference number of all the Slovak High Tatras routes (0930), and therefore starts off our Path Descriptions chapter. Because it is so long, we have divided it into seven sections, as shown below. We depart from our usual west-east policy here, since anyone wishing to follow the entire route will find it easier to start in the east where it is higher.

A) Veľké Biele Pleso - Skalnaté Pleso (for Tatranská Lomnica)
B) Skalnaté Pleso - Hrebienok (for Starý Smokovec)
C) Hrebienok - Sliezsky Dom
D) Sliezsky Dom - Popradské Pleso   F) Štrbské Pleso - Tri Studničky
E) Popradské Pleso - Štrbské Pleso   G) Tri Studničky - Podbanské

Fully opened in 1937, the Magistrála was the idea of the KČST (Klub Československych Turistov). Switchbacking along the southern slopes of the whole High Tatras range, Tatranská Magistrála now runs for 45 kilometres from Veľké Biele Pleso in the east, a tarn below the pass of Kopské Sedlo where the High Tatras give way to the White Tatras, to Podbanské, a village at the west end. On the way it passes other places which receive a mention in our gazetteer: Zelené Pleso, Skalnaté Pleso, Zamkovského Chata, Poľana Kamzík, Hrebienok, Velické Pleso, Batizovské Pleso, Popradské Pleso, Štrbské Pleso, Jamské Pleso, Tri Studničky.

Until 1978, when the White Tatras were put out of bounds to tourists, it continued on up to Kopské Sedlo and Hlúpy, then turned right to follow the ridge of the White Tatras to Skalné Vráta, before descending to finish at Tatranská Kotlina.

The route ranges in altitude from 940m at Podbanské to 2,020m at Sedlo pod Svišťovkou, a col close to the east end. At two points you come close to a minor summit: Ostrva (1,926m) and Veľká Svišťovka (2,037m), both of which can be reached by a short diversion.

Much of the route passes through the forest belt, but there are frequent open areas providing some of the best views across the Sub-Tatras Basin to the Low Tatras. Sometimes as you round a bend your breath is taken away by the magnificent sight of a clear tarn reflecting in almost mirror perfection the backdrop of a craggy Tatra peak. Tarns are a regular feature - the route links twelve, of varying sizes.

Using the fixed chain at Priečne Sedlo

Veľká Studená Dolina
Starolesnianské Pleso near Zbojnicka Chata

Separate sections of the Magistrála can be used to link routes from or to the resorts. While in general it offers fairly easy walking, there are several airy stretches across open rock, with some scrambling - these are pointed out in the path descriptions.

There is no lack of refreshment opportunities, since the Magistrála passes by or close to no fewer than four mountain chalets (Chata pri Zelenom Plese, Zamkovského Chata, Bilíkova Chata, Chata Kapitána Rašu), two mountain hotels (Sliezsky Dom, Chata Kapitána Morávku) and two cafeterias (Skalnaté Pleso, Hrebienok), as well as the villages of Štrbské Pleso and Podbanské.

The route is much higher at the east end than at the west end, so in general it is better to walk it from east to west. For this reason we have departed from our general west-east policy, which also happens to fit in with the numerical sequence of the information boards on our Section B (Skalnaté Pleso to Hrebienok), which is described on the maps as an "instructional path".

However, the route ascends and descends several times, alternatively dropping down into the valleys and rising up over passes and shoulders, so if you find it suits your plans better to walk from west to east, this may not make too much difference.

It takes around 15 hours of actual walking to cover the whole route - too much for one day, unless you are an exceptionally fit and experienced mountain walker. It is possible to do a tour along the whole route, though it would probably require $2^1/_2$ days. It is virtually impossible to book accommodation at the chalets at short notice, so for some nights you would probably have to come down to the resorts. This could be done by mountain lifts at Skalnaté Pleso (for Tatranská Lomnica) and Hrebienok (for Starý Smokovec).

A possible itinerary for such a tour, with two overnight stops at Starý Smokovec and Štrbské Pleso, would be:

Day 1: Bus to Biela Voda; walk to Veľké Biele Pleso to join Tatranská Magistrála to Hrebienok; funicular railway (or walk) down to Starý Smokovec (total walking time 6h 45m-7h 30m).

Day 2: Rack railway to Hrebienok; Tatranská Magistrála to Štrbské Pleso (total walking time 7h 15m).

Day 3: Tatranská Magistrála to Podbanské (infrequent buses back to other resorts; total walking time 3h 45m).

If you book early, overnight accommodation - sometimes only in dormitories - may be available at (with approximate walking times from the previous place in hours and minutes): Chata pri Zelenom Plese (3h 15m from Biela Voda via Veľké Biele Pleso), Zamkovského Chata (2h 45m), Bilíkova Chata (0h 45m), Sliezsky Dom (2h 00m), Popradské Pleso (3h 30m), Štrbské Pleso (1h 00m), Chata Kapitána Rašu (2h 15m) and Podbanské (1h 30m).

RED ROUTES

The main red route is the 45-kilometre Tatranská Magistrála (number 0930) - see above. Because it is so long, we have divided it into seven sections (0930A to 0930G), and these are described in the direction which is most recommended, ie. that which involves the least climbing. The other red routes are short ones to the summits of western High Tatras peaks.

Note: Red routes 0860 in the Western Tatras, and 0906 in the Spišská Magura, shown on some maps, are outside the scope of this book.

0930A: SKALNATÉ PLESO (1,751m) - VEĽKÁ SVIŠŤOVKA (2,037m) - ZELENÉ PLESO (1,545m) - VEĽKÉ BIELE PLESO (1,620m)

Grade: strenuous   Distance: 6km   Average gradient: 15%
S-N Height gain: 361m/loss 492m   Time: 2h 30m
N-S Height gain: 492m/loss 361m   Time: 3h 00m
Winter/spring: closed from Skalnaté Pleso; open from Zelené Pleso to Veľké Biele Pleso

The map indicates that this part of the route should be done from north to south - this makes using the one short length of chain easier by ascending it, and if you thus feel more comfortable you are advised to go north to south. However this seems to be generally ignored, and the majority of walkers go south to north for less height gain.

Most of this route is in open country with excellent views. It is very rocky - watch your step all the time! Some high parts are slightly exposed, and a short section through a gully is very steep and rocky, with fixed chains for support. Note: the section between Zelené Pleso and Veľká Svišťovka is closed from November to June inclusive.

From **Skalnaté Pleso** cable-car station (1,751m) go right to follow red waymarks (Tatranská Magistrála). The path climbs steeply at first above the tarn, then turns right to contour at around 1,900m for some time, with excellent views down to Tatranská Lomnica and Tatranské Matliare, and over the Sub-Tatras Basin. After crossing a stream it starts to climb steeply again to Sedlo pod Svišťovkou (Saddle below Svišťovka, 2,023m). The minor summit of **Veľká Svišťovka** (2,037m) is but a short distance to the east, and while it is not strictly accessible to walkers, being off the waymarked route, everybody seems to go there! (50-75 minutes)

From Sedlo pod Svišťovkou, the path continues at first on a well constructed but narrow ledge, with a long drop below. You pass a great lone slab of rock which makes a good background for photographs, then descend a long series of zigzags down a steep shoulder, with the green tarn of Zelené Pleso providing a subtly changing backdrop at each turn. There is a slight sense of exposure at

Veľké Biele Pleso (photo: Ian Mitchell)

some of the turns, where care is needed on crumbly rock, and to spot the waymarks. You eventually come to a rocky gully, which requires a scramble, but with minimal exposure and fixed chains for support. Below this the path levels out through dwarf pine, and passes a couple of small tarns before reaching **Zelené Pleso** (1,545m). (50-75 minutes)

From Chata pri Zelenom Plese the route continues north-eastwards, climbing gently through dwarf pine. Over to your right, you can clearly see the long zigzag path which brought you down from Svišťovka. You reach Trojrohé Pleso (Three Horned Tarn) - a lonely tarn, like a Scottish lochan, nestling in a hollow. Here you have a beautiful view of the White Tatras, with the triple-humped Košiare (2,011m) prominent. Finally you cross a wooden bridge over the tinkling brook called Kežmarská Biela Voda to reach **Velké Biele Pleso** (1,620m). (30 minutes)

0930B: SKALNATÉ PLESO (1,761m) - ZAMKOVSKÉHO CHATA (1,475m) - HREBIENOK (1,285m)

Grade: moderate	Distance: 4.5km	Average gradient: 11%
N-S Height loss: 476m	Time: 1h 30m	
S-N Height gain: 476m	Time: 2h 00m	
Winter/spring: open		

*This section is also an "instructional path", enhanced by interpretation boards telling you something about the territory you are passing - all in Slovak! Help is at hand, though: a summarised translation of each board appears below. Before you set off from **Skalnaté Pleso** (1,761m), go down to have a look at the tarn and the astronomical institute.*

From the exit at the top of the cable-car and gondola-lift from Tatranská Lomnica, go left (bearing 195) for a few hundred metres to the shell of Skalnatá Chata. Continue through open mountainside, passing Slnečá Vyhliadka (Sunny Viewpoint), where you can look out over Stará Lesna village, Poprad town and the Sub-Tatras Basin. You follow a narrow path, which at first contours at about 1,700m, then drops steeply through trees after 2km and swings round on bearing 320 to **Zamkovského Chata** (formerly Nálepkova Chata, 1,475m, refreshments). Green route 5812 joins here. (45 minutes)

From the door of Zamkovského Chata follow the path ahead (bearing 180) for 300m, dropping steeply to 1,400m. The path then swings right (bearing 270) to undulate at about this level, crossing by bridges over two streams fairly close together - both are branches of Malý Studený Potok - the second is the main one.

At the second bridge is **Obrovský Vodopád** (Giant's Waterfall). Shortly afterwards, the path drops steeply again and gradually bears left, eventually to bearing 140, and crosses a larger stream, Veľký Studeny Potok. Blue route 2907 joins here. Continuing in broadly the same direction, you first come to **Poľana Kamzík,** then progress downwards for a further 1km to reach the intersection with yellow route 8859 and **Hrebienok** (1,285m, refreshments). (45 minutes)

If you are starting from Hrebienok, the route to Skalnaté Pleso starts from behind the ski-slope control tower.

Now here is a summary of what it says on the boards:

1) The former chalet called Skalnatá Chata (now closed) stands on the site of the original shelter comprising a huge rock slab under which travellers could sleep. In 1877 the space was bricked up to provide more protection, and by 1918 this had been replaced by a concrete building.

2) You are crossing the ski-piste from Lomnické Sedlo to Štart - it is 2,000 metres long, with a drop of 990 metres. This area offers good winter sports possibilities, and the most important ski events in the High Tatras are held here. The barriers you can see are a protection against avalanches. Remember that you can only walk on the waymarked paths - please do not walk on the ski-piste or other areas.

3) This area is inhabited by marmots - large brown rodents related to squirrels, but more like badgers in shape and size. They dig burrows in which they hibernate; can be identified by their piercing, bird-like cry; and can sometimes be seen basking on rocks in the sun. Chamois and the rare rock eagle may also be seen here.

4) This area, called Škaredý Žľab (Ugly Gully), is particularly avalanche-prone in winter, and you can easily identify here several forms of erosion caused not only by them but by the combination of wind, water and the sun's heat. There are over 300 regular avalanche lines in the High Tatras.

5) The vegetation here is mainly dwarf pine, which helps to stabilise the mountainside and prevent erosion. Much of the mountainside that is now pasture was formerly covered by dwarf pine. Other trees and plants in this area include limba-fir, rowan, bilberries, wild raspberries, juniper, gentian, broom, greater woodrush and smallreed.

6) This is called Slnečná Vyhliadka (Sunny Viewpoint) with good reason. You are standing at 1,540m on the southern ridge that descends from Lomnický Štít, with an excellent view to the west of Veľká and Malá Studená Dolina (Great and Little Cold Valleys). The names hark back to the glacier that formed these valleys: at its greatest extent it was 220m thick and 9.8km long. As it receded, many tarns were formed. You are also at the upper limit of the pine forest zone; here the vegetation most commonly found is birch, rowan, willow and goat willow.

7) We are passing the upper forest zone where the trees grow to 15 metres. They include pine, limba-fir, larch, birch and rowan. Also to be found are greater woodrush, black honeysuckle, wood sorrel, purple coltsfoot, broad buckler fern, ragwort and hawkweed.

8) There is an inversion of the usual vegetation zones here. The glacier gouged out the mountainside, leaving great rock walls; the rock was then split by frost and tumbled downhill, resulting in ground suitable for dwarf pine at a lower level than usual. Further up, a zone of ordinary pine can be found.

9) The two streams near here (Veľký and Malý Studený Potok - see number 6) originate from springs at 2,128m and 2,017m respectively. The main stream is 19km long and its water is very pure. Salmon, common and brook trout, and bullhead swim in it. The birds on the bank include the dipper and white wagtail.

0930C: SLIEZSKY DOM (1,663m) - HREBIENOK (1,285m)

Grade: moderate (but with a short scramble)

Distance: 7km	Average gradient: 6%
W-E Height loss: 378m	Time: 1h 45m
E-W Height gain: 378m	Time: 2h 00m

Winter/spring: open (but a short section of scrambling requires care if icy)

This section, with exceptional views over to the Low Tatras, starts from outside

Sliezsky Dom hotel beside Velické Pleso (1,663m). At first you wind among scrub and rocks ahead (bearing 85) for a few hundred metres, then turn right (bearing 120) on a narrow path which climbs in 2km to 1,700m at Slavkovsky Pleso.

The tarn lies a little to the left of the path; the minor peak immediately above is Senná Kopa (1,848m); the great mass of **Slavkovský Štít** rears above that; and behind you is the Gerlach massif.

From the tarn, the path descends steadily for 3km to the junction with blue route 2906 (Starý Smokovec - Slavkovský Štít) and a further 1km to **Hrebienok.** On the way you must negotiate a short, steep stretch of path which involves scrambling and is a little exposed in places. It is mostly downwards, so if you prefer to scramble up, follow this section E-W. There is a good view of the Smokovec villages and Poprad from here.

If starting from Hrebienok, take the path between the big Ski Club hut (with cafe and giant scoreboard) and a white building.

0930D: SLIEZSKY DOM (1,663m) - OSTRVA (1,926m) - BATIZOVSKÉ PLESO (1,879m) - POPRADSKÉ PLESO (1,494m)

Grade: strenuous   Distance: 8.5km
Average gradient: 8% (but Ostrva to Popradské Pleso is 29%)
E-W Height gain: 263m/loss: 432m   Time: 3h 00m
W-E Height gain: 432m/loss: 263m   Time: 3h 30m
Winter/spring: closed (this sometimes applies in summer if there have been heavy snowfalls)

One of the tougher sections of the Tatranská Magistrála, especially if starting from Popradské Pleso. It is mostly above the tree-line, so you have constant views over the Sub-Tatras Basin, and you pass lonely Batizovské Pleso below Gerlachovský Štít.

From Sliezsky Dom by **Velické Pleso** the path contours at about 1,650m through dwarf pine and rock, then descends a little to the junction with route 8856 (yellow) - named on the signpost as Rázcestie pod Suchým (the junction below Suchý Vrch) at 1,720m. (30-35 minutes)

You then climb the shoulder of Suchý Vrch (Dry Hill), with views behind across the plain to Poprad town, up to **Batizovské Pleso** at 1,879m. (30-40 minutes)

From there, you descend gently for 10-15 minutes to the junction with yellow route 8855 (Rázcestie pod Končistou) at 1,850m, then follow a rocky, undulating path to the saddle (about 1,900m) below **Ostrva** (1,926m). The saddle has fine views, but can be very windy - there is more shelter at the summit. (70-80 minutes)

The path follows a long series of zigzags down the north slope of Ostrva to **Popradské Pleso.** (30-45 minutes)

0930E POPRADSKÉ PLESO (1,494m) - ŠTRBSKÉ PLESO (1,350m)

Grade: easy	**Distance: 4.5km**	**Average gradient: 4%**
N-S Height loss: 139m		**Time: 1h 15m**
S-N Height gain: 139m		**Time: 1h 25m**
Winter/spring: closed		

Starting from Chata Kapitána Morávku at **Popradské Pleso,** go past the kiosks and ascend to the junction with blue route 2902, and follow the red waymarks ahead. The path descends gently into the valley of **Mengusovská Dolina,** down which runs Hincov Potok, a trout-stream feeding the Poprad river. You cross this on a wooden footbridge, from which a charming view extends upstream. The large number of boulders in this area are the result of the frequent avalanches in winter - the reason for the closure of this path during that season! After climbing the south-eastern slope of Patria as far as about 1,500m, the path levels off and follows a ledge at this height for some time, with fine views across the valley. Soon after the path starts to descend, you reach the junction with green route 5805. (30-40 minutes)

Descend steadily to a point just before the road near Hotel Patria. Instead of joining the road, look for an inconspicuous white-red-white Magistrála waymark in the trees on your right, marking a path that leads steeply down to cross a stream by a wooden footbridge. Information boards tell you that dippers and woodpeckers may be seen in this area.

Now continue on to the main road, which you cross. Yellow route 8853 joins here and runs together with the Magistrála beside **Štrbské Pleso** tarn. Turn left along the tarnshore for Štrbské Pleso village. (See Gazetteer for directions on reaching the railway station from the tarn.)

If starting from Štrbské Pleso, look for the instructional sign at the north-east corner of the tarn - the route to Popradské Pleso starts from here.

0930F: ŠTRBSKÉ PLESO tarn (1,350m) - FURKOTSKÁ DOLINA (1,490m) - JAMSKÉ PLESO (1,447m) - TRI STUDNIČKY (1,140m)

Grade: easy	**Distance: 10km**	**Average gradient: 5%**
E-W Height gain: 140m/loss 350m		**Time: 2h 15m**
W-E Height gain: 350m/loss 140m		**Time: 2h 30m**
Winter/spring: open		

A gentle route, mostly in the forest zone, but passing the delightful Jamské Pleso, and with some good views over the plain.

The Tatranská Magistrála skirts the southern side of the tarn at **Štrbské Pleso.** Between the Kriváň and Solisko spa houses is a signpost, from which you follow the track with lamp-posts, rising into the forest on bearing 340.

The waymarking is a little patchy along here: ignore the coloured spots which indicate cross-country ski routes. At the fork of tracks, bear right, slightly uphill. At various track intersections, keep ahead.

After a little over 2km, mostly gently uphill, you pass the start of yellow route 8853. The Magistrála now continues upwards as a rough, stony track for a further 2km to the junction with route 2903 (blue) and the tarn of **Jamské Pleso** (1,447m).

The path contours beyond the tarn, initially on a narrow ledge, at around 1,500m for 2km. Then you come to a fork of tracks: ignore the obvious one that goes ahead downhill and take the one that contours round to the right through woodland. It soon starts to drop steeply and in another 2km you reach Chata Kapitána Rašu (1,180m, refreshments).

From the chalet you go down to the junction nearby with green route 5803; the two routes run together for several hundred metres, coming right down to the modern Cesta Slobody main road at one point. Follow the old road for a few hundred metres to visit the charming rural hamlet of **Tri Studničky** (1,140m).

0930G: TRI STUDNIČKY (1,140m) - PODBANSKÉ (940m)

Grade: easy	**Distance: 5km**	**Average gradient: 6%**
E-W Height gain: 35m/loss 235m		**Time: 1h 30m**
W-E Height gain: 235m/loss 35m		**Time: 2h 00m**
Winter/spring: open		

An easy route through the forest, but with some fine views of Kriváň, and of Bystrá, the highest Western Tatras peak.

From **Tri Studničky** (1,140m) you take the main track south for a short distance to the splendid hat-stand signpost, where you take a path up to the right into the woods, following the white-red-white Magistrála waymarks. Climbing gently for 1.5km, to about 1,175m, you eventually reach a new forest road, which may not be marked on your map. Turn left down the road for 100 metres, then turn right on to a path. Unfortunately when the forest road was built they omitted to re-paint red waymarks at the path junctions, but the great view of **Kriváň** up the road is some compensation.

You soon join a track heading downhill, passing a wooden shelter with a picnic table in a clearing. In a short distance you join another forest road, then when you reach a signpost beside another picnic table you turn right on to a track, with an enclosure nearby. After a few minutes, the track turns sharp left, then right at a loggers' clearing. Follow the track down to a meadow above the hamlet of **Nadbanské** (975m), and skirt the field to the road. This stretch is all well waymarked.

From Nadbanské you have a good view of two Western Tatras peaks, Kotlová (1,985m), and Bystrá (2,248m - highest in the Western Tatras); and another sighting of Kriváň behind you.

Turn right along the road through Nadbanské, then after bearing left in 100m turn right down a track to join the main road. Turn right on the path beside the road to cross the Belá river to **Podbanské** (940m, refreshments).

0931A: RÁZCESTIE POD TOMANOVOU DOLINOU (1,150m) - TOMANOVSKÉ SEDLO (1,686m)

Grade: moderate	Distance: 3.5km	Average gradient: 15%
E-W Height gain: 536m		Time: 1h 30m
W-E Height loss: 536m		Time: 1h 15m
Winter/spring: closed		

Rázcestie pod Tomanovou Dolinou means "the junction below Tomanová valley". Approaching from **Podbanské**, on reaching the junction you turn left and cross a bridge over Tomanovský Potok. The path leads at first through forest, then a meadow, before making a sharp left turn to climb steeply on a zigzag path through forest then dwarf pine beside the stream. You eventually reach the saddle on the border, Tomanovské Sedlo at 1,686m, with fine views both southwards over the tiny tarns which include Tomanovské Pleso, and westwards down the Polish Dolina Tomanowa to the refuge called Schronisko Ornak in the main valley of **Dolina Kościeliska.** A path descends into Poland, but remember that at present you are not allowed to cross into Poland.

0931B: RÁZCESTIE POD TOMANOVOU DOLINOU (1,150m) - ZADNÁ TICHÁ - SEDLO ZÁVORY (1,679m) - HLADKÉ SEDLO (1,994m)

Grade: moderate	Distance: 9km	Average gradient: 10%
W-E Height gain: 844m		Time: 2h 30m
E-W Height loss: 844m		Time: 2h 00m
Winter/spring: closed		

The first 2km of the route runs together with yellow 8851 on an asphalt road, as far as Rázcestie pod Kasprovým Vrchom. To your left are the rounded summits of the Červené Vrchy (Red Hills), the easternmost part of the Western

Tatras, accessible only from Poland. From the junction, the red route follows a track which is broad at first, then narrows as it climbs through meadows and thin forest into the upper part of Tichá Dolina (Zadná Tichá). Now on your right you can see the bulk of Veľká Kopa (2,052m) and its outlying minor summit, Magura (1,901m) - these form part of a finger of the High Tatras called Liptovské Kopy (the Stacks of Liptov). The main range of the High Tatras starts to your left, at **Ľaliové Sedlo.** The path becomes steeper, now through grass and rock, then swings left up to the broad saddle called Sedlo Závory (1,679m), where it is joined by green route 5801. Now you have a fairly moderate climb for an hour or so to **Hladké Sedlo** (Smooth Saddle; Gładka Przełecz in Polish), where the path ends at the border. From here you can see down into the beautiful **Dolina Pięciu Stawów Polskich** (Valley of Five Polish Tarns).

0932: RÁZCESTIE POD TEMNOSMREČINSKOU DOLINOU (1,580m) - NIŽNÉ TEMNOSMREČINSKÉ PLESO (1,674m)

Grade: easy	**Distance: 1.5km**	**Average gradient: 7%**
E-W Height gain: 94m		**Time: 1h 00m**
W-E Height loss: 94m		**Time: 0h 45m**
Winter/spring: closed		

Easy walking through Temnosmrečinská Dolina to the tarn of the same name. The path starts from the junction with green 5801, called Rázcestie pod Temnosmrečinskou Dolinou, at about 1,580m, here in forest. It very quickly reaches the dwarf pine for the remainder of the climb to the lower of the two quite large lakes, **Nižné Temnosmrečinské Pleso** at 1,647m. The waymarked route ends on its north-western shore - you cannot continue to the higher tarn. Shortly before the tarn, you can see far below to your right the waterfall called Vajanského Vodopád.

0933: RÁZCESTIE NAD ŽABÍM POTOKOM (1,600m) - RYSY (2,499m)

Grade: strenuous	**Distance: 4km**	**Average gradient: 23%**
SW-NE Height gain: 899m		**Time: 2h 45m**
NE-SW Height loss: 899m		**Time: 2h 00m**
Winter/spring: closed		

A popular route leading to Rysy, the highest summit on the waymarked route system, ie. for which you do not have to be accompanied by a mountain guide. It is strenuous and includes a fixed chain section, but is not difficult.

From blue route 2902, Rázcestie pod Žabím Potokom (junction above Frog Brook), the path climbs steeply, and quickly leaves the dwarf pine. A long series

Rysy summit (photo: Derek Goddard)

of zigzags leads to the southernmost of the Žabie Plesá (Frogs Tarns, 1,919m), then another set of zigzags including a great, steep slab of bare rock with two fixed chains (one up, the other down). More zigzags lead to **Chata pod Rysmi** (2,250m). (1h 45m).

The final section takes you first in just 15 minutes to the saddle called Váha (Weight, 2,337m) then on to the summit of **Rysy** (2,499m). (0h 30m). There are actually two summits - one each in Slovakia and Poland. Although you are allowed to visit either of these, you cannot continue on the path that descends into Poland.

0934: VYŠNÉ KÔPROVSKÉ SEDLO (2,180m) - KÔPROVSKÝ ŠTÍT (2,367m)

Grade: strenuous	**Distance: 1km**	**Average gradient: 19%**
S-N Height gain: 187m		**Time: 1h 30m**
N-S Height loss: 187m		**Time: 1h 30m**
Winter/spring: closed		

Kôprovský Štít is a comparatively easy summit to reach, with no fixed chains, and good views over three valleys - south-eastwards into Mengušovská Dolina, north-westwards into Temnosmrečinská Dolina, each with their tarns, and south-eastwards into Hlinská Dolina.

0935: CHATA POD SOLISKOM (1,830m) - PREDNÉ SOLISKO (2,093m)

Grade: moderate	Distance: 1.5km	Average gradient: 18%
S-N Height gain: 263m		Time: 0h 45m
N-S Height loss: 263m		Time: 0h 30m
Winter/spring: closed		

Predné Solisko is one of the easiest viewpoints to reach - especially if you use the chair-lift from Štrbské Pleso - so it can get very crowded. The route, which starts at the back of **Chata pod Soliskom,** is fairly steep, but boulders have been cleverly placed to provide steps for most of the way.

BLUE ROUTES
Note: Blue routes 2807 and 2809 in the Spišská Magura, and 2901 in the Western Tatras, shown on some High Tatras maps, are outside the scope of this book.

2836A: ŠTRBSKÉ PLESO (station 1,320m) - TATRANSKÁ ŠTRBA (900m) - STRBA (840m) - KOLESÁRKY (920m)

Grade: easy	Distance: 21km	Average gradient: 2%
N-S Height loss: 400m		Time: 1h 30m
S-N Height gain: 400m		Time: 1h 45m
Winter/spring: open		

A waymarked link between the High and Low Tatras, mostly on roads and beside the railway line. From **Štrbské Pleso** station, go left past the Panoráma Hotel where you join the track descending from the tarn. Turn left, downhill, and soon join the railway line as it passes under the road. You follow the line most of the way to **Tatranská Štrba,** crossing the road again in the forest, but at the next meeting with the road you turn left to cross the line and descend into the village. The route passes through Tatranská Štrba, and at the crossroads a branch leads off (right) to the station (called Štrba). It continues ahead down the road into the large village of **Štrba,** and on south to Suňava and eventually to Kolesárky in the Low Tatras.

2836B: ŠTRBSKÉ PLESO (1,350m) - CHATA POD SOLISKOM (1,830m) - FURKOTSKÁ DOLINA (1,800m)

Grade: moderate   Distance: 4km   Average gradient: 13%
SE-NW Height gain: 480m/loss 30m   Time: 1h 45m
NW-SE Height gain: 30m/loss 480m   Time: 1h 30m
Winter/spring: closed

A long, straight slog in the uphill direction, but this can be avoided by using the chair-lift which starts from beside the FIS Hotel 1km north of Štrbské Pleso. If you do decide to walk up, and need to make frequent stops to regain your breath, turn round for splendid views back over Štrbské Pleso tarn.

For instructions on reaching Štrbské Pleso tarn from the railway station, see the entry in the Gazetteer.

A blue arrow indicates the point where the path leaves the north-west corner of the tarn. After 50m, turn left (not waymarked), and you shortly reach a large clearing to your right. In winter this is abuzz with skiers and spectators, for it is the main practice area for **Štrbské Pleso**, the busiest ski resort in the Tatras, and nearby are two ski-jumps. Unless you are a keen student of winter sports architecture and rusty wire, you can ignore these and follow the ski-tow pylons for a long, straight, hard climb to the broad, cleared ski-piste. You will either be encouraged or frustrated by the sight of **Chata pod Soliskom,** which hovers endlessly above you. (60-90 minutes)

From the west end of the chalet buildings, follow the blue waymarks steeply downhill on a narrow, rocky path to Furkotská Dolina and the junction with yellow route 8853. (15-30 minutes)

2902A: TRI STUDNIČKY (1,140m) - VYŠNÉ KÔPROVSKÉ SEDLO (2,180m)

Grade: easy to Hlinská Dolina; moderate to Vysné Kôprovské Sedlo
Distance: 13km
Average gradient: 8% to Hlinská Dolina; 16% to Vyšné Kôprovské Sedlo
SW-NE Height gain: 1,200m/loss 160m   Time: 5h 00m
NE-SW Height loss: 1,200m/gain 160m   Time: 4h 15m
Winter/spring: open to Rázcestie pod Grúnikom (junction with green 5802)

The route starts to the left of the rustic buildings of **Tri Studničky** (1,140m), at first through meadows, then in forest as it crosses (at about 1,280m) Veľká Pálenica, the foot of the shoulder that descends south-west from Kriváň via the minor summit of **Grúnik**. The path now descends on big zigzags to meet green route 5802 at a junction called Rázcestie pod Grúnikom (1,120m), in the long valley called **Kôprová Dolina.** For the next 2km you gently climb an asphalt road, crossing and recrossing the brook (Kôprovský Potok) - there are picnic tables at several points. To your right you can see the impressive summit of **Kriváň;** to your left the lower but bulky massif of the Liptovské Kopy (Stacks of Liptov).

The road ends and you continue on a path through forest and meadows for 3km to the junction with green 5801 (Rázcestie pod Hlinskou Dolinou) at just over 1,400m. Your route turns right, descending at first to cross Kôprovský Potok, then climbing Hlinská Dolina with Hlinský Potok to your right. You emerge from the forest into the dwarf pine, with the massif of Hrubé (coarse) to your right. The path ascends several terraces through grass and rock, then steepens and zigzags to the saddle, Vyšné Kôprovské Sedlo (2,180m).

2902B: POPRADSKÉ PLESO station (1,250m) - POPRADSKÉ PLESO tarn (1,494m) - VYŠNÉ KÔPROVSKÉ SEDLO (2,180m)

Grade: easy to Popradské Pleso tarn; moderate to Vyšné Kôprovské Sedlo
Distance: 8.5km   **Average gradient: 7% to Popradské Pleso; 14% to Vyšné Kôprovské Sedlo**
S-N Height gain: 930m   Time: 3h 30m
N-S Height loss: 930m   Time: 3h 00m
Winter/spring: open as far as Rázcestie nad Žabím Potokom (1km beyond Popradské Pleso)

The first section of this route is a long slog up the service road to Popradské Pleso, but it is well used by walkers as the quickest way to reach the popular tarn, and beyond that (on paths mostly in dwarf pine and above the tree-line) the summit of Rysy.

From **Popradské Pleso** railway station (1,250m), turn right along the road (the old main road before the modern highway was built further south) for 150 metres to a left-hand bend, where the service road to the tarn (route 2902) goes right, past an electricity station. You follow this road all the way to the tarn, negotiating a considerable number of bends, and crossing the infant River Poprad twice - near the bottom and about halfway up. Before reaching the tarn, you reach the junction with yellow route 8854, which you can follow as an alternative route to the tarn via **Symbolický Cintorín.** A side-path leads down to the shore of the tarn, which you can follow if you require refreshment. (50-60 minutes)

You continue on a forest path, ascending gently, to emerge into the dwarf pine, then cross a stream to the point where the routes divide (Rázcestie nad Žabím Potokom (Junction above Frog Brook). The red route to Rysy (and most of the walkers) goes right; the blue route continues ahead in the dwarf pine, but soon comes to bare rock, which it climbs by means of short, steep zigzags.

The path now ascends gently to the huge tarn called **Veľké Hincovo Pleso,** largest in the Slovak Tatras, at 1,946m. The route turns left at the tarn, soon climbing steeply on more zigzags to the saddle, Vyšné Kôprovské Sedlo (2,180m).

2903: RÁZCESTIE BIELY VÁH (1,200m) - JAMSKÉ PLESO (1,447m) - KRIVÁŇ (2,494m)

Grade: strenuous	Distance: 6.5km	Average gradient: 20%
SE-NW Height gain: 1,294m		Time: 4h 15m
NW-SE Height loss: 1,294m		Time: 3h 30m
Winter/spring: open only as far as red route 0930 and Jamské Pleso		

A well graded path to the summit that is Slovakia's national symbol, with no fixed chains and some scrambling.

The bus stop at Rázcestie Biely Váh (1,200m, near the place called Na Striedku on the map) is the first one out of Štrbské Pleso in the direction of Podbanské and Liptovský Hrádok. Follow the blue waymarks up through the forest, crossing first the junction with green route 5803, then a stream - the infant Biely Váh, a tributary of Slovakia's longest river, the Váh. Ascending its valley, you cross back over the stream then cross red route 0930 - a few minutes to the left along the red route is **Jamské Pleso** - worth a detour. (45 minutes)

Continue climbing in the forest, above the valley called **Važecká Dolina,** reaching the tree-line near the minor summit of Jamy (Pits, 1,572m) which gives Jamské Pleso its name. You now begin the long ascent up the crest of a spur called Predný Handel, which leads first to the junction with green 5803 (Rázcestie pod Kriváňom), then in another 30 minutes to the summit of **Kriváň** (2,494m), with just a little scrambling.

2905: TATRANSKÉ ZRUBY (990m) - RÁZCESTIE POD SENNOU KOPOU (1,325m)

Grade: moderate	Distance: 2.5km	Average gradient: 14%
SE-NW Height gain: 335m		Time: 1h 00m
NW-SE Height loss: 335m		Time: 0h 45m
Winter/spring: open		

*A little used route linking the village of **Tatranské Zruby** to yellow route 8858, and thereby to Sliezsky Dom. It is straight and steep, and entirely in forest.*

2906: STARÝ SMOKOVEC (1,010m) - SLAVKOVSKÝ ŠTÍT (2,452m)

Grade: moderate	**Distance: 8km**	**Average gradient: 18%**
SE-NW Height gain: 1,442m		**Time: 4h 45m**
NW-SE Height loss: 1,442m		**Time: 3h 15m**
Winter/spring: closed		

Slavkovský Štít, dominating Starý Smokovec, is an obvious early target for walkers staying there, with excellent views as a reward. Do not underestimate this route - though appearing fairly short and innocuous on the map, it is a long, hard climb. There are no difficult parts, although at one point a short, narrow ridge is slightly exposed. The lower, forested part can be avoided by taking the funicular railway to Hrebienok, then using red route 0930 to the junction with blue route 2906. The upper part is either in dwarf pine or on open rock, with constant good views.

The route starts along a track to the left of the funicular railway station in **Starý Smokovec,** and follows the railway line for several hundred metres. The route then bears left, away from the track, and soon joins the fence of a water protection zone, which is fed by streams flowing from Päť Prameňou (Five Springs). Twisting and turning constantly, the path eventually reaches the junction with red route 0930. (30-45 minutes)

Continue ahead, following an earth-and-rock path which crosses the ski-pistes above **Hrebienok** before reaching a rocky verandah (with iron railing) called Slavkovská Vyhliadka (1,632m). From this exalted pulpit you can look out over the twin valleys of **Veľká and Malá Studená Dolina.** The highest summit in view is Lomnický Štít (2,632m), while Prostredný Hrot (Middle Point, 2,440m) pokes its head in on the left. (30-35 minutes)

Now among dwarf pine, another 30-minute climb brings you to a second viewpoint, from where you can see the green roof of Zamkovského Chata to the right, and look back to Hrebienok. In 15-20 minutes you reach a narrow ledge above the dwarf pine, with a view over Smokovec and other nearby villages. Another 15-20 minutes brings you to a thin ridge, slightly exposed, with the Sub-Tatras Basin on your left and Veľká Studená Dolina on your right. Continue climbing for an hour or so to reach the outlying summit of Nos (Nose, 2,283m), which lies up to your left and can be ascended quite easily. (90-120 minutes)

Summon up your strength and push on to reach the summit of **Slavkovský Štít** (2,452m). (40-60 minutes)

2907A: TATRANSKÁ LOMNICA (860m) - ZBOJNÍCKA CHATA (1,960m) - PRIELOM (2,288m)

Grade: moderate to Zbojnícka Chata; strenuous to Prielom

Distance: 14.5km	**Average gradient:**	9% to Zbojnícka Chata; 17% to Prielom
SE-NW Height gain: 1,428m		**Time: 5h 30m**
NW-SE Height loss: 1,428m		**Time: 4h 35m**

Winter/spring: open only as far as Zbojnícka Chata

This is a fairly easy route as far as Zbojnícka Chata, though at one point there is a short scramble with fixed chains. The passage over Prielom can be daunting in this direction, requiring an exposed descent using fixed chains. It is more easily tackled upwards, so would be better approached from the north (route 2907B below) or on green route 5806 via Poľský Hrebeň. It is advisable to avoid this route altogether if wet or icy.

The path starts near the Morava Hotel in **Tatranská Lomnica** (from the railway station, go past the shops then turn left, cross the main road and continue ahead up through the park). The route generally continues up the service road to Start, but a path cuts out one long bend. On the fourth bend after rejoining the road, the route bears left, beneath the gondola cableway and away from the road.

Eventually, after climbing a long series of steep stone steps through forest and semi-open meadows, you reach Studený Potok, which at this point cascades impressively for several hundred metres - **Vodopád Studeného Potoka** (Cold Brook Waterfall). You cross it on a curving wooden bridge, then climb to the junction with green route 5807 (1h 30m - 1h 45m). Refreshments are available at **Bilíkova Chata,** just 15 minutes' diversion to the left along green route 5807.

Continue climbing for 15 minutes on a broad path to **Polana Kamzík,** then a couple of minutes further on you cross red route 0930. The path continues, rocky but quite gently graded, through the forest in Veľká Studená Dolina, one of the main valleys in the Slovak High Tatras. On reaching the dwarf pine, it crosses the brook then climbs steeply. Care is needed, using sharp boulders as steps to cross a stream, then again to recross Veľký Studený Potok. The route then crosses an expanse of smooth rock, and a short scramble with fixed chains is encountered. In the valley below lie two small tarns - Vareškové Pleso (Stirring Stick Tarn) and Dlhé Pleso (Long Tarn, one of two so called in the High Tatras). A final steep ascent brings you to **Zbojnícka Chata** (1,960m, refreshments). (2h 00m - 2h 30m)

The path from the chalet starts fairly gently, but soon climbs steeply, becoming more so as you approach the saddle. A final push brings you to **Prielom** (2,288m). (75 minutes)

2907B: LYSÁ POĽANA (970m) - BIELOVODSKÁ DOLINA - KAČACIA DOLINA (1,300m) - PRIELOM (2,288m)

Grade: easy to Kačacia Dolina, then strenuous to Prielom
Distance: 15.5km   Average gradient: 3% to Kačacia Dolina;
                                        28% to Prielom
N-S Height gain: 1,318m   Time: 5h 45m
S-N Height loss: 1,318m   Time: 5h 00m
Winter/spring: open to Biela Voda

An easy valley route leads through forest and flowery meadows, with beautiful views of the peaks above, to some idyllic tarns at the foot of one of the most strenuous and formidable sections on the waymarked network - though this can be avoided by switching to green route 5806 via Poľský Hrebeň.

From the bus terminus at **Lysá Poľana** (970m, refreshments), walk towards the frontier station but turn left shortly before reaching it, along a side road which leads for some distance along **Bielovodská Dolina** (White Water Valley). The Biela Voda river on your right forms the border with Poland for several kilometres, and the notices on its banks warn you not to attempt to swim across! After 3 kilometres or so you pass, lying away from the road, a large foresters' chalet which is also a mountain rescue centre; there are some picnic tables and an ornamental water conduit. (40 minutes)

A kilometre further on is another, smaller foresters' hut, also with a picnic table, and yet another kilometre brings you to a bridge over the river, where the border swings away to the south-west. The picnic table here is the most pleasantly situated one on this route. In 1,500 metres you cross back to the east bank of the river - the picnic table on the far side has a roof. The forest road now gets rougher and narrower, but continues for some distance along the valley, climbing quite steeply for a while. Yet another picnic table is sited beneath the huge crag of Skorušniak on the far side of the valley. (90 minutes)

At times as a narrow path, at others as a broader track, the route now climbs more steeply, twisting and turning through the forest, then passing through a brief zone of dwarf pine, until the tarn called Litvorové Pleso is reached above the tree line. Some crags provide sheltered picnic spots beside the tarn. (70-90 minutes)

Zamrznuté Pleso (Frozen Tarn) is passed on the way to the junction with green route 5806 (Rázcestie pod Polským Hrebeňom, 30-40 minutes).

You now have the choice of turning right (easier route over Poľský Hrebeň. If you decide to continue to **Prielom,** be prepared for a strenuous and exposed climb using a series of fixed chains (45-60 minutes).

2908: ŠTART (1,140m) - SEDLO POD MALOU SVIŠŤOVKOU (1,490m) - SKALNATÉ PLESO (1,761m)

Grade: easy	**Distance: 8.5km**	**Average gradient: 8%**
SE-NW Height gain: 621m		**Time: 3h 00m**
NW-SE Height loss: 621m		**Time: 2h 15m**

Winter/spring: open only to Sedlo pod Malou Svišťovkou

From **Štart** (1,140m), the middle station of the cable-car from Tatranská Lomnica, go to your right along the path that is level at first, then alternately rises, falls and contours round the east side of the minor summit (not visible through the forest) of Malá Svišťovka (1,561m). 15 minutes after passing the junction with green route 5809, the path swings sharply left and climbs quite steeply to the saddle below Malá Svišťovka at about 1,490m, where you emerge into the dwarf pine. The route now goes up to the right, and you cross a stream on a wooden bridge before climbing steadily, still in dwarf pine, to **Skalnaté Pleso.**

2909: KEŽMARSKÉ ŽĽABY (920m) - TATRANSKÁ KOTLINA (765m)

Grade: easy	**Distance: 5km**	**Average gradient: 4%**
SE-NW Height gain: 20m/loss 155m		**Time: 1h 30m**
NW-SE Height gain: 155m/loss 20m		**Time: 1h 30m**

Winter/spring: open

A route through the forest linking the villages of Kežmarské Žľaby and Tatranská Kotlina. From the bus stop at **Kežmarské Žľaby,** you follow the blue waymarked track beside the holiday centre for a few hundred metres until you reach an asphalt road. Turn right along this, passing a reservoir. The road becomes a track, and eventually you reach the junction with green 5810 (Rázcestie Čierna Voda, 910m), which it joins to continue into **Tatranská Kotlina** - see green route 5810.

2911A: TATRANSKÉ MATLIARE (885m) - VEĽKÉ BIELE PLESO (1,600m) - KOPSKÉ SEDLO (1,749m)

Grade: easy to moderate	**Distance: 9.5km**	**Average gradient: 9%**
SE-NW Height gain: 864m		**Time: 3h 45m**
NW-SE Height loss: 864m		**Time: 2h 45m**

Winter/spring: open as far as Veľké Biele Pleso only

Though mostly in forest, this route leads to two very attractive spots at the meeting point of the High and White Tatras - Veľké Biele Pleso and Kopské Sedlo. It is one of the four routes that cross the main range (see also route 2911B below).

From the military sanatorium in **Tatranské Matliare,** follow the asphalt side road to a number of holiday centres, including "Metalurg" (refreshments), where yellow route 8864 joins from the left. It continues to climb, crossing several streams, until it joins the forest road bringing yellow route 8861 from Biela Voda. (40-60 minutes)

Routes 2911 and 8861 share the forest road for a while, climbing quite steeply close to the fast flowing Biela Voda Kežmarská (Kežmarok White Water) and crossing it at one point, until Šalviový Prameň (Sage Spring, 1,200m) is reached. There is a covered picnic table here. (20-30 minutes)

50 metres beyond Šalviový Prameň, the routes part: blue 2911 leaves the forest road to take a broad track off to the right, leading to another covered picnic table. The route then follows a steep and stony path, sometimes beside Biela Voda Kežmarská, crossing it from time to time on wooden bridges. There are some very pretty spots along here, some with a good view back to the forested saddleback hill called Stežky (1,529m). Eventually you reach the dwarf pine zone, then **Veľké Biele Pleso** (1,620m). (80-105 minutes)

From Veľké Biele Pleso, the path gradually becomes steeper, with some treacherous loose earth and rock near the top, to reach **Kopské Sedlo** (1,749m). (30-35 minutes)

2911B: JAVORINA (1,018m) - POD MURÁŇOM (1,100m) - KOPSKÉ SEDLO (1,749m)

Grade: moderate   Distance: 8km
Average gradient: 9% (11% Pod Muráňom to Kopské Sedlo)
NW-SE Height gain: 731m   Time: 3h 00m
SE-NW Height loss: 731m   Time: 2h 30m
Winter/spring: open to Pod Muráňom

This is one of just two waymarked routes that touch the White Tatras, albeit only the foothills, providing a unique opportunity to see the special plant-life of that area. For the first 2km it is shared with green route 5812. Most of the route is in open country, with good views and easy gradient, though it climbs quite steeply through the forested section. There are picnic tables at frequent intervals, including several covered ones. Most of this route (from Pod Muráňom upwards) is closed from November to June inclusive.

From the road junction at **Javorina** follow the minor road S beside the Javorinka river. Beyond the south end of the village, a dirt road continues to the forester's hut at Kubalová. (10 minutes)

Bear left here (another forest road leads off to the right). Soon the great, isolated slab of Muráň (1,890m), westernmost of the White Tatras peaks, towers ahead like a mini-Matterhorn. Then you see the pass of Kolový Sedlo, separating Jahňací Štít (on its left, 2,229m) and Zmrzlá Veža (2,310m). You pass on your right a water-treatment station, just before the path junction where blue 2911 and green 5812 separate (picnic tables). (25 minutes)

Blue 2911 turns left to cross the Javorinka river, still on a dirt road as far as **Pod Muráňom.** A stone track leads between meadows for several hundred metres, then climbs into the forest, shortly reaching a loggers' clearing with a covered picnic table. The forested hills to your right are Veľky and Malý Baboš; the evenly shaped peak to their left is Svišťovky, beyond which is Jahňací Štít. Curving round to the right is the valley of Javorová Dolina.

At a track junction by a stream, take the left fork (covered picnic tables) and enter the ravine of Zadné Meďodoly (Rear Coppermines) below the hill called Bránka (Little Gate). (15-20 minutes)

In another 15 minutes fork left, and in 20 minutes cross the stream to a small clearing (picnic tables), where a spring provides an opportunity to re-fill your bottle. (30-35 minutes)

You shortly reach more open country in the foothills of the White Tatras, with a clear view of the great whaleback of Havran (2,152m) ahead; flanked by Nový Vrch (1,999m) on its left, Ždiarska Vidla (2,146m) on its right (vidla = pitchfork). In July and August these meadows are ablaze with plants typical of alpine limestone terrain, such as edelweiss and gentian.

You climb steadily, escorted by tortoiseshell butterflies and little blue flying beetles, on a narrow and stony path, sometimes crossing the remains of last winter's avalanches. Ahead, you see for the first time your target - Kopské Sedlo - while to your right the brook called Meďodolský Potok tinkles through open grassland below. The path is not too steep, and requires little effort to reach **Kopské Sedlo.** (70-90 minutes)

GREEN ROUTES

Note: Green routes 5706 and 5707 in the Spišská Magura, and 5732 in the Low Tatras, shown on some High Tatras maps, are outside the scope of this book.

5801: RÁZCESTIE POD HLINSKOU DOLINOU (1,410m) - SEDLO ZÁVORY (1,879m)

Grade: strenuous	Distance: 2km	Average gradient: 24%
S-N Height gain: 469m		Time: 1h 30m
N-S Height loss: 584m		Time: 1h 15m
Winter/spring: closed		

From the junction with blue route 2902 (Rázcestie pod Hlinskou Dolinou, 1,410m), the path climbs through forest to the junction with red route 0932 (Rázcestie pod Temnosmrečinskou Dolinou). Here you turn left to climb steeply, at first through forest, but quickly emerging into the dwarf pine, up the valley of Kobylia Dolina. Near the top, now among rocks, you pass a tarn on your right (Kobylie Pleso). The path continues steadily up to Sedlo Závory (1,879m), a minor saddle, where it joins red route 0931.

5802: TICHÁ (980m) - RÁZCESTIE POD GRÚNIKOM (1,115m)

Grade: easy	**Distance: 4km**	**Average gradient: 4%**
W-E Height gain: 135m		**Time: 0h 45m**
E-W Height loss: 135m		**Time: 0h 45m**
Winter/spring: open		

This is a level, asphalt road which follows the south bank of Kôprovský Potok, and links yellow route 8851 at Tichá to the junction with blue route 2902 (Rázcestie pod Grúnikom).

5803A: ŠTRBSKÉ PLESO tarn (1,350m) - TRI STUDNICKY (1,140m)

Grade: easy	**Distance: 9km**	**Average gradient: 3%**
SE-NW Height loss: 210m		**Time: 2h 15m**
NW-SE Height gain: 210m		**Time: 2h 30m**
Winter/spring: open		

A gentle route through forest and meadows, running parallel to (and sometimes beside) the Cesta Slobody road. From the Solisko sanatorium at the south-west corner of **Štrbské Pleso** tarn, you turn left a little to enter the forest, then the route runs mostly slightly downhill or on the level, with an occasional short climb, all the way to Chata Kapitána Rašu (refreshments) and **Tri Studničky.** After 2km or so you cross a series of streams, among which is the junction with blue route 2903.

5803B: TRI STUDNIČKY (1,140m) - RÁZCESTIE POD KRIVÁŇOM (2,300m)

Grade: strenuous	**Distance: 4.5km**	**Average gradient: 30%**
SW-NE Height gain: 1,354m		**Time: 2h 00m**
NE-SW Height loss: 1,354m		**Time: 1h 30m**
Winter/spring: closed		

From **Tri Studničky**, at the junction with blue route 2902, you take the right-hand path, which at first climbs a valley, then more steeply up through forest to a series of zigzags leading to the grassy minor summit of **Grúnik** (1,576m) on the south-west shoulder of Kriváň. The route then climbs the shoulder, called Priehyba, at first through dwarf pine then on bare rock, and crosses a gully (Krivánsky Žľab) to reach the saddle below **Kriváň** at about 2,300m, where it meets blue route 2903 at Rázcestie pod Kriváňom.

5805: RÁZCESTIE NAD TRIGANOM (1,480m) - HINCOV POTOK (1,440m) POPRADSKÉ PLESO tarn (1,494m)

Grade: easy	**Distance: 2.5km**	**Average gradient: 4%**
S-N Height loss: 40m/gain 54m		**Time: 0h 45m**
N-S Height loss: 54m/gain 40m		**Time: 0h 45m**
Winter/spring: open		

This route comes into its own in winter, when the parallel section of red route 0930 is closed. However in spring it tends to get very wet, so at that time people wishing to reach Popradské Pleso tarn use blue route 2902 from Popradské Pleso station.

From the junction with red route 0930, the path descends steeply to Hincov Potok, crosses it, then rises steeply again to the junction with the asphalt service road (blue route 2902). Cross this and descend to **Popradské Pleso** tarn, then you can either turn left along the shore to Chata Kapitána Morávku (refreshments), or turn right for yellow route 8854 to **Symbolický Cintorín.**

5806A: NIŽNÉ HÁGY (910m) - DANIELOV DOM (1,000m) - TATRANSKÁ POLIANKA (1,010m)

Grade: easy	**Distance: 5km**	**Average gradient: 2%**
SW-NE Height gain: 100m		**Time: 1h 15m**
NE-SW Height loss: 100m		**Time: 1h 00m**
Winter/spring: open		

A gentle walk through the forest. From the bus stop at **Nižné Hágy,** walk north along the road for 100 metres, then turn right to follow the waymarks through the forest on a good path. After descending to cross a stream, it climbs again to a junction of forest roads - ignore these and bear right on a level grass path. In ten minutes you start climbing quite steeply to meet the Cesta Slobody road, which you cross then turn right on a pavement beside the road. The road now crosses a stream on a viaduct, but you follow the old road into **Tatranská Polianka.**

5806B: TATRANSKÁ POLIANKA (1,010m) - VELICKÉ PLESO (1,678m) - POĽSKÝ HREBEŇ (2,200m) - RÁZCESTIE POD POĽSKÝM HREBIENOM (2,100m)

Grade: moderate to strenuous	**Distance: 8.5km**
Average gradient: 14%	
SE-NW Height gain: 1,190m	**Time: 4h 00m**
NW-SE Height loss: 1,190m	**Time: 3h 30m**
Winter/spring: open only as far as Velické Pleso	

This route runs parallel to and crosses the service road, in forest and dwarf pine to Sliezsky Dom, and is then above the tree line to Poľský Hrebeň, passing two tarns. It becomes very steep as you approach the saddle, with a fixed chain section on bare rock - best avoided in wet or icy conditions.

From **Tatranská Polianka** railway station, cross the main road (Cesta Slobody) and go right a short distance to the parade of shops. Turn left here up a side road, which is the service road to Sliezsky Dom. It first passes to your left the big Wolkerov sanatorium (for respiratory ailments), then some way further up the waymarked route starts to make a number of short cuts on steep paths, avoiding the road's hairpin bends. A long road-avoiding stretch brings you to the junction with yellow route 8856, below Veľký Krížny Kopec (Big Cross Hill). (45-60 minutes)

Yellow route 8856 continues along the road, but for green 5806 you continue ahead on the footpath, beside Velický Potok, climbing steeply through the forest until the dwarf pine is reached, then the junction with yellow route 8858. A little way beyond this is **Velické Pleso** (1,663m, refreshments) and the junction with red route 0930. (1h 45-2h 00)

Continue beside the lake, at the north end of which is a cascade. You climb beside it on a zigzag path, known locally as Večný Dážď (Eternal Rain) from the spray. With Velické Potok to your left, the path now climbs steeply in two great stages up Kvetnica (Flower Valley - and it is a good place for flowers), to reach Dlhé Pleso (Long Tarn, 1,929m), and continues climbing to **Poľský Hrebeň** (2,200m). Just before the saddle is a 50-metre fixed chain. (2h 00m)

Beyond the saddle, the path drops steadily in a short distance to the junction with blue route 2907 (Rázcestie pod Poľským Hrebienom). (15 minutes)

5807: STARÝ SMOKOVEC (1,010m) - HREBIENOK (1,285m) - BILÍKOVA CHATA (1,255m) - VODOPÁD STUDENÉHO POTOKA (1,265m)

Grade: easy	**Distance: 3.5km**	**Average gradient: 9%**
S-N Height gain: 285m/loss 30m		**Time: 1h 00m**
N-S Height gain: 30m/loss 285m		**Time: 0h 35m**
Winter/spring: open		

The whole of this route runs as a broad, well defined path through the forest zone. It is not much used in the uphill direction, since the funicular railway can be used to save climbing. It is often used downhill, when the trains are crowded.

The route starts to the right of the funicular railway station in **Starý Smokovec,** then runs between the railway track and the service road all the way to **Hrebienok** (1,285m, refreshments). From time to time it joins the road. (45 minutes)

After Hrebienok, the path descends for a short distance down to **Bilíkova Chata** (1,255m, refreshments). (10 minutes)

The path continues level for a while, then climbs to meet blue route 2907, which joins from the right (5 minutes). For the best view of the cascade **(Vodopád Studeného Potoka)**, go for a short distance down route 2907, to the bridge.

5808: TATRANSKÁ LOMNICA (860m) - ŠTART (1,140m) - SKALNATÉ PLESO (1,761m)

Grade: moderate	**Distance: 6km**	**Average gradient: 15%**
SE-NW Height gain: 901m		**Time: 2h 00m**
NW-SE Height loss: 901m		**Time: 1h 30m**
Winter/spring: open		

Note: On older maps this route is shown in two separate sections - from Tatranská Lomnica to Štart and from Skalnaté Pleso to Lomnické Sedlo, with the Štart to Skalnaté Pleso section missing. The upper section to Lomnické Sedlo has since been closed to walkers unless accompanied by a mountain guide (see "Guided Routes" above), while the "missing" section has been reinstated.

The route starts under the pylons beside the Grandhotel Praha on the north side of **Tatranská Lomnica,** and winds its way up, crossing and recrossing the route of the cable-car, all the way to **Skalnaté Pleso** via the middle station at **Štart** (1,140m). It is in forest all the way, and gets steeper as you ascend.

5809: POĽANA POD MALOU SVIŠŤOVKOU (1,310m-1,240m)

Grade: easy	**Distance: 1km**	**Average gradient: 7%**
S-N Height loss: 70m		**Time: 0h 5m**
N-S Height gain: 70m		**Time: 0h 10m**
Winter/spring: open		

A short route through the forest, linking blue route 2908 to yellow route 8861.

5810: TATRANSKÁ KOTLINA (765m) - PLESNIVEC (1,340m) - VEĽKÉ BIELE PLESO (1,600m)

Grade: moderate   **Distance:** 10km   **Average gradient: 9%**
E-W Height gain: 835m   **Time: 3h 30m**
W-E Height loss: 835m   **Time: 3h 00m**
Winter/spring: open to Plesnivec only

Mainly in forest, this route is nevertheless of interest as one of the few that touch the White Tatras, with occasional good views. It is little used by comparison with those further west, and passes through bear territory! The first two kilometres are shared with blue route 2909. The lower part has seats at frequent intervals, but in 1992 was badly affected by a storm and may still be blocked by fallen trees at many points - diversions have been trodden out by other walkers.

The route (with blue and green waymarks) starts by the bus stop at the south-east end of **Tatranská Kotlina.** At first it follows a hard surfaced road, passing a TANAP office and mountain rescue centre (with picnic table) soon after the start. Near a custard-and-rust coloured, hacienda-style building, turn left along a path through trees to reach a forest road, with a black-painted sign-holder, and bear left along it. There has been some tree-felling in this area, and some of the waymarks may have disappeared - if in doubt, use your compass to follow bearing 225 as closely as possible. The forest road eventually reaches the point where routes 2909 and 5810 separate, called Rázcestie Čierna Voda (Black Water Junction). (30 minutes)

Turn right to follow a narrow earth path which climbs steadily through the forest, now with green waymarks only. Eventually it levels out and follows the contours, and comes to a series of zigzags at the top of which is **Plesnivec,** with a covered picnic table, a good view, and (50 metres further on) water from a pipe. (60-80 minutes)

The waymarks continue to the left from Plesnivec, and the path soon starts to climb steeply up a shoulder above Dolina Siedmich Prameňov (Valley of Seven Springs), then you cross the dry valley. You come to a ledge, where the path undulates for a while, with a fine view at one point down the valley and across the Sub-Tatras Plain. It then descends quite steeply for 100 metres or so, before climbing again to reach a broad, semi-open ledge with grass and dwarf pine. Here you are at the east end of the White Tatras, and to the south-east you have a good view of the forested, rounded minor summit of Stežky (1,529m). (30-40 minutes)

The route follows this ledge for several hundred metres, then re-enters the forest, where an unmarked track joins from the left. Leaving the forest again, and still climbing, you pass through a zone of dwarf pine and rowan, to the foot of **Predné Medodoly** (Front Coppermines). There is a picnic table at the top of the shoulder. (40-50 minutes)

After descending the far side of the moraine, the path crosses Napájadlový Potok (Water Brook) on a wooden bridge - the brook is often dry in summer and autumn - then gently ascends to **Veľké Biele Pleso.** (20 minutes)

5811: ŽDIAR (896m) - BIELA RIVER VALLEY - SKI TERRAIN (1,140m)

Grade: easy	**Distance: 3.5km**	**Average gradient: 7%**
E-W Height gain: 244m		**Time: 1h 00m**
W-E Height loss: 244m		**Time: 0h 45m**
Winter/spring: open		

Until the recent opening of the path across Široké Sedlo, this was an isolated route, little used in summer. Now it provides access to the only route across the White Tatras, and is linked thereby to the main High Tatras network.

The route starts by the Tatra trade union centre on the south side of the main road at **Ždiar**, following an asphalt road beside the Biela river. After 30 minutes, near the Magura trade union hotel, it leaves the road to bear left into the forest, crosses the river, then starts to climb more steeply. 15 minutes further on, you reach the junction with green route WT1 to Široké Sedlo (not shown on some maps), and continue ahead, climbing steadily and veering round to the right, eventually reaching Ždiar's ski terrain (Strednica). A final steep climb up a grassy slope, that takes you past the pylons of a ski-tow, brings you back to the main road at a point where the buses from Tatranská Lomnica to Lysá Poľana stop.

5812A: ZAMKOVSKÉHO CHATA (1,475m) - TÉRYHO CHATA (2,013m) - SEDIELKO (2,372m)

Grade: strenuous	**Distance: 5.5km**	**Average gradient: 17%**
SE-NW Height gain: 897m		**Time: 3h 30m**
NW-SE Height loss: 897m		**Time: 3h 00m**
Winter/spring: open as far as Téryho Chata		

A very well used route through one of the prettiest valleys in the Tatras, also linking two popular chalets. Together with 5812B, it is one of just three routes that cross the main High Tatras ridge. Sedielko, a pass on the main ridge of the High Tatras, is dangerous if there is much snow.

From **Zamkovského Chata** (1,475m), you climb Malá Studená Dolina, at first in the forest, but soon you come to the dwarf pine and a rock face called Vieľký Hank (Great Slope), which you climb on steep zigzags, passing a yellow wall which is very popular with climbers. The path then turns right to Malý Hank (Little Slope), with more zigzags, to reach **Téryho Chata** (refreshments) in its idyllic location beside Pät Spišskych Plies (Five Tarns of Spiš). The route continues, now together with yellow 8860 for a while, on stony ground to cross a stream and go round the rock wall. At the parting with the yellow route, take the right-hand path up a small grassy kettle (the geological type), passing **Modré Pleso** (Blue Tarn), highest in the all of the Tatras at 2,192m, then steeply on rock to the saddle of **Sedielko** (2,372m).

5812B: JAVORINA (1,018m) - JAVOROVÁ DOLINA - ŽABIE JAVOROVÉ PLESO (1,886m) - SEDIELKO (2,372m)

Grade: moderate to Žabie Javorové Pleso; strenuous to Sedielko
Distance: 12km   **Average gradient: 9% to Žabie Javorové**
                                  Pleso; 25% to Sedielko
N-S Height gain: 1,354m   **Time: 5h 00m**
S-N Height loss: 1,354m   **Time: 4h 15m**
Winter/spring: open only to Rázcestie pod Muráňom

*This route provides easy walking for the most part, up the valley of **Javorová Dolina** and beside the Javorinka river, with good views of the high peaks above, but gets steep towards the top.*

From **Javorina,** the start with blue route 2911 (q.v. for a description as far as Rázcestie pod Muráňom). From the junction, you continue along the forest road for another kilometre or so. Then the valley starts to climb quite steeply, and the road becomes a track, passing through forest and meadows. In 3km, still climbing steeply, you reach the dwarf pine and have a great view of the long ridge leading up to Javorový Štít. The path crosses the infant Javorinka river, now in the upper part of the valley which is called Zadná Dolina, and climbs to a grassy terrace. At the head of the valley is the tarn called Žabie Javorové Pleso, after which the path zigzags steeply to **Sedielko.**

5WT1: BELIANSKY POTOK (930m) - ŠIROKÉ SEDLO (1,830m) - KOPSKÉ SEDLO (1,749m)

Grade: moderate   **Distance: 4km**   **Average gradient: 24%**
N-S Height gain: 900m/loss 81m   **Time: 3h 00m**
One way traffic (N-S only)
Winter/spring: closed

This route was reopened in 1993 after a 15-year closure for ecological reasons - see the section on the White Tatras in the General Description chapter. It is quite steep, but not difficult. To use this route, you must pay a nominal fee, which is collected at the start. Note that the waymarks on this route are slightly different, in that the white-green-white bands are diagonal. No official number has been allocated, so to fit in with our system we call it 5WT1.

From the junction with green route 5811 beside Beliansky Potok (the upper part of the Biela river), you follow and sometimes cross Rigľový (Rigeľský) Potok, the stream that occupies the valley called Monková Dolina, climbing steeply to the top of the pine forest. On the way, you pass a meadow with picnic tables and a spring (2h 00m).

Continuing through the dwarf pine, you reach **Široké Sedlo** (dry saddle), a splendid viewpoint (30 minutes), then continue a little higher to the left as you traverse under the peak called Hlúpy (stupid). At a second (unnamed) saddle, above the valley called Predné Medodoly Dolina, you can see the front part of the White Tatras. Heading south, you descend to **Kopské Sedlo** and blue route 2911 (30 minutes).

YELLOW ROUTES

Note: Yellow route 8712 in the Spišská Magura, shown on some High Tatras maps, is outside the scope of this book.

8851: PODBANSKÉ (940) - TICHÁ (980m) - RÁZCESTIE POD TOMANOVOU DOLINOU (1,150m) - SUCHÉ SEDLO (1,985m)

Grade: easy to Rázcestie p.T.D.; moderate to Suché Sedlo
Distance: 16km   Average gradient: 2% to Rázcestie p.T.D.;
                                    14% to Suché Sedlo
SW-NE Height gain: 40m   Time: 5h 30m
NE-SW Height loss: 40m   Time: 4h 30m
Winter/spring: open only as far as Tichá

This is one of the most remote routes in the High Tatras. It is mostly on an asphalt road, but you are rewarded with beautiful views of mountains in both the High and Western Tatras. Though according to the map the valley of Tichá Dolina lies in the Western Tatras (Zapadné Tatry), it is locally considered to belong to the High Tatras. This route does in fact lead almost to the high saddle, Ľaliové Sedlo, which is generally accepted as the point where the High meets the Western Tatras.

From the car park at **Podbanské,** you cross the bridge over the Belá river, then turn left along an asphalt road leading to the Horárén (mountain lodge)

Tichá, and the junction with blue route 5802. On the opposite side of the river is a big trade union holiday centre called Permon. The road is virtually flat, and after Tichá, where it bears left into Tichá Dolina, though it does climb you hardly notice the gradient. At Tichá you are almost surrounded by mountains, with Kriváň dominant to the east. To the west are the first peaks of the Western Tatras.

As you ascend Tichá Dolina, a beautiful panorama unfolds with the rounded peaks of the **Červené Vrchy** (Red Hills) ahead - also in the Western Tatras. At Rázcestie pod Tomanovou Dolinou you join red route 0931, and the two routes coincide for the next 2km. At the next junction, Rázcestie pod Kasprovým Vrchom, the asphalt finishes and the routes part. The yellow goes left across a meadow, then goes into the forest and starts to climb steeply, including a long zigzag section leading towards the summit of Beskyd (2,012m). Just short of it, the path bears left and heads for Suché Sedlo (Dry Saddle, 1,985m). Regrettably it is dry in every sense, since the facilities within a stone's throw at the top of the cable-car at Kasprowy Wierch, just in Poland, are out of bounds to those on the Slovak side.

8853A: ŠTRBSKÉ PLESO tarn (1,350m) - VODOPÁD SKOK (1,700m) - BYSTRÉ SEDLO (2,314m)

Grade: moderate (to Vodopád Skok); **strenuous** (to Bystré Sedlo and Vyšné Wahlenbergovo Pleso) (chains) **Distance: 7km**
Average gradient: 12% to Vodopád Skok; **31%** to Bystré Sedlo; **17%** to Vysné Wahlenbergovo Pleso
SE-NW Height gain: 964m/loss 169m
Time: 3h 30m to Bystré Sedlo; **4h 00m** to Vyšné Wahlenbergovo Pleso
Winter/spring: open only as far as Vodopád Skok

Note: Bystré Sedlo can only be crossed from east to west, to ensure one-way traffic on a stretch of fixed chain, so those wishing to complete the whole of route 8853 as a circuit from Štrbské Pleso can only do so in an anti-clockwise direction. In winter and spring, the upper part from Vodopád Skok to Bystré Sedlo and from there down to the junction with red route 0930 is closed. The lower part of this route from Štrbské Pleso to Vodopád Skok is open all year, and can be followed in both directions. If there is much snow, the upper part around Bystré Sedlo can be dangerous.

From Hotel FIS, north of **Štrbské Pleso** tarn, follow the asphalt road northwards; this shortly finishes and you continue ahead on a path which climbs through forest, then dwarf pine, with some zigzags and views down into **Mlynická Dolina.** Having left the dwarf pine, you soon come to the impressive waterfall called Vodopád **Skok.** Above Skok you encounter the first chains, and a small tarn called Pleso nad Skokom. Higher up, you pass through a cluster of small tarns, then another series of steep zigzags leads to a traverse across a gully with more chains and on up to **Bystré Sedlo** (Sharp Saddle, 2,314m). There are many loose rocks here, so you must walk with great care. From the saddle, you have excellent views of the surrounding peaks, valleys and tarns.

8853B: ROUTE 0930(R) (1,475m) - FURKOTSKÁ DOLINA (1,710m) - VYŠNÉ WAHLENBERGOVO PLESO (2,145m) - BYSTRÉ SEDLO (2,314m)

Grade: strenuous	**Distance: 3km**	**Average gradient: 23%**
SE-NW Height gain: 670m		**Time: 2h 30m**
NW-SE Height loss: 670m		**Time: 1h 45m**
Winter/spring: closed		

This route is exceptionally steep in places, but leads to the pretty valley called Furkotská Dolina with its tarns named after a Swedish botanist.

From the junction with red route 0930 at 1,475m, follow the yellow waymarks, at first on an earthy, gently graded path through the forest, but soon becoming ever steeper and rockier as it reaches the dwarf pine. Here it comes close to Furkotský Potok, and this is followed to the junction with blue route 2836 - this is the point referred to as Furkotská Dolina on signposts, at 1,710m. Looking back you have a fine vista over the Sub-Tatras Basin, with the villages of Tatranská Štrba and Štrba in clear view. (35-45 minutes)

The path continues steeply in dwarf pine, but now leaving Furkotský Potok far below, and eventually climbs sharply the moraine of **Nižné Wahlenbergovo Pleso** (2,053m), which you pass on its right. (50-75 minutes)

A second steep moraine leads to **Vyšné Wahlenbergovo Pleso** (20-30 minutes), then a series of zigzags takes you to **Bystré Sedlo** (2,314m) - see route 8853B, and remember that you cannot continue in this direction beyond the saddle (one way - up only - on the chains).

8854: ROUTE 2902B (1,500m) - SYMBOLICKÝ CINTORÍN (1,525m) - POPRADSKÉ PLESO (1,494m)

Grade: moderate	**Distance: 1.5km**	**Average gradient: 5%,**
		but very steep in parts with chains
S-N Height gain: 25m/loss 31m		**Time: 0h 30m**
N-S Height gain: 31m/loss 25m		**Time: 0h 30m**
Winter/spring: this route is normally open from 15 June to 31 December		

From the junction with blue route 2902, the path descends a little to cross the infant river Poprad, then reascends and soon begins to climb quite steeply. There is a very steep section just before you reach the **"Symbolic Cemetery"**, with fixed wires for support. The path through the cemetery itself is also quite steep in places.

The path descends back over the river to the shore of Popradské Pleso, which it follows for 500 metres to Chata Kapitána Morávku.

8855: NIŽNÉ HÁGY (910m) - VYŠNÉ HÁGY (1,085m) - BATIZOVSKÉ PLESO (1,879m)

Grade: moderate	Distance: 7km	Average gradient: 14%
S-N Height gain: 969m		Time: 3h 15m
N-S Height loss: 969m		Time: 2h 45m
Winter/spring: open		

A steep path mostly through forest, providing a link from the Tatranská Magistrála to the tram station at Vyšné Hágy.

From the forest lodge at **Nižné Hágy,** opposite green route 5806, you go left along an asphalt road past some apartment houses, then ascend past more apartments, still on the road, until you reach Cesta Slobody (Freedom Highway) at **Vyšné Hágy** tram station. Follow the old road to the left for a short distance, then turn right to cross the tram line near a forest lodge. You climb through the forest, with the stream called Malý Šum to your right, to reach a meadow with a spring and picnic tables. The path now steepens, and eventually you cross a stream to reach the dwarf pine; then on up to the Tatranská Magistrála (red route 0930D, which you follow for some 500 metres to **Batizovské Pleso.**

8856: RÁZCESTIE PRI VELICKOM MOSTE (1,250m) - RÁZCESTIE POD SUCHÝM VRCHOM (1,720m)

Grade: moderate	Distance: 4km	Average gradient: 12%
SE-NW Height gain: 470m		Time: 1h 15m
NW-SE Height loss: 470m		Time: 1h 00m
Winter/spring: open		

A route linking the Tatranská Magistrála (red 0930D) with green route 5806. It provides a short cut for walkers on the Tatranská Magistrála wishing to avoid Sliezsky Dom, whose service road is followed for much of this route.

The route starts from a roofed picnic table at 1,250m, where route 5806(G) crosses the service road to Sliezsky Dom beside Velický Potok, and below Veľký

Krížny Kopec (Big Cross Hill). This point is known as Rázcestie pri Velickom Moste (junction at the bridge over Velický brook). It uses the service road for almost two kilometres, until a very sharp right-hand hairpin bend is reached. (25-30 minutes)

Leaving the road on a rocky path to the left, it soon leaves the forest zone and enters the dwarf pine, with good views down to the plain. Climbing steadily you reach the junction with red route 0930 at a point named on the signpost as Rázcestie pod Suchým Vrchom (junction below Dry Hill) at 1,720m.

8857: POĽSKÝ HREBEŇ (2,200m) - VÝCHODNÁ VYSOKÁ (2,428m)

Grade: moderate	**Distance: 1km**	**Average gradient: 23%**
W-E Height gain: 228m		**Time: 0h 45m**
E-W Height loss: 228m		**Time: 0h 30m**
Winter/spring: closed		

A very steep, but short and not difficult, route leading to a popular viewpoint at the heart of the High Tatras.

The route starts from green route 5806 at the saddle called **Poľský Hrebeň** at 2,200m. There is a series of short and steep zigzags, then you traverse a terrace to reach the summit of **Východná Vysoká** (2,428m).

8858: STARÝ SMOKOVEC (1,010m) - RÁZCESTIE POD SENNOU KOPOU (1,325m) - RÁZCESTIE NA VELICKEJ POĽANE (1,560m)

Grade: moderate	**Distance: 4.5km**	**Average gradient: 10%**
SE-NW Height gain: 450m		**Time: 2h 15m**
NW-SE Height loss: 450m		**Time: 1h 45m**
Add 15 minutes to these times for Sliezsky Dom		
Winter/spring: open		

A useful route linking Starý Smokovec with the Tatranská Magistrála at Sliezsky Dom on Velické Pleso.

The route starts 200 metres east of the rack railway station along the back road in **Starý Smokovec,** close to Hotel Bystrina. It climbs steadily through the forest, crossing the ski-lift track and several streams, to meet blue route 2905 coming from Tatranské Zruby at Rázcestie pod Sennou Kopou (junction below Senna Stack). It then steepens to reach the dwarf pine, and the junction with green route 5806, known as Rázcestie na Velickej Poľane (junction below Velické meadow), 500 metres south of **Velické Pleso** and Sliezsky Dom.

8859: TATRANSKÁ LESNÁ (905m) - RÁZCESTIE PRI VODOPÁDOCH STUDENÉHO POTOKA (1,255m)

Grade: easy **Distance: 3.5km** **Average gradient: 10%**
SE-NW Height gain: 350m **Time: 1h 30m**
NW-SE Height loss: 350m **Time: 1h 15m**
Add 15 minutes to these times for Bilíkova Chata or Hrebienok
Winter/spring: open

A romantic route through the forest between the tramline and the beautiful cascade called Vodopád Studeného Potoka. It provides a useful link to Hrebienok and Bilíkova Chata.

The path starts opposite the tram station at **Tatranská Lesná** (905m), climbing quite steeply at first, while the brook called Studený Potok twists and tinkles below to your right. The path levels out where it runs beside the brook, then climbs steeply again, finally passing the cascade of **Vodopád Studený Potok** to reach the junction with green route 5807, understandably known as Rázcestie pri Vodopádoch Studeného Potoka (junction at Cold Brook Cascade). Refreshments are quite near at hand at **Bilíkova Chata,** 15 minutes' level walk to your left along green 5807.

8860: TÉRYHO CHATA (2,013m) - PRIEČNE SEDLO (2,352m) - ZBOJNÍCKA CHATA (1,960m)

Grade: strenuous **Distance: 5km** **Average gradient: 23%**
 to Priecne Sedlo; 11% to Zbojnícka Chata
NE-SW Height gain: 339m/loss 392m **Time: 3h 00m**
Winter/spring: closed
Note: This route can only be followed in one direction (NE-SW)

A popular but demanding route, always above the tree-line, crossing the saddle of Priečne Sedlo. There are excellent views all the time, especially from the saddle. The approach to this is very steep, with a long stretch of fixed chains in three separate sections - at weekends in high season there are often queues for these.

From **Téryho Chata** (2,013m, refreshments), the route starts off sharing with green 5812, for about 1.5km, then turns left to climb steeply to **Priečne Sedlo** (2,352m) - the last section includes the fixed chains. (1h 30m)

Descending from the saddle, you pass several tarns, including one of the largest in this group, Sivé Pleso (Grey Tarn). After crossing Veľký Studený Potok (Great Cold Brook), you climb again briefly to join blue route 2907 at **Zbojnícka Chata** (1,960m, refreshments). (1h 30m)

8861: BIELA VODA (910m) - ŠALVIOVY PRAMEŇ (1,200m) - ZELENÉ PLESO (1,545m) - KOLOVÉ SEDLO (2,118m) - JAHŇACÍ ŠTÍT (2,229m)

Grade: easy (to Zelené Pleso); strenuous to Jahňací Štít

Distance: 9.5km **Average gradient:** 9% to Zelené Pleso; 27% to Jahňací Štít

SE-NW Height gain: 1,319m **Time: 5h 00m**
NW-SE Height loss: 1,319m **Time: 4h 15m**
Winter/spring: open only as far as Zelené Pleso

A route of two moods: one gentle and full of anticipation, mostly in the forest, to reach the beautiful emerald tarn of Zelené Plesso; one stern as you leave the tarn, mostly on open rock, to face the stiff climb to Jahňací Štít. Since Zelené Pleso is one of the loveliest spots in the High Tatras, with a welcoming chalet, the lower part of this route is well used - even in winter, both by cross-country skiers and by local people going to skate on the tarn. The upper section includes some short fixed chains in an exposed situation.

From the bus stop at **Biela Voda** (915m, no refreshments), follow the dirt road up through the forest to the junction with blue route 2911, with which it runs together for a while. (30 minutes)

The road continues, still in the forest, crossing the Biela Voda Kežmarská river, to **Šalviový Prameň** (1,200m), where the two routes part company. (30 minutes)

Yellow route 8861 stays on the dirt road, which shortly turns left to re-cross the river. Now with the river on your right, you soon reach the junction with green route 5809, and continue climbing steadily through the forest, eventually reaching the dwarf pine zone, having turned left out of the main valley into Dolina Zeleného Plesa. The river is replaced on your right by the brook, Zelený Potok, which naturally leads you unerringly to **Zelené Pleso** and its chalet (1,545m, refreshments). (2h 30m)

Leaving the chalet, you start to climb steeply behind it on a narrow path, at first continuing among dwarf pine. You reach Červená Dolina (Red Valley) which has several small tarns including Červené Pleso (Red Tarn), the largest. After skirting its southern shore you continue climbing with Jastrabia Veža (Hawk Tower) to your left. At the valley head you use several short lengths of fixed chain to surmount the wall. You follow a ridge to a saddle, then cross a sequence of ribs and gullies to the summit of **Jahňací Štít** (2,229m). (1h 30m)

8862: TATRANSKÁ KOTLINA (765m) - BELIANSKA JASKYŇA (855m)

Grade: easy	**Distance: 1.5km**	**Average gradient: 6%**
E-W Height gain: 90m		**Time: 0h 20m**
W-E Height loss: 90m		**Time: 0h 15m**
Winter/spring: open		

*A short but steep access route to the fascinating cave of **Belianska Jaskyňa.** It starts from the back of the car park at the north end of **Tatranská Kotlina** (765m, refreshments).*

8864: TATRANSKÁ LOMNICA Grandhotel Praha (900m) - TATRANSKÁ MATLIARE Metalurg (910m)

Grade: easy	**Distance: 1km**	**Average gradient: 1%**
SW-NE Height gain: 10m		**Time: 0h 20m**
NE-SW Height loss: 10m		**Time: 0h 20m**
Winter/spring: open		

*A route through the forest, linking the bottom station of the cable-car at **Tatranská Lomnica** to blue route 2911 just outside **Tatranské Matliare,** by the Metalurg holiday centre. This route is fairly new, and may not be marked on older maps.*

SELECTED TIMINGS

This section provides a quick-reference guide to selected walking times. Taken from a variety of sources, they are approximate, and intended to provide a rough guide only - always allow extra time for your journey, in case of unforeseen difficulties. By adding together the various sections, these tables can be used to compute the total times for your own routes.

Of course, people walk at differing speeds. On your first day of walking, you can compare your own times with those shown to get an idea of whether you are faster or slower. This is only for your information; there is no point in racing the signposts!

Note: Vielké Biele Pleso is sometimes shown on the signposts as Kežmarská Chata (a chalet that no longer exists). Velické Pleso is usually referred to as Sliezsky Dom, the mountain hotel there.

**Remember that: routes beginning with
"0" = red, "2" = blue, "5" = green, "8" = yellow.**

FROM/to	Time	Via routes
BATIZOVSKÉ PLESO to:		
Hrebienok	3h 00m	0930
Popradské Pleso	2h 15m	0930
Sliezsky Dom	1h 15m	0930
Tatranská Polianka	2h 00m	0930, 8856, 5806
Vyšné Hágy	1h 30m	0930, 8855
BIELA VODA to:		
Jahňací Štít	5h 15m	8861
Veľké Biele Pleso	2h 45m	8861, 2911
Zelené Pleso	2h 45m	8861
BYSTRÉ SEDLO to:		
Chata pod Soliskom	2h 15m	8853, 2836
Štrbské Pleso	3h 00m	8853, 0930
CHATA POD RYSMI to:		
Popradské Pleso	2h 00m	0933, 2902
Rysy	1h 00m	0933
Sedlo Váha	0h 15m	0933
Štrbské Pleso	3h 00m	0933, 2902, 0930
CHATA POD SOLISKOM to:		
Bystré Sedlo	2h 45m	2836, 8853
Nižné Wahlenbergovo Pleso	1h 30m	2836, 8853
Predné Solisko	0h 45m	0935
Štrbské Pleso	1h 15m	2836
FURKOTSKÁ DOLINA to:		
Bystré Sedlo	2h 30m	8853
Chata pod Soliskom	0h 30m	2836
Nižné Wahlenbergovo Pleso	1h 15m	8853
Štrbské Pleso	1h 15m	8853, 0930
HREBIENOK to:		
Bilíkova Chata	0h 05m	5807
Polana Kamzík	0h 15m	0930 (0h 20m on 5807)
Slavkovský Štít	4h 00m	0930, 2906
Sliezsky Dom	2h 00m	0930
Starý Smokovec	0h 45m	5807
Tatranská Lesná	1h 30m	5807, 8859
Tatranská Lomnica	1h 45m	5807, 2907
Zamkovského Chata	0h 45m	0930
Zbojnícka Chata	2h 45m	0930, 2907
JAMSKÉ PLESO to:		
Kriváň	3h 30m	2903
Biela Voda west (bus stop)	0h 45m	2903
Štrbské Pleso	1h 00m	0930
Tri Studničky	1h 30m	0930

FROM/to	Time	Via routes
JAVORINA to:		
Hrebienok	8h 45m	5812, 0930
Kopské Sedlo	3h 00m	2911
Sedielko	5h 15m	5812
Starý Smokovec	9h 30m	5812, 0930, 5807
Tatranská Lomnica	6h 30m	2911, 8864
Téryho Chata	6h 15m	5812
Veľké Biele Pleso	3h 30m	291
KEŽMARSKÉ ŽĽABY to:		
Plesnivec	2h 30m	2909, 5810
Tatranská Kotlina	1h 30m	2909
Veľké Biele Pleso	3h 00m	2909, 5910
KOPSKÉ SEDLO to:		
Javorina	2h 30m	2911
Skalnaté Pleso	3h 00m	2911, 0930
Veľké Biele Pleso	0h 30m	2911
Zelené Pleso	1h 00m	2911, 0930
LYSÁ POĽANA to:		
Hrebienok	8h 45m	2907, 5807
Poľský Hrebeň	5h 15m	2907, 5806
Prielom	5h 45m	2907
Sliezsky Dom	7h 00m	2907, 5806
Starý Smokovec	9h 30m	2907, 5807
Tatranská Lomnica	10h 00m	2907
PLESNIVEC to:		
Kežmarské Žľaby	2h 30m	5810, 2909
Tatranská Kotlina	2h 00m	5810
Veľké Biele Pleso	1h 30m	5810
POD MURÁŇOM to:		
Javorina	0h 45m	2911/5812
Kopské Sedlo	2h 15m	2911
Sedielko	4h 30m	5812
Tatranská Lomnica	5h 45m	2911, 8864
Téryho Chata	5h 45m	5812
Veľké Biele Pleso	2h 45m	2911
PODBANSKÉ to:		
Hladké Sedlo	5h 30m	8851, 0931
Kriváň	4h 00m	0930, 5803
Štrbské Pleso	3h 45m	5803 (4h 00m on 0930)
Suché Sedlo	5h 30m	8851
Tri Studničky	1h 30m	0930
POLANA KAMZIK to:		
Hrebienok	0h 25m	2907, 5807

FROM/to	Time	Via routes
Lysá Poľana	8h 30m	2907
Obrovský Vodopád	0h 20m	2907, 0930
Prielom	3h 45m	2907
Skalnaté Pleso	1h 45m	2907, 0930
Tatranská Lomnica	1h 30m	2907
Téryho Chata	2h 30m	2907, 0930, 5812
Zbojnicka Chata	2h 30m	2907

POĽSKÝ HREBEŇ to:

Sliezsky Dom	1h 45m	5806

POPRADSKÉ PLESO (tarn) to:

Kôprovské Sedlo	2h 15m	2902
Popradské Pleso (station)	0h 50m	2902
Rysy	3h 15m	2902, 0933
Sliezsky Dom	3h 30m	0930
Štrbské Pleso	1h 15m	0930
Veľké Hincovo Pleso	1h 30m	2902

POPRADSKÉ PLESO (station) to:

Veľké Hincovo Pleso	2h 30m	2902
Popradské Pleso (tarn)	1h 00m	2902
Rysy	4h 15m	2902, 0933

PRIELOM to:

Poľský Hrebeň	1h 00m	2907, 5806

RÁZCESTIE NA MAGISTRÁLE (junction 0930/2906) to:

Hrebienok	0h 15m	0930
Slavkovský Štít	4h 15m	0930, 2906
Sliezsky Dom	1h 45m	0930
Starý Smokovec	0h 30m	5807

RÁZCESTIE POD FURKOTSKOU DOLINOU (Junction 0930/8853) to:

Bystré Sedlo	3h 15m	8853
Jamské Pleso	0h 30m	0930
Kriváň	3h 00m	0930, 2903
Podbanské	3h 15m	0930
Štrbské Pleso	0h 30m	0930
Tri Studničky	1h 45m	0930
Vyšné Wahlenbergovo Pleso	2h 30m	8853

RÁZCESTIE POD KONČISTOU (junction 0930/8855) to:

Batizovské Pleso	0h 15m	0930
Sliezsky Dom	1h 15m	0930
Vyšné Hágy	1h 15m	8855

RÁZCESTIE POD SUCHÝM VRCHOM (junction 0930/8856) to:

Batizovské Pleso	0h 30m	0930
Hrebienok	2h 30m	0930
Popradské Pleso	3h 00m	0930

FROM/to	Time	Via routes
Sliezsky Dom	0h 30m	0930
Tatranská Polianka	1h 30m	8856, 5806

RÁZCESTIE POD POĽSKÝM HREBEŇOM (junction 2907/5806) to:

Kačacia Dolina	1h 15m	2907
Lysá Poľana	4h 15m	2907
Poľský Hrebeň	0h 15m	5806
Prielom	0h 45m	2907
Sliezsky Dom	1h 00m	5806
Zbojnícka Chata	1h 45m	2907

RÁZCESTIE PRI VODOPÁDOCH STUDENÉHO POTOKA (junction 2907/5807) to:

Bilíkova Chata	0h 15m	5807
Hrebienok	0h 20m	5807
Polana Kamzík	0h 15m	2907
Stará Lesná (rly station)	1h 30m	5807, 8859
Starý Smokovec	1h 00m	5807
Tatranská Lomnica	1h 30m	2907
Téryho Chata	2h 45m	2907, 0930, 5812
Zbojnícka Chata	2h 45m	2907

RÁZCESTIE ČIERNA VODA (junction 2909/5810) to:

Kežmarské Žľaby	1h 00m	2909
Plesnivec	1h 30m	5810
Tatranská Kotlina	0h 30m	2909/5810
Veľké Biele Pleso	3h 00m	5810

RÁZCESTIE BIELA VODA (junction 2911/8861) to:

Biela Voda	0h 30m	8861
Jahňací Štít	4h 00m	8861
Kopské Sedlo	2h 45m	2911
Tatranské Matliare	0h 45m	2911
Veľké Biele Pleso	2h 15m	2911
Zelené Pleso	1h 30m	8861

RÁZCESTIE NA VELICKEJ POLANE (junction 5806/8856) to:

Batizovské Pleso	1h 30m	8856, 0930
Sliezsky Dom	1h 00m	5806
Tatranská Polianka	0h 30m	5806

ŠALVIOVÝ PRAMEŇ to:

Biela Voda	1h 00m	8861
Jahňací Štít	3h 30m	8864
Kopské Sedlo	2h 15m	2911
Tatranská Lomnica	1h 30m	2911, 8864
Veľké Biele Pleso	1h 45m	2911
Zelené Pleso	1h 45m	8864

SKALNATÉ PLESO to:

Hrebienok	1h 30m	0930

FROM/to	Time	Via routes
Obrovský Vodopád	1h 00m	0930
Šalviový Prameň	1h 30m	2908, 5809, 8861
Štart	1h 30m	5808 (2h 15m on 2908)
Sedlo pod Malou Svišťovkou	0h 30m	2908
Tatranská Lomnica	2h 15m	5808
Veľká Svišťovka	1h 15m	0930
Zelené Pleso	2h 15m	0930
SLIEZSKY DOM to:		
Batizovské Pleso	1h 15m	0930
Hrebienok	2h 00m	0930
Poľský Hrebeň	2h 00m	5806
Starý Smokovec	2h 00m	5806, 8858
Tatranská Polianka	1h 30m	5806
Vyšné Hágy	3h 00m	0930, 8855
ŠTART to:		
Šalviový Prameň	1h 30m	2908, 5809, 8861
Skalnaté Pleso	2h 00m	5808
Skalnaté Pleso	3h 00m	2908
Tatranská Lomnica	0h 30m	5808
Zelené Pleso	2h 30m	2908, 5809, 8861
STARÝ SMOKOVEC to:		
Bilíkova Chata	0h 50m	5807
Hrebienok	0h 45m	5807
Slavkovský Štít	5h 00m	2906
Sliezsky Dom	2h 30m	8858, 5806
ŠTRBSKÉ PLESO (tarn) to:		
Bystré Sedlo	3h 20m	8853
Jamské Pleso	1h 00m	0930
Junction 0930/8853	0h 30m	0930
Kôprovský Štít	4h 15m	0930, 2902, 0934
Kriváň	3h 30m	0930, 2903
Podbanské	3h 45m	0930/5803
Popradské Pleso	1h 05m	0930
Rysy	4h 20m	0930, 2902, 0933
Sliezsky Dom	4h 35m	0930
Tri Studničky	2h 15m	0930/5803
Veľké Hincovo Pleso	2h 35m	0930, 2902
Vodopád Skok	1h 20m	8853
Vysné Kôprovské Sedlo	3h 45m	0930, 2902

From Štrbské Pleso station add five minutes

TATRANSKÁ KOTLINA to:		
Belianska Jaskyňa	0h 40m	8862
Kežmarské Žľaby	1h 30m	2909
Plesnivec	2h 00m	5810

FROM/to	Time	Via routes
Veľké Biele Pleso	3h 30m	5810
TATRANSKÁ LESNÁ to:		
Bilíkova Chata	1h 45m	8859
Hrebienok	2h 15m	8859, 5807
Poľana Kamzík	2h 00m	8859, 5807
TATRANSKÁ LOMNICA to:		
Bilíkova Chata	2h 00m	2907, 5807
Hrebienok	2h 15m	2907, 5807
Javorina	6h 30m	8864, 2911
Kopské Sedlo	4h 00m	8864, 2911
Polana Kamzík	2h 00m	2907
Šalviový Prameň	2h 00m	8864, 2911
Skalnaté Pleso	2h 45m	5808
Štart	0h 45m	5808
Zamkovského Chata	2h 30m	2907, 0930
Zbojnícka Chata	4h 00m	2907
Zelené Pleso	3h 30m	8864, 2911, 8861
TATRANSKÁ POLIANKA to:		
Batizovské Pleso	3h 00m	5806, 8856, 0930
Lysá Poľana	8h 30m	5806, 2907
Nižné Hágy	1h 00m	5806
Poľský Hrebeň	4h 00m	5806
Sliezsky Dom	2h 00m	5806
Štôla	1h 15m	5806
TATRANSKÉ MATLIARE to:		
Kopské Sedlo	3h 45m	2911
Šalviový Prameň	1h 30m	2911
Veľké Biele Pleso	3h 15m	2911
Zelené Pleso	3h 15m	2911, 8861
TATRANSKÉ ZRUBY to:		
Sliezsky Dom	2h 15m	2905, 8858, 5806
TÉRYHO CHATA to:		
Hrebienok	1h 45m	5812, 0930
Javorina	5h 30m	5812
Priečne Sedlo	1h 30m	8860
Sedielko	1h 30m	5812
Starý Smokovec	2h 15m	5812, 0930, 5807
Zamkovského Chata	1h 00m	5812
Zbojnícka Chata	3h 00m	8860
TRI STUDNIČKY to:		
Hladké Sedlo	4h 30m	2902, 5801, 0931
Kriváň	2h 30m	5803
Nižné Temnosmrečinské Pleso	4h 15m	2902, 5801, 0932

FROM/to	Time	Via routes
Podbanské	1h 30m	0930
Štrbské Pleso	2h 15m	5803 (2h 30m on 0930)
TRIGAN (junction 0930/5805) to:		
Popradské Pleso	0h 30m	0930
Popradské Pleso	0h 45m	5805
Rysy	3h 45m	0930, 2902, 0933
Štrbské Pleso	0h 30m	0930
Veľké Hincovo Pleso	2h 00m	0930, 2902
VEĽKÉ BIELE PLESO to:		
Biela Voda	2h 00m	2911, 8861
Javorina	2h 30m	2911
Skalnaté Pleso	2h 30m	0930
Tatranská Kotlina	3h 30m	5810
Tatranské Matliare	2h 15m	2911
Zelené Pleso	0h 30m	0930
VYŠNÉ HÁGY to:		
Batizovské Pleso	2h 30m	8855
Popradské Pleso	4h 30m	8855, 0930
Sliezsky Dom	3h 30m	8855, 0930
ZAMKOVSKÉHO CHATA to:		
Hrebienok	0h 45m	0930
Javorina	7h 15m	5812
Poľana Kamzík	0h 30m	0930
Sedielko	3h 15m	5812
Skalnaté Pleso	1h 00m	0930
Starý Smokovec	1h 15m	0930, 5807
Téryho Chata	1h 45m	5812
ZBOJNÍCKA CHATA to:		
Hrebienok	2h 30m	2907, 0930
Kačacia Dolina	3h 00m	2907
Lysá Poľana	6h 00m	2907
Poľana Kamzík	2h 30m	2907
Poľský Hrebeň	2h 15m	2907, 5806
Prielom	1h 15m	2907
Tatranská Lomnica	4h 00m	2907
ZELENÉ PLESO to:		
Biela Voda	2h 30m	8861
Jahňací Štít	2h 30m	8861
Kopské Sedlo	1h 00m	0930, 2911
Skalnaté Pleso	2h 00m	0930
Tatranské Lomnica	3h 00m	8861, 2911, 8864
Veľká Svišťovka	1h 15m	0930
Veľké Biele Pleso	0h 30m	0930

HIGHEST SUMMITS
(above 2,300m)

* = shared with Poland
+ = accessible to walkers
G = accessible to walkers with a qualified mountain guide
C = accessible by cable-car

The translations are in some cases very rough. Many summits are simply named after the nearest villages in the plain below.
Note: Gerlachovská Veža, here shown separately, is generally regarded as part of Gerlachovský Štít and not counted in the order of peaks.

Summit	Translation	Height
Gerlachovský Štít (G)	Gerlachov Peak	2,655m
Gerlachovská Veža	Gerlachov Tower	2,642m
Lomnický Štít (G) (C)	Lomnica Peak	2,632m
Zadný Gerlach	Hinder Gerlach	2,630m
Ľadovy Štít	Icy Peak	2,627m
Pyšny Štít	Haughty Peak	2,623m
Malý Ľadový Štít	Little Icy Peak	2,602m
Kotlový Štít	Kettle Peak	2,601m
Vysoká	High	2,560m
Kežmarsky Štít	Kežmarok Peak	2,558m
Končista	The One at the End	2,535m
Baranie Rohy	Ram's Horn	2,526m
Český Štít	Czech Peak	2,500m
Rysy *+	Gashes	2,499m
Kriváň +	The Crooked One	2,494m
Spišsky Štít	Spiš Peak	2,481m
Bradavica	Wart	2,476m
Snehový Štít	Snow Peak	2,465m
Široká Veža (G)	Broad Tower	2,461m
Ganek (Goral dialect)	Verandah	2,459m
Batizovský Štít	Batizovce Peak	2,456m
Slavkovský Štít +	Slavkov Peak	2,452m
Prostredný Hrot	Middle Sharp	2,440m
Veľký Mengušovsky Štít *	Great Mengusovce Peak	2,438m
Čierny Štít	Black Peak	2,434m
Kvetnicová Veža	Flowerpot Tower	2,433m
Hrubý Vrch	Rough Hill	2,428m
Východná Vysoká +	East High	2,428m
Zlobivá	The Infuriating One	2,426m

Summit	Translation	Height
Litvorový Štít	Litvorov Peak	2,423m
Kolový Štít	Stake Peak	2,418m
Javorový Štít	Maple Peak	2,417m
Satan (G)	Satan	2,416m
Huncovský Štít	Huncovce Peak	2,415m
Furkotský Štít	Furkotsky Peak	2,405m
Veľké Solisko	Big Sun Point	2,404m
Vychodný Mengušovský Štít *	East Mengusovce Peak	2,398m
Popradský Ladový Štít	Poprad Icy Peak	2,396m
Štrbský Štít	Štrba Peak	2,395m
Prostredný Mengušovský Štít *	Middle Mengusovce Peak	2,393m
Svišťový Štít	Marmot Peak	2,382m
Zadná Bašta	Hinder Lookout	2,380m
Čubrina *	No translation	2,378m
Divá Veža	Wild Tower	2,376m
Veľká Ľadová Veža	Great Icy Tower	2,376m
Kôprovský Štít +	Dill Peak	2,367m
Predná Bašta	Front Lookout	2,366m
Východná	The Eastern One	2,356m
Kôpky	Little Stack	2,354m
Slavkovská Kopa	Slavkov Stack	2,346m
Žabia Veža	Frog Tower	2,340m
Malý Kriváň	Little Crooked One	2,334m
Hlinská Veža	Earthy Tower	2,330m
Velický Štít	Velicky Peak	2,320m
Veľká Granátova Veža	Great Garnet Tower	2,313m
Zmrzlá Veža	Frozen Tower	2,310m
Štrbské Solisko	Štrba Sun Point	2,302m
Svinica *+	Porcine	2,300m

TRAVEL

To and from the Slovak High Tatras

Note: Since the break-up of Czechoslovakia, the structure of links with other countries has been in a state of flux, and the details that follow are subject to change.

The easiest way to reach the Slovak side of the Tatras is by air. The region has its own airport, located 4 kilometres north-west of the centre of Poprad. It is marked on the map as Airport Tatra (Letisko Tatry), but is confusingly known to the airlines as Tatry-Poprad, and referred to in local timetables as Poprad-Tatry!

The airport is very convenient for the High Tatras, being just 10 kilometres from Starý Smokovec, 16 kilometres from Tatranská Lomnica, and 27 kilometres from Štrbské Pleso (10-30 minutes by taxi). Flights from Prague by CSA Czechoslovak Airlines take about an hour, usually including a stop at Bratislava en route. There are sometimes direct charter flights to Poprad from places outside Slovakia.

There are flights by CSA and other airlines to Prague from all parts of Europe, and from other continents. Bratislava is served from Munich, Stuttgart and Zurich by various airlines

You may find it more convenient to fly to Kraków in Poland (see below) which has direct flights from London, and where self-drive cars can be hired. From Kraków to Starý Smokovec by car takes about three hours. Or you can fly to Vienna, whose airport has a direct bus connection to Bratislava.

By rail, there are direct main line train services to Poprad from Prague (these depart from the stations called Hlavní Nádrazí and Holešovice) and Bratislava; also from Budapest. Trains from Prague and Bratislava also call at the main line station called Štrbské Pleso which is actually situated in the village of Tatranská Štrba, and not to be confused with the rack railway and tram station in Štrbské Pleso itself! Trams, a rack railway and buses provide connections to all the High Tatras resorts.

Long distance buses run direct to the High Tatras resorts from Bratislava and Budapest.

A long distance bus comes to Poprad and Starý Smokovec from Budapest in Hungary. From Poland, you have to come by train or bus to Zakopane, then take a local bus to Lysá Poľana on the Slovak border, from where buses run to Tatranská Lomnica and Starý Smokovec. Alternatively, some of Zakopane's minibuses (see the section on transport within Poland) are allowed to cross into Slovakia.

Within the Slovak High Tatras

An electric tramway along the foot of the mountains links Poprad with Tatranská Lomnica, Starý Smokovec and Štrbské Pleso. There are stations at all the villages and hamlets along the line, and most of these are starting points for walking routes into the mountains. This line forms the spine of an excellent network of trams and buses which are inexpensive and generally reliable, letting you easily start some of your walks from one resort and finish at another.

An electric rack railway links the main line station at Tatranská Štrba (called Štrbské Pleso) with the village of Štrbské Pleso itself. A diesel-hauled line links Tatranská Lomnica with a station called Studený Potok (close to Veľká Lomnica) on the line from Poprad to Kežmarok.

Bus services run parallel to the railway lines, and some of these continue to the more remote High Tatras villages of Tatranská Kotlina, Ždiar and Javorina, as well as Lysá Poľana on the border with Poland. The buses are faster and cheaper, but can be so crowded that it sometimes seems impossible to get on

- yet you usually can! Many visitors prefer to use the trains which are slow, but more spacious and rarely crowded.

Times of services are displayed at all the railway stations and at the main bus stops. They are usually shown as a list of departure times for the various destinations, though full train timetables are also displayed at main stations.

A useful booklet, *Everyman's Guide to the High Tatras,* can be bought at local bookshops and tourist offices. It contains bus and train times for the High Tatras resorts, as well as other information about the mountains and resorts. Also included is a translation of the restrictions that apply to some of the bus and train services.

At present there are no return, season or rover tickets - you must buy single tickets for each journey.

Mountain Transport

Inexpensive mountain lifts of various kinds provide a means of avoiding some of the hard work of climbing through the forest zone. They are always busy, especially at weekends and during August, so you should allow plenty of time.

From Štrbské Pleso two chair-lifts operate: to Chata pod Soliskom, and to the Interski ski-jumps (both 08.30-17.00 daily; 20-minute ride).

From Starý Smokovec, a funicular railway runs for nearly two kilometres up to Hrebienok (06.35-19.45 daily except Friday 08.45-19.45; 7-minute ride).

The busy tram station at Starý Smokovec (photo: Derek Goddard)

From Tatranská Lomnica (Grandhotel Praha), a cable-car climbs four kilometres to Skalnaté Pleso (07.00-18.00 daily except Tuesdays; 25-minute ride). Confusingly, the middle station is called Štart. This lift is so busy that, when you buy a ticket, you are also given a coupon bearing a "flight number"; you must then look out for this number to light up on the indicator board above the departure gate before you can board. It is not possible to reserve places, so the best thing is to give yourself plenty of time and be as early as possible at the ticket office.

From Skalnaté Pleso there is a cable-car to Lomnický Štít (operates all year; 25-minute ride); and a chair-lift to Lomnické Sedlo (summer only; 08.00-18.00 daily; 9-minute ride).

At the end of the summer and winter seasons, usually in November and April/May, all the mountain transportation is closed for several weeks for overhaul. Note that the "funicular", which is shown on maps as operating from the west side of the Tatranská Lomnica to Skalnaté Pleso, is likely to be out of action for some years.

By Car

A motorway runs from Prague eastwards to Brno, then a main road takes you further east to Trenčín, where you join the road linking Bratislava north-east to Poprad and on to Košice - this is gradually being improved to motorway standard. For Štrbské Pleso, turn off at Tatranská Štrba; for Starý Smokovec and Tatranská Lomnica, turn off at Poprad. Approaching from Poland, you should head first for Kraków, then south-east to Nowy Targ and on to cross into Slovakia at Lysa Poľana. From there it is a short drive to Tatranská Kotlina, where you turn right along Cesta Slobody (Freedom Highway) which links all the High Tatras resorts.

Cars can be rented in Poprad (see under Shopping and Local Services, below).

Private vehicles are banned at all times from side roads leading up into the mountains. They may only be parked in the official car parks, shown on the maps, where a small charge is made.

Passports & Visas

The following requirements are those that applied in March 1993. You are advised to check the latest position with your travel agent, airline or a consulate of Slovakia.

All visitors to Slovakia need a valid full passport. Short-term passports and identity cards are not accepted. Nationals of European Union and Scandinavian countries, the USA and Canada do not need visas for Slovakia. Visitors from most other countries will probably need a visa, obtainable in advance from the nearest Slovak consulate.

DIVERSIONS

If some members of your party do not wish to walk, or in the unlikely event that you need a change from walking, or have enough energy left for night-life, here are some suggestions. You can get more details from your hotel reception or local travel agencies in the High Tatras.

Sightseeing Excursions

- Raft sailing on the River Dunajec, beside the border with Poland to the north-east. Includes lunch and a visit to Červený Kláštor - the Red Monastery.
- Walking in Slovensky Raj (Slovak Paradise). Completely different from the High Tatras, in a limestone range to the south-east called Slovenské Rudohorie (Slovak Ore Mountains) - quite demanding with ladders and chains. Lunch is included.
- Low Tatras. You can visit the spectacular Demänovské limestone caves, and take a chair-lift to the summit of Chopok (2,024m), one of the highest in the range. Lunch is included.
- Tour of Spiš. You will often see this word included in place names to the east and south-east of the High Tatras. It refers to an ancient Germanic people, of which there are many traces in the architecture and culture of this region. Lunch is included.
- Tour into Poland, including Zakopane (see the Gazetteer in the Polish section) and Nowy Targ, which has an interesting market on Thursdays.
- Sightseeing flights from Airport Tatra, Poprad: a splendid way to admire the High Tatras in good weather.

    You can easily visit Poprad and Kežmarok (see Gazetteer) on your own using public transport.

Museums & Art Galleries

Starý Smokovec: Galleria Villa Flóra
Horný Smokovec: Tatranská Galléria
Tatranská Lomnica: TANAP (National Park) Museum
Ždiar: Museum of Folk Architecture

Poprad: Podtatranské Muzeum
Kežmarok: Castle Museum

Sports etc:

Cycle/mountain bike hire: Sportcentrum, Horný Smokovec; T-Ski and Tatrasport Adam, Starý Smokovec.
Fitness centre: Hotel FIS, Štrbské Pleso; near Parkhotel, Nový Smokovec; Hotel Slovakia, Tatranská Lomnica.
Minigolf: Parkhotel, Nový Smokovec (summer only).
Saunas: FIS and Patria Hotels, Štrbské Pleso; Grandhotel, Starý Smokovec; Hotel Bellevue, Horný Smokovec; Hotels Odborár and Slovakia, Tatranská Lomnica;

Hotel Slovan and Grandhotel Praha, Tatranská Lomnica.
Swimming pools: Hotel Patria, Štrbské Pleso; Grandhotel, Starý Smokovec; Hotel Bellevue, Horný Smokovec; Hotels Odborár, Slovakia and Urani, Tatranská Lomnica.
Tennis: Štrbské Pleso; Tatranská Lomnica; Dolný Smokovec.
T-Ski and other local travel agencies (see Appendix 3) can also arrange horse-riding, tennis, paragliding and mountain climbing.

Dining with Entertainment:
Štrbské Pleso: Slovenka Restaurant, Hotel Patria (live folk music)
Štrbské Pleso: Cengalka, Hotel Panoráma (taped folk music)
Nový Smokovec: Hubertus Club, Villa Dr. Szontag (gipsy music)
Nový Smokovec: Koliesko Wine Bar (taped folk music)
Stará Lesná: Zbojnícka Koliba (gipsy music)
Tatranská Lomnica: Zbojnícka Koliba (gipsy music)
Tatranská Lomnica: Koliba, Eurocamp FICC (live folk music)

Night Clubs (music and dancing):
Štrbské Pleso: Vatra Bar, Hotel Patria
Nový Smokovec: Wine Bar, Parkhotel
Starý Smokovec: Crystal Bar, Grandhotel
Starý Smokovec: Albas Disco
Horný Smokovec: Lucullus Restaurant, Hotel Bellevue
Stará Lesna: Night Club, Hotel Horizont
Tatranská Lomnica: Country Bar, Hotel Slovakia; Night Club, Grandhotel Praha.

Theatres & Cinemas
Starý Smokovec; Tatranská Lomnica; Poprad

SHOPPING AND LOCAL SERVICES

Here is a summary of facilities available in the High Tatras area. Many shops will show outside the English word for the service offered, but we give the Slovak equivalent in brackets in case of need. Little if any English is spoken in the shops, but German is widely understood. Generally, shops are open Mondays to Fridays from 8am to 12 noon, and from 2pm to 6pm; Saturdays from 8am to 1pm.

Poprad has a wide range of shops for all general purposes.

Supermarkets/Foodshops (Potraviny):
Štrbské Pleso: by the railway station (open Sundays)
Starý Smokovec: on the main road (Cesta Slobody)

Tatranská Lomnica: by the railway station
There are also small supermarkets or groceries selling a limited range of food at Podbanské, Tatranská Štrba, Tatranská Polianka, Sibír (Nový Smokovec), Dolný Smokovec, Horný Smokovec, Stará Lesná, Eurocamp, Ždiar.

Post Offices (Pošta):
Štrbské Pleso: turn right outside the tram station for 50 metres (open Monday to Friday 8am to 6pm; Saturday 8am to 2pm).
Starý Smokovec: turn left outside the tram station for 50 metres (open Monday to Friday 8am to 12 noon: Saturday 8am to 10am).
Tatranská Lomnica: turn right outside the station for 50 metres (open Monday to Friday 8am to 4pm; closed Saturday).
Ždiar: on the main road near the filling station.
Poprad: turn left outside the railway station for 80 metres.

Travel Agencies (Cestovná Kancelaria)
Usual opening hours are Monday to Friday 9am to 5pm; Saturday 9am to 12 noon.
We particularly recommend T-Ski, whose director is co-author Renáta Nárožná! Their offices are at the funicular railway station in Starý Smokovec and at the railway station in Strbské Pleso.

Štrbské Pleso: T-Ski	(phone 0969-92253)
Starý Smokovec: T-Ski	(phone 0969-3200)
Starý Smokovec: Satur	(phone 0969-2515/2710)
Nový Smokovec: Slovakoturist	(phone 0969-2827)
Tatranská Lomnica: Satur	(phone 0969-967428/967451)
Tatranská Lomnica: Júlia	(phone 0969-967947)
Ždiar: Goralturist	(phone 0969-98179)
Poprad: Satur	(phone 092-23262/23651/23287)

Currency Exchange (Valuta):
All hotels and travel agencies offer currency exchange facilities. There are banks at Starý Smokovec and Poprad. The VUB bank at Poprad has an automatic cash machine which accepts Mastercard and Eurocard, and the SSS bank at Stary Smokovec has one which accepts Visa.

Department Stores (Obchodný Dom)
Štrbské Pleso (Prior)   Tatranská Lomnica (Javor)
Starý Smokovec (Mladost)   Poprad (Prior)

Bookshops (Knihy)
The following also sell maps:

Štrbské Pleso (next to Prior department store)
Horný Smokovec (Slovenská Kniha)
There is also a bookshop in Tatranská Lomnica and several in Poprad.

Pharmacies (Farmacia):
In Štrbské Pleso, Starý Smokovec, Tatranská Lomnica, Ždiar and Poprad.

Souvenirs (Suveniry)
Slovakia, Starý Smokovec (glassware, traditional leather and woollens)
Vila Flóra, Starý Smokovec (ceramics)
Bell-Glas, Starý Smokovec (glassware)
Úľuv, Tatranská Lomnica (traditional handmade products)
The department stores in Štrbské Pleso, Starý Smokovec and Tatranská Lomnica
also stock glassware and other products.

Camera Film (Fotografia)
T-Ski, Starý Smokovec, and department stores.

Sport Shops (Sport):
Štrbské Pleso: T-Ski Sport-time
Starý Smokovec: Sportcentrum, Tatrasport Adam
Horný Smokovec: Sportcentrum
Tatranská Lomnica: Šerpabazar, Sportcentrum
Most of the above hire out cycles and walking equipment. Cycles can also be
hired at T-Ski in Starý Smokovec.

Tourist Information
A tourist information centre is due to open in summer 1994 at the Služby Dom
(House of Services) near Starý Smokovec railway station. Otherwise you can
usually obtain tourist information from your hotel reception or from travel
agencies (see Appendix 3).

Taxis (Taxi)
Can be arranged through your hotel reception, and can be found at:
Starý Smokovec: at the bus station   (phone 0969-2525)
Tatranská Lomnica: in the car park   (phone 0969-967237)
Poprad: Rádiotaxi   (24 hours, phone 092-24624)

Car Rental:
Poprad: Hertz, at Airport Tatra   (phone/fax 092-64647);
Exclusive Cars, c/o Hotel Gerlach   (phone 092-22530, fax 092-22439).

Car Repair/Service Stations:
Starý Smokovec: Verejnoprospešné Služby
Tatranská Lomnica: Eurocamp
Poprad: Motocentrum; J & P Servis.

Filling Stations
Tatranská Štrba, Nový Smokovec, Tatranská Lomnica, Ždiar. There is also a 24-hour filling station in Poprad.

National Park Offices
TANAP, 05960 Tatranská Lomnica (phone 0969-967951; fax 0969-967248). Also information offices at Podbanské, Popradské Pleso, Skalnaté Pleso, Tatranská Kotlina and Javorina. Information about the national park can also be provided at the mountain rescue centre (see Appendix 6).

Mountain Guides
Horská Služba, Starý Smokovec   (phone 0969-2820 or 2855).

OTHER USEFUL INFORMATION

Here are some more little snippets of information, which do not fit in under any of the foregoing headings:

Currency
Since 1993 Slovakia has its own currency, the Slovak koruna (crown, abbreviated to SK). You can only obtain Slovak currency inside Slovakia, and you are not allowed to take out more than Ks 100. You must therefore transact all your currency exchange inside Slovakia, and in order to avoid having too much left over at the end of your holiday you should not change too much at once.

If you are flying to Slovakia via Prague, you may also need a small amount of Czech currency; if via Kraków, Polish currency - these can be bought at the respective airports.

You can exchange your currency at hotels, travel agencies and banks. If travelling between Poland and Slovakia or vice versa, there is a currency exchange office at the Lysá Poľana frontier station.

Meals
Food and drink in cafes, mountain chalets and restaurants are very inexpensive. Meat tends to be quite spicy. Vegetarians may struggle to find much other than pizzas, cheese and egg dishes. Specialities include bryndza (sheep cheese), bryndzové halušky (sheep cheese noodles), zemiaková placka (potato pancakes)

and Slovenská pochúťka (Slovak titbits -pies filled with spiced pork or beef and onions).

Phoning Home from Slovakia

Dial the following prefixes, then the area code (* = without preliminary 0), then the individual number:
Australia 0061; New Zealand 0064; South Africa 0027; UK 0044 *; USA/ Canada 001.

Tipping

At your discretion, a small tip may be given for good service to waiters, bartenders, taxi drivers, receptionists, room-cleaning staff and hairdressers. The generally accepted amount is 5 percent. In a restaurant, the minimum is 3 crowns, maximum 50 crowns.

Cost of Living

Public transport and food are very inexpensive. Hotel accommodation is quite moderately priced. Clothes and luxury goods are not such good value.

Toilets

Men = Muži or Páni
Women = Ženy or Dámy
There is sometimes a guardian who collects a nominal charge.

Electricity

220 volts.

GAZETTEER

Baranie Rohy (Ram's Horns, 2,526m). A distinctive peak, very popular with climbers, to the north of Téryho Chata in Malá Studená Dolina.

Batizovce (750m). A large village in the Sub-Tatras Basin to the south-west of Starý Smokovec. It was founded by a nobleman called Botyz or Batiz, who was granted the land in 1264 by King Bela IV of Hungary. There are two manor houses and two churches (one catholic, one evangelical).

Batizovské Pleso (Batizovce Tarn, 1,879m). A pretty tarn to the north of Vyšné Hágy, surrounded by some of the highest Tatra summits: Končistá (2,535m), Batizovský Štít (2,456m), Gerlachovsky Stít (2,655m) and Kotlový Štít (2,601m).

Belianska Jaskyňa (White Cave, 885m). A large limestone cave above Tatranská Kotlina in the White Tatras, of which about 1 kilometre is open to the public - the only publicly accessible one in the Slovak High, White or Western

Tatras. The entrance is at 885 metres, and you descend 112 metres to 773 metres. Discovered in the 1880s, this was one of the first caves to be electrically lit, in 1896, and the lighting certainly enhances the stalactites and other limestone formations. Guided tours take place all year round, daily except Mondays. They last about an hour, and you should allow 20 minutes each way from the village.

Belianska Kopa (1,832m). A minor summit above Kopské Sedlo, lying to the north-west of Tatranská Lomnica between the High and White Tatras. It used to be a much used sheep pasture, before livestock was banned from the national park.

Biela Voda (White Water, 920m). The starting point of yellow route 8861, on Cesta Slobody (Freedom Highway) north-east of Tatranská Lomnica. There is a bus stop but no other facilities here.

Bielovodská Dolina. The longest valley (10km) on the north side of the Slovak High Tatras, and one of the prettiest in the area, falling through many terraces. It is named after the river called Biela Voda (white water), and for much of its length forms the border with Poland, with the customs post of Lysá Poľana on its banks.

Bilíkova Chata (Bilík Chalet, 1,255m, telephone 0969-2439). A very popular chalet, owned by the Sokopo company, to the north of Starý Smokovec, from which it is easily accessible, either on foot or with the rack railway. Originally a simple hut, built in 1875, it was enlarged and rebuilt in 1934, and then operated as a mountain resort called Studeno Potocké Kúpele for some years. After World War II, it was renamed after Captain Pavel Bilík of the Starý Smokovec border patrol, who was executed at Kežmarok by the Nazis in 1944. The chalet was refurbished in 1993, and has accommodation for tourists in twin-bedded rooms (which share a shower between two rooms) as well as some suites.

Bradavica (wart, 2,476m) A peak to the north-west of Starý Smokovec that is clearly visible from Veľká Studená Dolina, and accessible to walkers with a guide.

Brnčalova Chata - see Zelené Pleso.

Bystré Sedlo (fresh saddle, 2,314m). A pass to the north-west of Štrbské Pleso, connecting the Mlynichá and Furkotská valleys. It was once much used by shepherds and hunters.

Červené Vrchy (red peaks, in Polish Czerwone Wierchy). The name reflects the autumnal colour of the grass that covers this range of rounded summits. They lie at the east end of the Western Tatras, rising above Tichá Dolina to the north of Podbanské. In the past they attracted shepherds, whose flocks were banned from the national park area in the 1950s; and miners who were unsuccessful in their attempts to find copper.

Česká Dolina. A hanging valley above the south end of the long Bielovodská

Dolina, on the north side of the High Tatras. Containing two small tarns (České Pleso and Zmrzlé Pleso), it is inaccessible to walkers, but can be viewed from the saddle called Váha on the way to Rysy.

Chata Kapitána Morávku - see Popradské Pleso.

Chata Kapitána Nálepku - see Zamkovského Chata.

Chata Kapitána Rašu - see Tri Studničky.

Chata Plesnivec - see Plesnivec

Chata pod Rysmi (Chalet below Rysy, 2,250m, no telephone). The highest chalet in the Tatras, in a superb position 250m below Rysy summit. Built in 1932, and owned by Slovenské Karpaty, the Slovak national sports association, it is open to walkers from May to October only, but also in winter to climbers and mountain skiers in good snow conditions. You can hardly miss the giant karabiner (an item of climbing equipment) - one of the biggest in the world at about 60 centimetres (two feet) long - suspended from the eaves outside. Accommodation for those wishing to stay the night is provided in one large dormitory.

Chata pod Soliskom (1,830m, Chalet below Solisko, no telephone). A very popular chalet to the north-west of Štrbské Pleso, from which it is easily reached by chair-lift. Owned by the FIS Hotel at the foot of the chair-lift, it is the starting point for the short climb to Predné Solisko. There is also a cafe called Bivák Club in the chair-lift building, and both are alive in winter with skiers, since this is the top of the main ski-slope at Štrbské Pleso.

Chata pri Zelenom Plese - see Zelené Pleso

Čierny Štít (black peak, 2,434m). A triangular peak to the north of Starý Smokovec, rising from three valleys: Čierna Javorová Dolina, Veľká Zmrzlá Dolina and Malá Zmrzlá Dolina. Its south wall is very popular with climbers.

Dolný Smokovec (890m). A large but attractive village, which lies hidden in the forest away from the main roads, 2 kilometres south-east of Starý Smokovec. Its name means Lower Smokovec, from dolina (valley). There is a supermarket, a greengrocer (zeleninar), the Chata Valaska restaurant and the To-Ja Chinese Restaurant. The pretty wooden church was built at the beginning of the twentieth century. There is a large children's sanatorium for the treatment of tuberculosis and other respiratory diseases. Dolný Smokovec has a station on the railway from Poprad to Starý Smokovec. The village is served by bus from Starý Smokovec.

Encian - see Skalnaté Pleso

Furkotský Štít (2,405m). A triangular peak at the head of Furkotská Dolina, and above Bystré Sedlo, to the north-east of Štrbské Pleso. Immediately below to the south is the tarn called Vyšné Wahlenbergovo Pleso. In previous centuries its slopes were visited by poachers and miners. The first tourist to reach the summit was a Pole, Kazimir Przerwa-Tetmajer, in 1890. More recently the summit was used as a measuring point by army cartographers.

Ganek (2,459m). A group of three summits to the south-east of Rysy - easily visible from the saddle called Váha. It is well known to climbers for its gallery.

Gerlachov (791m). A village in the Sub-Tatras Basin to the south-west of Starý Smokovec. Founded in the late thirteenth century by a merchant called Gerlach, it became a centre for the distillation of sembra oil, once used in spa treatments but now banned. In 1876 the village was destroyed by fire. It is now a typical agricultural village, and has an evangelical church.

Gerlachovský Štít (Gerlachov Peak, 2,655m). The highest mountain in the High Tatras, Slovakia and the whole Carpathian range; also the highest point in Europe north of the Alps. For long a target of hunters and botanists, its first known ascent was made by Johan Still in 1874. The peak is now accessible to walkers only if accompanied by a local mountain guide.

Grúnik (1,576m). A minor summit on an outcrop on the south-western slope of Kriváň. During World War II, it held a partisan bunker, and in January 1945 was the site of a major battle. The bunker has been reconstructed as a memorial, and can be visited (from green route 5803) but is difficult to find.

Havran (2,152m). The highest summit of the White Tatras.

Hladké Sedlo (smooth saddle, 1,993m). A pass on the border with Poland to the north-west of Štrbské Sedlo. From here, you can look out over the upper part of the beautiful Dolina Pięciu Stawów Polskich (valley of five Polish tarns). The first recorded visit was in 1827 by Albrecht von Sydow.

Hlúpy (stupid, 2,061m). A broad, grassy summit in the centre of the White Tatras. The Tatranská Magistrála used to cross it until the closure of the White Tatras to walkers in 1978.

Horný Smokovec (950m). The upper and newest part of Smokovec ("horný" from "hora", mountain). There are two bookshops (but only Slovenská Kniha sells walking maps), a sports shop (selling walking and climbing equipment), the Slovakoturist travel agency (providing information and currency exchange). Refreshments are available in the *denný bar* of Penzion Polana, and in the Hotel Bellevue and Hotel Šport. The sanatorium is for children with respiratory ailments. On the south side of the railway line is the only youth hostel (Juniorhotel) in the High Tatras. Buses and trains from Starý Smokovec to Tatranská Lomnica stop here.

Hrebienok (little crest, 1,285m). A collection of buildings on a short ridge above Starý Smokovec. It is a major starting point for walkers, lying at the top of the rack railway from Starý Smokovec, which was completed in 1908. As well as the station building (which contains toilets and telephone in the departure hall - "vchod"), there is the Ski Club (offering refreshments), while Bilíkova Chata (see above) is just a few minutes' walk away. The building under reconstruction (as at 1993) is a trade union recreation centre. In winter, this is a beehive for skiers, and the service road from Starý Smokovec doubles as a toboggan run.

Huncovský Štít (2,415m). A peak to the east of Lomnický Štít, visible from Skalnaté Pleso. It is thought to be one of the first Tatras summits to be climbed - this was during the seventeenth century. The name comes from the village in whose parish the peak used to lie - Huncovce, near Kežmarok.

Jahňací Štít (Lamb Peak, 2,229m). The easternmost peak in the High Tatras, first climbed by the Scotsman, Robert Townson, in 1793.

Jamské Pleso (1,447m). An idyllically located tarn on the Tatranská Magistrála, north-west of Štrbské Pleso. Tree-cover is thin, allowing fine views both down over the plain and up to the peaks from the scattering of picnic tables among the scrub. The minor peak to the north-west is Jamy (pits, 1,572m), from which the lake takes its name. To the north, Sedielková Kopa (little saddle stack, 2,062m can be seen). On the east side of the tarn once stood Nedobrého Chata, built in 1936 by Gustav Nedobrý, but burned down in 1943 during the partisan uprising.

Jastrabia Veža (Hawk Tower, 2,139m). This is the great, dark grey crag that soars above Zelené Pleso (q.v.). It is also known as Karbunkulová Veža (emerald tower) for its part in the legend of how Zelené Pleso got its name.

Javorina (1,018m). A quiet village at the west end of the White Tatras, beside the Javorinka river, named after the village. Both take their name from Javorová Dolina (see below). Javorina lies 2.5 kilometres east of the Polish border, and was one of the earliest settlements in the Tatras, having been established in 1759 for the mining of iron ore. In the village centre is a post office and a TANAP information office. There are two churches; in the churchyard of the wooden one is the grave of Jaroslav Votruba, a notable painter of Tatras scenes.

The wooden church, and a nearby hunting lodge near the Hotel Polana, also of wood, were once part of the estate of a nobleman of the Prussian Hohenlohe dynasty. During the nineteenth century, he bought the whole of Javorina parish and developed it into his conception of a forest village. He built the church and lodge, and tried to set up a nature reserve with animals from other countries, but they could not survive in the different environment. In 1936, the estate was returned to the state.

Refreshments can be obtained 500m north of the village, up the hill towards Lysá Poľana, at the Bufet pod Rogov, just inside the entrance to the modernistic Hotel Poľana, which lies at the spot marked as Pri Bránke on the map, and has a restaurant. Buses to Lysá Poľana from Poprad, Starý Smokovec and Tatranská Lomnica stop at Javorina.

Javorová Dolina (maple valley). A quiet valley, 8 kilometres long, running south from Javorina. From the sixteenth century until the 1950s it was sheep rearing country. During the eighteenth century it was the scene of frantic activity, as prospectors came to hunt a rumoured source of cinnabar, which turned out to be false. The Hohenlohe estate (see Javorina) brought tourists to the valley in the nineteenth century.

Javorový Štít (2,417m). A steep-sided pinnacle of a peak at the head of Javorová Dolina, north-west of Starý Smokovec. It was first climbed by Antonia and Karl Englisch, together with their local guide Jan Hunsdörfer, in 1897.

Kačacia Dolina (duck valley). The upper part of Bielovodská Dolina, lying just off the waymarked network, since blue route 2907 turns off before reaching this area. It lies at the top of a moraine, which also holds in the tarn of Kačacie Pleso. A stream falls from the tarn as a waterfall - Hviezdoslavov Vodopád, named after a nineteenth-century Slovak poet called Hviezdoslav. According to a local legend, the valley is the home of a very special duck, which each Midsummer's Day lays a golden egg at the foot of the waterfall, then spends the rest of the year in the mountains. More prosaically, the tarn does attract a large migrant duck population.

Kežmarok. A historic small town near the east end of the High Tatras, just off the walking maps, about 13 kilometres south-east of Tatranská Lomnica. It is easily accessible direct by bus from all the Tatras villages; or by train from Starý Smokovec via Poprad, or from Tatranská Lomnica via Studený Potok. The imposing castle is open for guided tours on the hour, and contains a museum dedicated to artisan activities. The town hall has a Renaissance bell-tower, and there is a small cultural museum. The old wooden, Protestant church, built in 1717 without any help from metal (even nails were avoided), is closed at the time of writing, awaiting restoration; however, a modern one in oriental style, also Protestant, can be visited.

Kežmarská Chata. See Veľké Biele Pleso.

Kežmarské Žľaby (Kežmarok Gullies, 920m). A hamlet on Cesta Slobody (Freedom Highway). There is a field study centre for children, but no facilities for walkers.

Kežmarsky Štít (Kežmarok Peak, 2,558m). The tenth highest summit in the High Tatras, adjoining Lomnický Štít. Its first recorded ascent was in 1615, by David Frölich from Kežmarok.

Končistá (2,535m). One of the more prominent Tatras peaks, as seen from the Sub-Tatras basin. It lies above Batizovské Pleso, north-east of Štrbské Pleso, and the name is a dialect word meaning "end" (of the range).

Kôprová Dolina. One of the longest Tatras valleys, at 11 kilometres, running north-eastwards from Podbanské in the western part of the High Tatras. It was visited during the fifteenth and sixteenth centuries by miners from Liptov seeking gold and antimony, and later by hunters and shepherds. During the early part of the twentieth century, there was a chalet called Vatra (bonfire).

Kôprovský Štít (2,367m). One of the easier peaks in the Tatras, though it requires a lengthy approach. It lies to the north of Štrbské Pleso, close to the border with Poland, and has beautiful views over three valleys, two of them lake-filled.

Kopské Sedlo (stack saddle, 1,749m). The "official meeting point" of the High and White Tatras, and therefore the easternmost point of the High Tatras. There are actually two saddles here - the northernmost is the higher one. Together they cover a broad, grassy expanse where three valleys meet: Zadné Meďodoly, Predné Meďodoly and Dolina Bielych Plies. This area was once the location of some unsuccessful copper mines.

Kopské Sedlo is one of the best viewpoints in the Tatras, reached by easy routes, yet the distance from the nearest transport ensures that it rarely gets crowded. If not too windy it makes a great picnic spot, and there is a table at the lower, southernmost saddle, which also has an excellent view down Dolina Bielych Plies to the Sub-Tatras Basin. Three White Tatras peaks are visible from here are: Havran (2,152m), Hlúpy (2,061m), and Košlare (2,011m) with its three distinctive humps; close by to the south-east with a green, rounded summit, is Belianská Kopa (1,832m); to the south is Kežmarský Štít (2,558m), and to the south-east with its lone pinnacle is Jahňací Štít (2,229m).

Kotlový Štít (2,601m). The peak that hides Gerlachovský Štít from the Sub-Tatras Basin. It is the eighth highest in the Tatras.

Kriváň (The Crooked One, 2,494m). Though only fifteenth in the overall peaking order, this is the second highest summit on the Tatras waymarked network. The distinctive and imposing curved shape that gave rise to its name is best seen from Podbanské and Pribylina (a village to the south-west of Podbanské on the way to Liptovské Hrádok). This peculiarity proved irresistible to early climbers, who included the Scotsman Robert Townson in 1793 (the first recorded ascent), the Swedish naturalist Göran Wahlenberg in 1813, and King Friedrich August II of Saxony in 1840. Kriváň has become the national symbol of Slovakia, because it can be seen from such a great distance. In 1841, a pilgrimage to the summit by Slovak writers and poets took place, and since 1955 this has been commemorated with an annual pilgrimage at the end of August.

Ľadovy Štít (icy peak, 2,627m). The fourth highest summit in the High Tatras, it dominates the head of Malá Studená Dolina behind Téryho Chata, to the north-west of Starý Smokovec. The first recorded climb was by the Irishman, John Ball, in 1843.

Ľaliové Sedlo (lily saddle, 1,947m). The official meeting point of High and Western Tatras, therefore the westernmost point of the High Tatras. It lies to the north of Tri Studničky, on the border between Slovakia and Poland. Though on one of the waymarked routes in Poland (where it is known simply as Liliowe, and the altitude is given as 1,952m), it is accessible to walkers from Slovakia only if accompanied by a local mountain guide, using an unwaymarked path that

Lomnický Štít: the astronomical and meteorological station (photo: Jeston Price)

starts from Sedlo Závory.

Litvorová Dolina (marked on maps as Litvorová Kotlina). Once a popular sheep pasture, this high valley and its tarn are now much visited by walkers crossing the saddles of Poľský Hrebeň and Prielom. The name comes from a locally occurring herb called litvor.

Lomnické Sedlo (Lomnica saddle, 2,189m). An easily visited saddle at the top of the chairlift from Skalnaté Pleso, north-west of Tatranská Lomnica. There are spectacular views over the Sub-Tatras Basin and over the Pät Spišských Plies (five Spis tarns). A formerly waymarked path to it, shown on older maps (an extension of green route 5808, is no longer accessible to walkers, as it has been obliterated by the popular ski slope that descends from here.

Lomnický Štít (Lomnica Peak, 2,634m). The second highest summit in the Tatras, whose first recorded ascent was by the Scotsman, Robert Townson, on 17 August 1793 with two local hunters as his guides. At that time it was thought to be the highest Tatras peak by the local Spiš people, who called it Dedko (grandfather), while its slightly lower neighbour Kežmarský Stít was Babka (grandmother). Since 1940, it has been served by cable-car from Tatranská Lomnica (with a change at Skalnaté Pleso), and is accessible on foot only if accompanied by a local mountain guide. At the summit are a refreshment kiosk, an astronomical and meteorological station of the Slovak Academy of Science, and the highest post office in Slovakia! (You can have your postcards sent from here.)

Lučivná (799m). A village and climatic spa in the Sub-Tatras Basin, lying midway between Štrba and Svit. There is a sanatorium for children with tuberculosis and other respiratory diseases.

Lysá Poľana (bald meadow, 970m). A small settlement which has grown up around the customs post on the border with Poland, beside the river called Biela Voda in Slovak or Białka in Polish (both mean or imply White Water). In Polish the initial "L" of Łysa has the line, making the pronunciation "weesa". There is a buffet on the Slovak side by the bus stop. Buses come from Poprad, Starý Smokovec and Tatranská Lomnica in Slovakia; and from Zakopane in Poland. If you wish to continue your journey by bus on the far side of the border, you must cross the border on foot.

Malá Studená Dolina (little cold valley). A comparatively short (4 kilometres) but much visited valley in the central High Tatras, north of Starý Smokovec. There are two popular chalets: Zamkovského Chata at the foot, and Téryho Chata at the head, and the upper part contains the Pät Spišských Plies (five Spiš tarns).

Matejovce - see Poprad.

Mengušovce (810m). A village to the south-west of Starý Smokovec, with fine views of the High Tatras. It was founded in the thirteenth century as part of the estate of the neighbouring village of Batizovce. The village has an attractive Roman Catholic church.

Mengušovská Dolina. A much used valley climbing northwards from Štrbské Pleso, past the popular tarn of Popradské Pleso, towards Velké Hincovo Pleso (largest tarn in the Slovak High Tatras) and Rysy summit.

Mlynica (688m). A small village in the Sub-Tatras Basin, lying between Tatranská Lomnica and Poprad. Founded in the thirteenth century by immigrants from Saxony, it became the first Protestant village in the Špis region - nowadays there is a catholic as well as a Protestant church. In the second half of the nineteenth century it provided many mountain guides for excursions into the Tatras. Mlynica is also the name of the stream that flows through Štrbské Pleso to join the River Poprad at Svit.

Mlynická Dolina. The 6-kilometre long valley in which Štrbské Pleso lies. In its upper part can be found the beautiful Skok waterfall and a large number of small tarns. Now a popular ski terrain in winter, it was formerly much used for sheepgrazing.

Modré Pleso (Blue Tarn, 2,190m) The highest tarn in the Slovak High Tatras. It lies just below the saddle called Sedielko, at the head of Malá Studená Dolina to the north of Starý Smokovec.

Nadbanské (970m). A peaceful hamlet lying just to the east of Podbanské, at the foot of the west slope of Kriváň. Its name means "above the mine" (compare Podbanské), and derives from the coppermines that existed here until the nineteenth century. There are no facilities here for walkers.

Nálepkova Chata - see Zamkovského Chata.

Nižné Hágy (910m) (Lower Hágy). A hamlet between Vyšné Hágy and Stôla, served by the bus from Štrbské Pleso to Poprad via Svit.

Nižné Rakytovské Pleso (Low Rakytov Tarn, 1,323m). The lowest tarn in the Slovak High Tatras, situated 2 kilometres west of Štrbské Pleso - it is the larger of the two tarns shown there.

Nižné Temnosmrečinské Pleso (Lower Spruce Tarn, 1,674m). A large and pretty tarn at the end of the waymarked path along Kôprová Dolina, to the north-west of Štrbské Pleso.

Nižné Wahlenbergovo Pleso (Lower Wahlenberg Tarn, 2,053m). A tarn passed on the waymarked route along Furkotská Dolina, north-west of Štrbské Pleso.

Nová Lesná (New Forest, 746m). A village lying a little to the east of the main road between Stary Smokovec and Poprad, with panoramic views of the High Tatras. It has for many years been the home of leading Tatras guides, including Jan Still, one of the first people to reach the summit of Gerlachovský Štít.

Nová Polianka (New Polianka, 1,00m). A hamlet on Cesta Slobody (Freedom Highway) between Starý Smokovec and Štrbské Pleso. There is a post office, and walkers can slake their thirst in the Tomi Bar, situated in the Vojenský Ústav Dýchacich Chorob (Military Institute for Respiratory Ailments).

Nový Smokovec (New Smokovec, 1,000m). The western part of the Smokovec community. Nový Smokovec was established in the second half of the nineteenth century by the physician Dr Mikuláš Szontagh, after whom one of the hotels, Villa Dr Szontagh, is named - it doubled as his home and a sanatorium for his richest patients. The buildings called Europa and Branisko are sanatoria. You cannot help but notice the hulking great sanatorium called Penzák, looming up behind the railway station. Built in 1925, it had in its heyday a worldwide reputation for luxury. Of more modest proportions, but almost as noticeable, is the circular Park Hotel with a minigolf course at its centre. Nearby is a hotel called MS-70, which was built as the press centre for the World Nordic Ski Championships in 1970. In winter, the terrain above Nový Smokovec, called Jakubková Lúka (Jacob's Meadow) is alive with downhill skiers. At the west end of the resort is an estate called Sibír, which means Siberia!

Nové Štrbské Pleso (New Štrba Tarn, 1,305m). This small, artificial tarn was created in the late nineteenth century out of the swamp that previously occupied the land to the south-east of Štrbské Pleso. There are several hotels, including one (Hotel Baník) beside the lake, where refreshments can be obtained.

Obrovský Vodopád (Giant's Waterfall, 1,400m). The bridge over Malý Studený Potok (Little Cold Brook) provides an excellent view of the waterfall. From here until the late nineteenth century a smugglers' path led into Poland. Note how the trees nearby cling almost impossibly to the rock face.

Ostrva (1,984m). A minor summit dominating Popradské Pleso, from which red route 0930 zigzags up the north slope to a saddle below the summit at 1,926m. The broad summit itself, though not on the waymarked route, is easily accessible to and generally visited by walkers for the panoramic views.

Pät Spišských Plies (Five Spiš Tarns). A group of small and pretty tarns at the head of Malá Studená Dolina, to the north of Stary Smokovec. They are best viewed from the saddle called Sedielko. Nearby is the chalet Téryho Chata.

Plesnivec (Edelweiss, 1,350m). Shown as Chata Plesnivec on signposts. There is a chalet here, actually the only one in the White Tatras. It was built in 1935 for use by walkers, but since 1955 has been used only as a TANAP research base. However, outside is a covered picnic table, and you can replenish your water-bottle at a spring a little way along the waymarked path in the uphill direction. The chalet could do with some restoration, but commands a fine view down Dolina Siedmich Prameňov (Seven Springs Valley) to the Sub-Tatras Basin. During the second half of the eighteenth century, this valley was the home of a gold prospector called Drechsler.

Pod Muráňom (Below Muráň, 1,100m). A forester's house and mountain rescue centre near the foot of Javorová Dolina, 2 kilometres south-east of Javorina. Muráň is the distinctive slab of a mountain, the westernmost summit of the White Tatras, that rears above the farm.

Granaty, from Czarny Staw Gasienicowy

Chata pri Zelenom Plese
Schronisko Kondratowa

Podbanské (Below the Mine, 940m). A quiet village at the foot of Kôprová Dolina between the High and Western Tatras. Nowadays left in peace from main road traffic by a bypass, it has a relaxed atmosphere, though a series of battles of the Slovak National Uprising were fought here during 1944-45. In the village centre, refreshments can be obtained at Krčma pod Kriváňom (Tavern below Kriváň), and there is a grocery (potraviny). Refreshments and meals can also be obtained at Hotel Kriváň - from the village centre take the path up the hill behind Krčma pod Kriváňom. At the main road junction is a TANAP information office.

Buses from Štrbské Pleso to Liptovský Hrádok go via Podbanské - the bus stops are 50 metres south of the main road junction. No timetable is displayed by the stops, but times are shown in the *Everyman's Guide*, or you can get them either from the TANAP information office or from Hotel Kriváň reception. There is a car park by the main road junction.

Podspády (Underslope, 912m). A quiet village on the Javorinka river on the north side of the White Tatras, 5 kilometres from the Polish border. At the village centre is Chata Muráň, with a restaurant and grocery. Buses from Poprad to Lysá Poľana stop at Podspády, and go via Starý Smokovec and Tatranská Lomnica.

Poľana Kamzík (Chamois Meadow, 1,295m). A clearing a little to the north of Hrebienok. There was a chalet here (Chata Kamzík) until the early 1980s, but its sewage started to cause hygiene problems for the villages below, so it had to be closed. The raised foundations remain, and provide a popular picnic site in a sunny location. The original chalet, the first in the Slovak Tatras, was built in 1863. This well wooded area abounds in limba-fir, rowan (mountain ash) and bilberries.

Poľský Hrebeň (Polish Ridge, 2,200m). A saddle on the main ridge of the High Tatras, to the north-west of Starý Smokovec, linking the valleys called Velická Dolina and Bielovodská Dolina. Its name comes from use by Polish smugglers in past centuries.

Poprad (672m). The main commercial centre for the Tatras region, with a population of around 52,000. It is a busy town with a pedestrianised central area of shops and restaurants. Though never of any historical significance, there is a historic old quarter (Spišská Sobota, see below), and the suburbs of Veľká, Matejovce and Stráže pod Tatrami, formerly separate villages, are also worth exploring. The town developed as a result of the railway line to Košice, opened in 1871.

Among the buildings of interest are the Renaissance bell tower, the Gothic church of St Juraj, and the Sub-Tatras Museum. Another good reason for a visit is the stunning view of the whole High Tatras range from various points in the town, including the airport (which was funded by Bata, the famous shoe manufacturer). There are frequent train and bus connections to and from all the main Tatras resorts in Slovakia - the trains to Starý Smokovec and Štrbské Pleso leave from the high level part of the railway station.

Popradské Pleso (Poprad Tarn, 1494). A large tarn which is the popular target of an easy stroll from Štrbské Pleso. It has long been on the tourist trail, with a first recorded mention by the local naturalist, David Frölich, during the first half of the seventeenth century. There is now a railway station named after it, though this is an hour away on foot - see blue route 2902. The tarn is in a beautiful setting beneath the towering summit of Ostrva, but the collection of refreshments kiosks, and the throng of customers, on the west shore may be a detraction for some. It is sometimes called Malé Rybie Pleso (Little Fish Tarn).

The Poprad river, which issues from the tarn, flows through the town of the same name, then continues through Poland to join the Dunajec and then the Vistula into the Baltic Sea; all the streams further west feed the Váh, a tributary of the Danube, which of course flows to the Black Sea.

The mountain hotel on the west shore of the tarn is one of the most visited chalets in the Slovak High Tatras. Called Chata Kapitána Morávku, or sometimes Chata pri Popradskom Plese, it provides meals and refreshments all year round, and can accommodate about 100 people in bedrooms and small dormitories. It is owned by Interhotel, and has developed from a log cabin built in 1879. Captain Morávka was killed in 1945 while leading a Slovak partisan reconnaissance patrol.

Predné Meďodoly (Front Coppermines). A gently sloping valley between the High and White Tatras. For long an idyllic sheep pasture, during the seventeenth and eighteenth centuries both this and Zadné Meďodoly (Back Coppermines) became the scene of copper-mining activities.

Predné Solisko (Front Solisko, 2,093m). A minor summit which, being one of the easiest nigh viewpoints to reach in the High Tatras, with the help of the chairlift, tends to get very crowded. There are two higher Solisko summits: Štrbské (Štrba, 2,302m), which can be seen looking north-west from Predné, and Veľké (Great, 2,404m) which is out of sight beyond Štrbské Pleso. To the south is a splendid view over Štrbské Pleso to the Sub-Tatras Basin. Other summits in view are: Satan (bearing 20, 2,416m); Patria (bearing 85, 2,203m); Kriváň (bearing 290, 2,494m); Krátka (bearing 300, 2,370m).

Priečne Sedlo (Transverse Saddle, 2,352m). A deep saddle between Široká Veža and Priečna Veža, to the north-west of Starý Smokovec. It is well used, being on a popular route between the valleys of Malá and Veľká Studená Dolina. From here can be seen the summits of Slavkovský Štít and Bradavica, and there are fine views over the two valleys with their chalets (Zbojnícka Chata and Téryho Chata).

Prielom (Crack, 2,288m). An aptly named pass, literally a crack in the mountains, to the north-west of Starý Smokovec. It is difficult to negotiate, with steep drops and fixed chains on both sides.

Prostredný Hrot (Middle Edge, 2,440m). A summit to the north of Starý Smokovec, above Téryho Chata. Although off the waymarked network, it can be visited with a mountain guide, and is not difficult to reach.

Rysy (Gashes, 2,499m). On the border between Poland and Slovakia, this popular summit is the highest in Poland, and the highest in Slovakia on the waymarked network, ie. that can be reached without a mountain guide. For the origin of the name see the Polish section of the Gazetteer. Vladimir Ilyich Lenin is supposed to have climbed Rysy, and there used to be a plaque to record this feat, but it has now been removed and there seems to be some doubt about the veracity of this story anyway.

Sedielko (Little Saddle, 2,372m). The highest saddle on the waymarked route network in the Tatras. It lies to the north of Starý Smokovec, and has good views over the Pät Skišských Plies (Five Spiš Tarns) and Zadná Dolina, the upper part of Javorová Dolina.

Široké Sedlo (Dry Saddle, 1,830m). The central saddle of the White Tatras range, situated between the peaks of Ždiarska Vidla (Ždiar's Pitchfork, 2,146m) and Hlúpy (Stupid, 2,061m). The saddle was recently made accessible to walkers for the first time since 1978. Southwards from here you have a marvellous view of the easternmost peaks of the High Tatras, dominated by Jahňací Štít in the foreground and Lomnický Štít in the background. North-east lies the village of Ždiar, with the Spišská Magura range behind it. Beyond, in good weather, you can see the Pieniny mountains in Poland.

Skalnaté Pleso (Rocky Tarn, 1,751m). A tarn at the top station of the cable-car and gondola-lift from Tatranská Lomnica, which is a little higher than the tarn at 1,761m. In the huge and rather ugly buildings, known as Encián (Gentian), once a mountain hotel, there are a restaurant and *denný bar*. The buildings near the tarn belong to the Slovak Astronomical Institute. A few hundred metres south of the cable-car station, along red route 0930B, is the shell of Skalnatá Chata, a primitive former mountain bothy - see information board 1 in the path description for this route.

Skok, more properly Vodopád Skok (Jump Waterfall, 1,780m). An impressive waterfall in Mlynická Dolina to the north of Štrbské Pleso, from some parts of which it is visible. Nearby is a tarn called Pleso Nad Skokom (Tarn above Skok).

Slavkovský Štít (Slavkov Peak, 2,452m). The fourth highest peak on the waymarked route network in the Slovak High Tatras, named after a village near Poprad. A major earthquake several thousand years ago (see also Vodopád Studeného Potoka) is thought to have dislodged the top of Slavkovský Štít, which until then was probably the highest in the Tatras. This was the target of one of the earliest recorded ascents, by Juraj Buchholz in 1664.

From the summit, there is a grandstand view over the Sub-Tatras Basin, while other major peaks in sight are: Gerlachovský Štít (bearing 265, 2,655m); Bradavica (bearing 280, 2,476m); Javorový Štít (bearing 335, 2,417m); Široká Veža (due north, 2,461m); Prostredný Hrot (bearing 15, 2,440m); Lomnický Štít (bearing 30, 2,632m).

Sliezsky Dom - see Velické Pleso.

Spišská Sobota (680m). Now one of the oldest parts of Poprad, this was once the wealthiest town in the Sub Tatras Basin in its own right, until the rise of Poprad itself in the late nineteenth century. There are many relics of that glorious time, including Renaissance houses, Gothic churches and memorials galore.

Stará Lesná (Old Forest, 740m). A one-street village to the south of Tatranská Lomnica. At its north end are Hotel Horizont (restaurant) and Hotel Ceva (snack bar, coffee shop and swimming pool). The church dates from the thirteenth century, but was rebuilt in the Baroque style in the eighteenth century. Some buses from Tatranská Lomnica to Kežmarok go via Stará Lesná.

Štart (1,120m). The middle station of the cable-car and chair-lift from Tatranská Lomnica to Skalnaté Pleso. There are no facilities here for walkers.

Starý Smokovec (Old Smokovec, 1,010m). The administrative centre of the whole High Tatras region, joined to Nový Smokovec and Horný Smokovec (see above) to form the community that you will sometimes see written as Smokovce (the plural form). Hiding in the forest 1.5 kilometres to the south-west is the separate village of Dolný Smokovec (see above). You can understand why this location was chosen as a recuperation centre: there is a healthy, clean feeling about the place, imbued by the scent of pine trees. Starý Smokovec is the oldest resort in the High Tatras, established in 1793. The oldest remaining building is Vila Flóra (1839), now a ceramics shop and art gallery.

In the upper part of the village is the imposing Grand Hotel, built in 1904. Many of the buildings that look like hotels in Starý Smokovec are in fact trade union holiday centres or sanatoria, some of which are beginning to open to tourists. In the upper part of the village, near the Grand Hotel, are the catholic church, built in 1894, the bottom station of the funicular railway to Hrebienok (see above), and the sports centre, under construction that (as in 1993) may yet take several years to finish, due to lack of funds.

In the lower part is the railway station, a busy junction with trains in three directions to Poprad, Tatranská Lomnica and Štrbské Pleso. Close by you will find the post office, supermarket and other shops, restaurants, bars, and the Policlinic (health centre). A pleasant tree-lined pedestrian thoroughfare (unnamed) leads westwards to Nový Smokovec, passing the huge Palace sanatorium.

Štôla (860m). A typical old village of the Sub-Tatras Basin, lying just off the road from Vyšné Hágy to Mengušovce. It was once a centre of manufacture of sembra pine oil, used in local sanatoria. The heart of the village, with its church, lies on a side road to the west of the main road. There is a post office, a small general store and a buffet; also a sanatorium. Buses from Štrbské Pleso to Poprad via Svit stop at Štôla.

Štrba (827m). A large village in the Sub-Tatras Basin, founded in the thirteenth century. It developed following the building of the railway line to Košice, and was especially noted as a base for carriage drivers.

Štrbské Pleso (Štrba Tarn, 1,320-1,355m). A sprawling mountain resort, the highest community in Slovakia, established in 1873 beside the tarn above the town of Štrba, hence the name. Most facilities of use to walkers are grouped around the railway station: supermarket, open-air market and refreshments (*denný bar*, kiosks, and restaurants). The modern, split-level station also contains toilets, a spacious waiting room and left luggage facilities. Most of the buildings in the resort are modern - some unfortunately rather too functional in design. At the north end of the village are the Patria and FIS Hotels, near the ski-slopes. Near the Hotel Patria, a side road leads to a long, white building, Sanatorium Helios, described as a "natural climatic spa".

Štrbské Pleso is served by train from Poprad and Starý Smokovec, by rack railway from Tatranská Štrba, and by bus from Poprad, Starý Smokovec, Podbanské and many other places in Slovakia. Private vehicles are banned from the village; there is one car park on the approach road from Cesta Slobody (Freedom Highway), and another at the railway station.

This is Slovakia's leading winter sports resort - the World Nordic Championships were held here in 1970. The main ski facilities, dominated by two ski-jumps, are located on the north side of the tarn.

To reach the tarn from the railway/bus station, go to the right of the supermarket, then climb the steps leading up to a road, which you cross, and continue ahead for 50m to the tarn. To reach the station from the south-east corner of the tarn, go to the left of a white electricity sub-station, cross the road then go down the steps.

A footpath completely encircles the tarn itself (1,350m), which contains several rare species of fish. At the south-west corner of the tarn are two spa establishments called Kriváň (formerly the Grand Hotel) and Solisko, where refreshments can be obtained. There are good views here: to one side over the tarn towards Vysoká and its neighbouring peaks; to the other over the plain of Liptovská Kotlina. On the western shore is a small peninsula, whose seats provide a pleasant resting place, and on which is located a memorial (inscribed "česť ich pamiatke", "in their memory") to the Slovak national heroes Jan Rašo (killed 26.9.44) and Štefan Morávka (killed 14.1.45), after whom two nearby mountain chalets were named.

See also Nové Štrbské Pleso.

Studený Potok (Cold Stream). One of the main streams in the High Tatras, flowing south-east to the River Poprad at Veľká Lomnica. It is formed by its tributaries where they merge on leaving the valleys of Malá Studená Dolina and Veľká Studená Dolina. Studený Potok is also the name of the railway station at Veľká Lomnica, where the line from Tatranská Lomnica meets the one from Poprad to Kežmarok and beyond.

Svinica (Porcine, 2,300m). The westernmost peak in the High Tatras, lying on the border with Poland.

Svit (717m). A small industrial town in the Sub-Tatras Basin to the south of Starý Smokovec. Svit was built in 1936 by the shoe manufacturers, Bata, and its name comes from the initials of the factory complex: Slovenská Viskozová Továreň (Slovakian Viscose Factory).

Symbolický Cintorin (Symbolic Cemetery, 1,540m). A memorial near the tarn called Popradské Pleso to those who gave their lives while in the mountains. No-one is buried here, there are just plaques and crosses, often decorated with flowers. There is a small chapel, which has a single bell inscribed in Slovak, "In memory of the dead, a warning to the living". The "cemetery", started in 1936, was the idea of Otakar Stafl, a painter of the Prague Academy, who was also for a while the manager of the chalet at Popradské Pleso. It is normally open from mid-June to December only, since the paths leading to and through it are quite steep and icy in winter and spring. At the end of September each year, the cemetery is the scene of the Mountain Rescue Service Day ceremony, in honour of the people who perform this valuable task.

Tatranská Kotlina (Tatras Basin, 760-765m). A resort at the east end of the White Tatras, established in 1881. On the south side of the road in the village centre is a modern complex containing a supermarket, post office and pub, serving a number of sanatoria. Nearby is a coffee bar (Kaviareň Carda), and at the north end of the village, at the foot of the path leading to Belianska Jaskyňa (see above), is a car park, buffet and a small store. 1 kilometre south, at the main road junction, is Penzion Limba which has a restaurant.

Tatranská Lesná (905m). A small holiday resort on the railway line between Starý Smokovec and Tatranská Lomnica, with two trade union holiday homes (Jánošík and Karpatia), but no facilities for walkers. There is no car park.

Tatranská Lomnica (850-860m). A spacious village, one of the largest resorts in the High Tatras, with many facilities and excellent transport connections. It has developed around a central park on the hillside. The hotels Grandhotel Praha, Horec (Gentian) and Slovan are on the upper side of the park; others (Lomnica, Slovakia and Odborár) are near the railway/bus stations on the lower side. The resort recently celebrated its centenary, having been established in 1893 with the construction of the Hotel Lomnica. The large, modern Morava building on the upper side of the park is a trade union holiday centre.

Tatranská Lomnica is a winter sports resort: lifts take skiers up to 2,190 metres at Lomnické Sedlo, and there are ski jumps at the west end of the village. At the east end is the TANAP (National Park) Museum; this has an interesting display of Tatras wildlife, and an excellent audio-visual show once or twice daily, with an English commentary. The village offers a good choice of refreshment facilities, including a pizzeria (by the railway station) and a pub (by the bus station). The railway station is the terminus of lines from Poprad via Veľká Lomnica, and from Starý Smokovec. Buses link the village with all parts of the High Tatras, Poprad, Kežmarok and many other nearby towns in Slovakia. There are two car parks on the west side of the village.

Tatranská Polianka (1,005-1,010m). A small spa, 3 kilometres south-west of Starý Smokovec, founded in 1885. In its early days it became a leading ski resort, and the first international race took place here, but there are now no ski facilities left. At the village centre is a parade of shops, including a post office, a small supermarket, the HB Cafe-Restaurant and a bistro. Buses and trains between Starý Smokovec and Štrbské Pleso stop here, and there is a car park.

Tatranská Štrba (827m). A village to the south of Štrbské Pleso, which has developed around its railway station on the main line from Bratislava to Košice - this is in fact the highest main-line railway station in Slovakia, though confusingly it is called Štrbské Pleso. A rack railway to Štrbské Pleso itself also starts here. In the village is Tatranský Lieskovec (Tatras Hazelnut), a complex of apartments for people working in the High Tatras resorts.

Tatranské Matliare (885m). A small but long established holiday resort on the north-east side of Tatranská Lomnica, with a couple of trade union holiday centres, Hutník and Metalurg, where refreshments can be obtained. The former luxury Hotel Esplanade is now an army health centre, also offering refreshments to the public. Buses from Starý Smokovec and Tatranská Lomnica to Lysá Poľana stop here. Cars may be parked at Hutník and Metalurg.

Tatranské Zruby (Tatras Log Cabins, 990m). Since 1923 a rest centre for the military to the south-west of Nový Smokovec, but tourists are welcome at its Koliba Titris night spot, where traditional trout meals are served accompanied by folk music. Buses and trains between Starý Smokovec and Štrbské Pleso stop here. There is no car park.

Téryho Chata (Téry's Chalet, 2,015m, telephone 092-24900, open all year). An isolated chalet at the head of Malá Studená Dolina, near Päť Spišských Plies (Five Spis Tarns). Built in 1899, and named after Dr Edmund Téry (1856-1917), a Slovak doctor, mountaineer and pioneer of tourism development in the Tatras, the chalet is now owned by Slovenské Karpaty, the Slovak national sports association.

Tri Studničky (Three Little Wells, 1,180m) A charming and peaceful rural hamlet, built on a slope in the foothills of Kriváň, well away from the main road. TANAP (national park authority) has a base here. Close by to the south is a splendid example of a typical Tatras "hatstand" signpost. There are no facilities for walkers in the hamlet, but 1 kilometre south is Chata Kapitána Rašu, a mountain chalet where refreshments are available. It is named after Jan Rašo, a partisan who was killed during a battle of the Slovak National Uprising on 26 September 1944 (a memorial can be seen on the main road nearby), and replaces the original chalet, then called Važecka Chata, which was burned down during the battle.

Važec (792m). A village in the Liptov Basin to the south-west of Štrbské Pleso, from which it can be reached by train or bus. It was founded in the thirteenth century, but rebuilt in 1931 after having been destroyed by fire. On the south-west side of the village is Važecká Jaskyňa, a 400-metre long limestone cave, which is open to the public.

Važecká Dolina. A valley on the south side of Kriváň, once a popular walking route to the summit (the uncoloured path can still be seen on the map), but now a strict nature reserve.

Velické Pleso (1,663m). A quietly situated tarn, lying at the foot of Gerlachovský Štít. At its south end is Sliezsky Dom (Silesian House, 1,670m, telephone 092-22590, open all year), a spacious mountain hotel owned by the Interhotel company. It provides meals and refreshments, also accommodation in bedrooms and a dormitory. The present building, opened in 1968, has several predecessors - the first, built in 1874, was destroyed by an avalanche. The name comes from the Silesian section of the Hungarian Carpathian Association, which built one of the early chalets.

Veľká Lomnica (639m). A large village in the Sub-Tatras Basin to the south-east of Tatranská Lomnica - just outside the bottom right-hand corner of the *Vysoké Tatry* 1:50,000 map. It is one of the oldest settlements in the area, having been established by a Slavonic tribe in the seventh century on the site of a neolithic settlement.

Veľká Studená Dolina (Great Cold Valley). One of the most visited valleys in the High Tatras, 5.5 kilometres long, lying close to the north of Starý Smokovec. Hrebienok, the upper terminus of the rack railway, lies above its southern slopes. The broad head of the valley contains no less than 27 small tarns, at the centre of which lies the popular chalet called Zbojnicka Chata. Until 1901, when it was acquired by the state, the valley belonged to the parish of Stará Lesná.

Veľká Svišťovka (Great Little Marmot, 2,037m). A fairly easily accessible minor summit at the east end of the High Tatras, with fine views of the White Tatras, across the Sub-Tatras Basin, and down to Zelené Pleso. The distinctive summit on bearing 35 is Bujačí Vrch (Bull Hill, 1,946m), the easternmost of the White Tatras. On bearing 310 is Jahňací Štít (2,229m) in the High Tatras.

Velké Biele Pleso (Great White Tarn, 1,612m). A magical, yet rather melancholy spot, on the way to Kopské Sedlo, north of Tatranská Lomnica. The largest of several tarns in Dolina Bielych Plies (White Tarns Valley), it is a splendid place for a picnic, with several tables, and a view up to the pass of Kopské Sedlo (1,749m) and the minor summit of Belianská Kopa (White Stack, 1,832m). Some of the tables have been placed on the foundations of the former Kežmarská Chata (Kežmarok Chalet), which was dismantled when the White Tatras were closed to visitors in 1978. The foundations, plus some piles of bricks and the nameplates, are all that remain. The name of the chalet lives on though, as it still appears on some signposts.

Veľké Hincovo Pleso (1,946m). The largest and deepest tarn in the Slovakian High Tatras, lying close to the border with Poland at the foot of Kôprovský Štít, north of Štrbské Pleso. It covers about 20 hectares, is 53 metres deep, and contains 4 million cubic metres of water.

Veľký Slavkov (677m). A large village in the Sub-Tatras Basin, lying a little to the east of the main road from Poprad to Starý Smokovec. It was established by Germanic people in the thirteenth century, and its Gothic church dates from this period. There is also an Evangelical church of the eighteenth century.

Veľký Studený Potok (Great Cold Stream). At the bridge on red route 0930B, a few minutes' walk beyond Polana Kamzik to the north of Starý Smokovec, it is the tradition that, if you like it here, and throw a coin from the footbridge into the brook, you will return! The coins are collected to help with chalet maintenance, if possible before the Spring - otherwise the torrent of meltwater carries them to an unknown fate further downstream. For most of the year, the water here is very blue, clear and soft; this is because of its purity, coming from the granite rock with no mineral salts. In May and early June, though, it turns to a blue-grey foam, from melted snow.

Vodopád Studeného Potoka (Cold Stream Waterfall). A pretty series of cascades at the confluence of the two streams that form Studený Potok, to the north of Starý Smokovec. Two minutes' walk along red route 0930 from here, towards Hrebienok, you can see a large, flat and rocky open area, which thousands of years ago was the bed of a lake, until a violent earthquake removed the moraine that dammed it, allowing the water to escape (see also Slavkovský Štít).

Východná Vysoká (Eastern Great One, 2,428m). The fourth highest summit on the waymarked route network in Slovakia, with excellent views. It lies above the saddle called Poľský Hrebeň, to the north-west of Starý Smokovec.

Vyšné Hágy (Upper Hágy, 1,085-1,125m). A settlement to the east of Štrbské Pleso, consisting almost entirely of an extensive sanatorium complex that specialises in the cure of tuberculosis and respiratory ailments. It can be the starting point for walks, but there are no facilities for walkers here. Buses and trains between Štrbské Pleso and Starý Smokovec stop here, as do buses from Štrbské Pleso to Poprad via Štôla. There are several car parks along Cesta

Slobody (Freedom Highway) on the west side of the village.

Vyšné Wahlenbergovo Pleso (Upper Wahlenberg Tarn, 2,157m). The second highest tarn in the Slovakian High Tatras, situated to the north-west of Štrbské Pleso. It is named after Göran Wahlenberg (1780-1851), a Swedish naturalist who explored the High Tatras and described its plantlife in his book *Flora Karpatorum Principalium.*

Vysoká (2,560m). One of the most imposing mountains in the High Tatras with its twin peaks, eminently visible to the north-east from Štrbské Pleso. Its first recorded ascent was in 1874 by the Hungarian, Mor Dechy, accompanied by local guides.

Žabí Kôň (Frog Horse, 2,291m). A relatively low peak on the west side of Rysy, but locally famous as the place where climbers take their "graduation test", since it is a notoriously difficult climb.

Zamkovského Chata (Zamkovsky Chalet, 1,475m, telephone 0969-2636, open all year). A very popular chalet, situated above Malý Studený Potok to the north of Starý Smokovec, within easy reach of the rack railway at Hrebienok. It was built in 1943, and named after Štefan Zamkovský (1908-1961), a well known Tatras mountaineer and guide. After World War II, it was renamed Nálepkova Chata (shown on some maps as Chata Kapitána Nálepku), after Captain Ján Nálepka who came from this area but was killed in battle in Russia in 1943. In 1991 it reverted to the original name. The chalet has now been returned to the Zamkovský family and offers refreshments and accommodation in four- and five-bed dormitories. The leaseholder at the time of writing, Laco Kulanga, is famous for the huge supply loads that he backpacks up to the chalet on a wooden frame - on one record occasion 207 kilograms, the equivalent of a whole family of mother, father and two children!

Zbojnícka Chata (Highwaymen's Chalet, 1,960m, no telephone, open all year). An isolated chalet in a lake-filled hanging valley above the head of Veľká Studená Dolina, north-west of Starý Smokovec. It takes its name from a nearby minor peak called Zbojnícky Chrbát (Highwayman's Back). The original chalet, dating from 1907, was substantially rebuilt in 1984. Now owned by Slovenské Karpaty, it offers refreshments (including a delicious, spiced lemon tea) and accommodation for 18 people in a single dormitory. The outside toilets are rather primitive.

Ždiar (896m). A large village on the east side of the White Tatras, that straggles along the southern slopes of the Spišská Magura hills. It has many attractive shuttered wooden houses in the style of the Goral (mountain) people, who also inhabit the neighbouring region in Poland. There is a museum here called Ždiarsky Dom, devoted to the architecture and lifestyle of the Goral people. Also a supermarket, a small store, three restaurants, and the Goralturist travel agency which provides information and currency exchange.

Ždiarska Vidla (2,146m). The second highest summit in the White Tatras.

Zelené Pleso (Green Tarn, 1,545m). One of the loveliest places in the High Tatras, it is a popular resort for walkers, and with local people who come here to skate on the ice in late autumn. The water is actually green because the light is affected by the way the mountains rise on three sides - but the legend is more romantic: A princess, it seems, fell asleep beside the tarn. She wore a ring containing a huge emerald stone, which caught the eye of a hawk. This felonous bird, perched on the great crag on the north side of the tarn, swooped down, removed the jewel and returned to its perch, but on the way dropped the emerald into the tarn. It could not be recovered, and the water turned green. The crag is called Jastrabia Veža, which means Hawk Tower.

Chata pri Zelenom Plese (Chalet at Green Lake, 1,545m, telephone 0969-967420) is one of the most spectacularly situated chalets in the High Tatras. Built in 1924, it was renamed after World War II Brnčalova Chata, after Albert Brnčal, a celebrated mountaineer, teacher and Slovak nationalist who was killed in an accident at nearby Jastrabie Sedlo. The original name was resumed in 1991, but old maps may still show the previous name. Owned by Slovénská Karpaty, it offers refreshments, and (if you book well in advance) accommodation in dormitories.

Overlooking Dolina Roztoki, from the traverse below Niźnia Kopa (see p187)

The Polish Tatras

LATER HISTORY

The Podhale region, that is the plains and valleys on the north side of the Tatras, remained relatively uninhabited, at least as far as any recorded history is concerned, until the thirteenth century. It seems that the mountains were too much of a barrier to be surmounted by people living to the south, while those to the north relied too much on sea trade to venture so far from the Baltic Sea and the navigable rivers that feed it.

The earliest known settlement in the area was at Nowy Targ, established in the thirteenth century. Zakopane, first mentioned in a document dated 1578, may date from the fifteenth century.

In 1766, a foundry was established at Kuźnice, which means "smithy" in Polish, immediately to the south of Zakopane, using iron ore mined in the Tatras. It closed down in 1878, but the great waterwheel from that period still remains, close to the cable-car station.

In 1769, Poland ceased to exist as a state, as it was partitioned between Prussia, Russia and Austria-Hungary - the Podhale region then became part of the Austro-Hungarian Empire until the end of World War I, after which the state of Poland was recreated.

Austro-Hungarian rule was considered to be quite lenient, and the Polish language was allowed to continue in use. At this time, Zakopane became isolated from the rest of Poland. By the mid nineteenth century, its different culture, dialect and beautiful scenery attracted intellectuals from all over Europe. Some of the current buildings in the street in Zakopane called Koscieliska date from this period, as does the Old Church (Stary Kościół) of circa 1846.

Before the advent of accurate maps, the exact line of national borders was in many places a vague notion in the minds of civil servants, and travellers in the eighteenth century were able to roam much of Europe with little hindrance. Thus the earliest recorded ascents of the Polish Tatras peaks were by those whose names we have already encountered in the section on the early conquests on what is now the Slovak side: in 1793 by the Scot, Dr Robert Townson, and in 1843 by the Irishman, John Bull, both accompanied by local hunters. Other summits were first climbed by local explorers such as David Frölich in the early nineteenth century.

At that time, the area was generally considered abroad to be part of Hungary, and Townson's illustrated book, *Travels in Hungary*, published in

1797, became one of the classic works about the Tatras.

The greatest spur to the development of the Podhale came with the railway line from Kraków to Zakopane, opened in 1899. Until then, it took two days to cover this journey using horse-drawn vehicles. Thereafter, Zakopane quickly developed as a popular health resort.

1939 brought the invasion of Poland by the Nazis, and after World War II Poland became virtually a satellite of the Soviet Union. The rise of the Solidarity movement in the 1980s eventually led to the overthrow of the communist regime in 1989.

INTRODUCTION TO THE WALKING

Note: Most of the Polish Tatras are shown on the Slovenská Kartografia or Freitag & Berndt maps of the Slovak Tatras, but the names are shown in their Slovak equivalents. Since this may confuse, for walking on the Polish side you are advised to obtain the Polish map, which in any case is at a larger scale (see chapter on maps above).

Zakopane, the main base in the Polish Tatras, is well located for exploration of both the Western and High Tatras on their Polish sides, so we cover both in this book. In fact, Zakopane lies in the foothills of the Western Tatras, in an area called Podhale (which means "below the mountain pastures") where horse-drawn carts are still an everyday sight. The High Tatras are within easy reach, but to explore the main part of the range you really first need to take a bus or cable-car.

There are fewer summits than in Slovakia, and they are not so high, though Rysy on the border can also be reached from Poland, and at 2,499m is the country's highest peak. But the lakes are bigger than in Slovakia, there are excellent views of Slovakia's mountains, and Orla Perć (Eagle's Perch), linking several high peaks, is the most challenging ridge route accessible without a guide in the High Tatras. (By the time you read this, Orla Perć may have been taken off the waymarked network - some parts of the route have been badly eroded and there have been a number of accidents there in recent years. However you will still be able to tackle it with a mountain guide - see above.)

All of Poland's highest summits are to be found here in the Tatras, and most are accessible without a guide, being well waymarked. Świnica (2,301m), Kozi Wierch (2,291m), Granaty (2,235m) and Krzyżne (2,113m) all provide rewarding targets for experienced walkers, and several high passes can be reached, such as Mięguszowiecka Przełęcz (2,307m) and Wrota Chałubińskiego (2,022m).

Giewont, a Western Tatras peak known as the "Sleeping Knight", though of relatively low altitude by Tatras standards, will provide a fairly challenging test early in your holiday, with some scrambling and fixed chains. It has two peaks at 1,894m and 1,728m - the higher one supports a huge iron cross - and is eminently visible from Zakopane.

There is also some fine ridge walking in the Western Tatras, easily accessible from Zakopane. A splendid 8-kilometre walk, not too difficult, runs along the frontier ridge through the Czerwone Wierchy (Red Peaks). At present this route is only accessible from the Polish side. From Ciemniak in the west to Świnica in the east, it switchbacks at around 1,900m to 2,300m with outstanding views into both Poland and Slovakia.

Waymarks in the Polish Tatras are similar to those on the Slovak side, ie. two white bands sandwiching a third band of the route's colour as shown on the map. A difference from Slovakia, though, is the use of spots of the appropriate colour to mark each end of the route.

ROUTE SUGGESTIONS

Routes marked (*) include a fixed chain or wire.

1) POLANA HUCISKA (982m) - CHOCHOŁOWSKIE SCHRONISKO (1,150m) - WOŁOWIEC (2,063m) and return

Grade: easy to Chochołowskie Schronisko; moderate to Wołowiec.
Distance: 20km   **Average gradient:** 4% to Chochołowskie Schronisko; 17% to Wołowiec.
Height gain: 1,083m   **Height loss:** 1,083m   **Time:** 6h 45m
Refreshments: Chochołowskie Schronisko

From Polana Huciska car park follow routes:
501 (green) to Chochołowskie Schronisko and on to Wołowiec, and return. The last 500 metres to Wołowiec summit are on a blue route coming from Slovakia. You can use this, but remember that you are not allowed to descend into Slovakia.

Being more remote from Zakopane, Dolina Chochołowska is a quiet valley. It is also very pretty, and from Wołowiec you have fine views into Slovakia.

2) POLANA HUCISKA (982m) - CHOCHOŁOWSKIE SCHRONISKO (1,150m) - WOŁOWIEC (2,063m) - JARZĄBCZY WIERCH 2,137m) - STAROROBOCIAŃSKY WIERCH 2,176m) - RACZKOWA PRZEŁĘCZ 1,959M) - DOLINA STAROROBOCIAŃSKA - POLANA HUCISKA (982m)

Grade: strenuous   **Distance:** 28km   **Average gradient:** 13%
Height gain: 1,822m   **Height loss:** 1,822m   **Time:** 10h 00m
Refreshments: Chochołowskie Schronisko

From Polana Huciska follow routes:

501 (green) to Wołowiec (see note in route suggestion 1 regarding the final section to Wołowiec summit;

002 (red) to Raczkowa Przełęcz;

503 (green) to Siwa Przełęcz;

902 (black) to Straznicówka;

501 (green) to Polana Huciska.

An arduous route suitable only for walkers with stamina, with several ups and downs but no difficult walking. You will be rewarded with one of the finest ridge walks in the Tatras with views into Poland and Slovakia.

3) KIRY (927m) - DOLINA KOŚCIELISKA - SCHRONISKO ORNAK (1,100m) and return

Grade: easy	Distance: 12km	Average gradient: 3%
Height gain: 173m	Height loss: 173m	Time: 2h 30m
Refreshments: Schronisko Ornak		

From Kiry follow routes:

504 (green) to Schronisko Ornak and return

This is a pleasant and easy stroll, and because of that and its proximity to Zakopane usually very crowded. There are several options for side trips to caves and waterfalls.

4) ZAKOPANE (830m) - DOLINA STRĄŻYSKA - CZERWONA PRZEŁĘCZ (1,303m) - SARNIA SKAŁA (1,377m) - DOLINA BIAŁEGO - ZAKOPANE (830m)

Grade: moderate	Distance: 13km	Average gradient: 9%
Height gain: 547m	Height loss: 547m	Time: 4h 00m
Refreshments: Zakopane		

From the Old Cemetery in Zakopane centre follow the side street called Kasprusie (shortly becomes Strążyska) southwards for 2km until you reach the national park boundary. Then follow routes:

008 (red) to Polana Strążyska

901C (black) to Czerwona Przełęcz and Białe

(optional side trip from Czerwona Przełęcz to Sarnia Skała)

807 (yellow) to Zakopane

A good short route to test your legs; mostly in forest but with a good view over Zakopane from Sarnia Skała.

5) KUŹNICE (1,015m) - POLANA KALATÓWKI (1,198m) - POLANA KONDRATOWA (1,335m) - GIEWONT (1,895m) - PRZEŁĘCZ W GRZYBOWCU (1,311m) - POLANA MLYNISKA - ZAKOPANE (830m)

Grade: strenuous   Distance: 15.5km   Average gradient: 13%
Height gain: 880m   Height loss: 1,065m   Time: 6h 30m
Refreshments: Kalatówki Schronisko; Kondratowe Schronisko (there is sometimes a mobile drink-seller at the foot of Giewont)

From Kuźnice follow routes:
206 (blue) (*) to Kalatówki, Kondratowa and Giewont
008 (red) (*) to Przełęcz w Grzybowcu, Polana Mlyniska and Zakopane
There are no difficulties on this route until the final ascent to Giewont, though it is very steep in places; those unwilling to tackle the fixed chains to and from the summit can wait at the foot. Splendid views from Giewont over Zakopane and Podhale, though the summit is likely to be crowded.

6) KASPROWY WIERCH (1,987m) - ZIELONY STAW (1,672m) - KARB (1,853m) - KOŚCIELEC (2,158m) - CZARNY STAW GĄSIENICOWY (1,620m) SCHRONISKO MUROWANIEC (1,505m) - KUŹNICE (1,015m)

Grade: moderate to strenuous
Distance: 13.5km   Average gradient: 15%
Height gain: 486m   Height loss: 1,456m   Time: 4h 30m
Refreshments: Kasprowy Wierch; Schronisko Murowaniec; Kuźnice

From Kasprowy Wierch cable-car station go south-east for 300 metres to Sucha Przełecz then follow routes:
811 (yellow) to foot of chair-lift
908 (black) to Zielony Staw
208 (blue) to Karb
909 (black) (*) to Kościelec and return to Karb
515 (green) to Czarny Staw Gąsienicowy
207 (blue) to Schronisko Murowaniec and on to Kuźnice
A route with some testing sections expecially on the ascent from Karb to Kościelec which has fixed chains and some exposed sections - those wishing to avoid them can wait at Karb. Most of it is downward and above the treeline, with good views of the Eagle's Perch summits from Kościelec. As an alternative to route 207 (blue), the final descent to Kuźnice can be made on 810 (yellow) which is mostly in meadows rather than forest.

7) KASPROWY WIERCH (1,987m) - ORLA PERĆ/EAGLE'S PERCH (highest point ŚWINICA (2,301m) - SCHRONISKO MUROWANIEC (1,505m) - KUŹNICE (1,015m)

Grade: difficult   Distance: 20km   Average gradient: 15%
Height gain: 977m   Height loss: 1,917m   Time: 11h 30m*
Refreshments: Kasprowy Wierch; Schronisko Murowaniec

From Kasprowy Wierch cable-car station go south-east for 300 metres to Sucha Przełęcz then follow routes:
009 (red) (*) to Świnica and on to Krzyżne
812 (yellow) to Schronisko Murowaniec
207 (blue) to Kuźnice
The most exciting route in the Polish Tatras, with spectacular, constantly changing views. Suitable only for more experienced mountain walkers with lots of stamina and a good head for heights.
There are at least a dozen ups and as many downs, mostly quite short, but with frequent fixed chains, scrambling and exposure.
* To avoid such a long day, you would be well advised to consider spending a night at Schronisko Murowaniec, allowing the route to be divided into two.
Note: This ridge route has become badly eroded and dangerous in some places, and at the time of writing there was a possibility that it would be removed from the waymarked network. In this case, the route as a whole would still be accessible with a mountain guide (see above), and some of its peaks could still be reached direct using other routes.

8) KASPROWY WIERCH (1,987m) - SCHRONISKO MUROWANIEC (1,505m) CZARNY STAW GĄSIENICOWY (1,620m) - SKRAJNY GRANAT (2,225m) - SCHRONISKO MUROWANIEC (1,505m) - KUŹNICE (1,015m)

Grade: strenuous   Distance: 15.5km   Average gradient: 16%
Height gain: 771m   Height loss: 1,743m   Time: 6h 00m
Refreshments: Kasprowy Wierch; Schronisko Murowaniec; Kuźnice

From Kasprowy Wierch cable-car station go south-east for 300 metres to Sucha Przełęcz then follow routes:
811 (yellow) to Schronisko Murowaniec
207 (blue) to Czarny Staw Gąsienicowy
813 (yellow) (*) to Skrajny Granat (Granaty north peak) and return to Czarny Staw Gąsienicowy
207 (blue) to Schronisko Murowaniec and on to Kuźnice
An opportunity to sample the Eagle's Perch without having to face the more

exacting sections of that route. There is only one short fixed chain on the final approach to Skrajny Granat, where it is also very steep.

9) KASPROWY WIERCH (1,987m) - ŚWINICA (2,301m) - ZAWRAT (2,159m) WIELKI STAW (1,665m) - WODOGRZMOTY MICKIEWICZA (1,100m) - PALENICA BIAŁCZAŃSKA (990m)

Grade: strenuous   **Distance: 15km**   **Average gradient: 13%**
Height gain: 428m   **Height loss: 1,425m**   **Time: 5h 30m**
Refreshments: Kasprowy Wierch. Also Schronisko Przedni Staw 10 minutes off route from Wielki Staw.

From Kasprowy Wierch cable-car station go south-east for 300 metres to Sucha Przełecz then follow routes:
009 (red) to Świnica and Zawrat
209 (blue) to Wielki Staw
517 (green) to Wodogrzmoty Mickiewicza
010 (red) and road to Palenica Białczańska
Another chance to view the Eagle's Perch from close quarters at Świnica and Zawrat. Most of the route is not difficult, but the section around Świnica and Zawrat is steep and exposed in places. On the descent to Palenica Białczańska you pass Wielki Staw, one of the largest tarns in the Tatras, and two picturesque waterfalls.

10) PALENICA BIAŁCZAŃSKA (990m) - WODOGRZMOTY MICKIEWICZA (1,100m) - DOLINA PIĘCIU STAWÓW POLSKICH (Valley of Five Polish Tarns) - SZPIGLASOWA PRZEŁĘCZ (2,114m) - MORSKIE OKO (1,406m) - WODOGRZMOTY MICKIEWICZA (1,100m) - PALENICA BIAŁCZAŃSKA (990m)

Grade: strenuous   **Distance: 21km**   **Average gradient: 4% on road sections; 20% on paths**
Height gain: 1,124m   **Height loss: 1,124m**   **Time: 7h 15m**
Refreshments: Morskie Oko; also at Przedni Staw which is 10 minutes off route.

From Palenica Białczańska follow the road to Wodogrzmoty Mickiewicza then routes:
517 (green) to Wielki Staw
209 (blue) and
814 (yellow) (*) to Szpiglasowa Przełęcz and on to Morskie Oko

011 (red) to Wodogrzmoty Mickiewicza
then road to Palenica Białczańska
This route ascends one of the most beautiful valleys in the Tatras - the Valley of Five Polish Tarns; passes two of its largest tarns (Wielki Staw and Morskie Oko); and you see two picturesque waterfalls. It is not particularly difficult, though there is one fixed chain as you approach Szpiglasowa Przełęcz. Much of it is on traffic-free roads (closed to public vehicles because of landslips), but horse-drawn buses are available.

11) PALENICA BIAŁCZAŃSKA (990m) - WODOGRZMOTY MICKIEWICZA (1,100m) - MORSKIE OKO (1,406m) - RYSY (2,499m) and return by same route

Grade: strenuous   **Distance: 28km**   **Average gradient: 4% on road sections; 22% on paths**
Height gain: 1,509m   **Height loss: 1,509m**   **Time: 10h 45m**
Refreshments: Morskie Oko

From Palenica Białczańska follow the road to Wodogrzmoty Mickiewicza then routes:
011 (red) to Morskie Oko
012 (red) to Rysy
Return by same route
This is the least strenuous way to reach Poland's highest summit, especially if you take the horse-drawn bus for the first and last 7km along the road. Because of Rysy, and the presence of the beautiful tarn Morskie Oko with its popular refuge, this is one of the more crowded routes in the Polish Tatras.

12) ZAKOPANE (830m) - GUBAŁÓWKA (1,117m)

Grade: easy   **Distance: 4 to 17km**   **Average gradient: 4% to 14%**
Height gain: 287-460m   **Height loss: 287-460m**   **Time: 1h 00m to 4h 30m**
Refreshments: Gubałówka; Zakopane

Gubałówka is the ridge that overlooks Zakopane from the north with a splendid panorama of the Polish Tatras. It is easily reached by rack railway or chair-lift, and there are several refreshment facilities. Consequently the whole ridge resembles a seaside promenade at high altitude, with telescopes and other entertainments into the bargain. However, some of the walking routes to it are quite steep and not crowded, and a visit is well worth while for the views and a change from the mountains.

There are several options, varying from 4 to 17km. The following combination is recommended to give, at 17km, a full day's walking, though there are several short-cut possibilities. From Zakopane railway station go south for 800 metres along Jagiellońska street to the church, then follow routes:

808 (yellow) to Harenda
809 (yellow) to Furmanowa and on to Gubałówka
906 (red) to Pałkówka
806 (yellow) to Zakopane

PATH DESCRIPTIONS

RED ROUTES

Take care not to confuse these routes, marked by broken red dashes on the Tatrzański Park Narodowy map, with the ski routes, which are marked either as solid red lines or broken lines with arrows, and cannot be used by walkers.

001: POLANA TRZYDNIÓWKA (1,080m) - TRZYDNIOWIAŃSKI WIERCH (1,758m) - DOLINA WYŻNIA CHOCHOLOWSKA (1,160m)

Grade: moderate	**Distance: 8km**	**Average gradient: 16%**
NE-SW Height gain: 678m/loss 598m		**Time: 3h 15m**
SW-NE Height gain: 598m/loss 678m		**Time: 3h 15m**
Winter/spring: closed		

A long, horeshoe-shaped route in the foothills of the Western Tatras. It is mostly in forest, but comes into the open at the top of Trzydniowiański Wierch (1,758m), where there are good views of the ridge known as Długi Upłaz to the south. This route is little used, and some parts, especially in the dwarf pine, can be overgrown. It provides access to the ridge by linking with green route 502.

Both ends of the route join different points along green route 501 in **Dolina Chochołowska.** Approaching from the north, you reach the first point 10 minutes after passing through the gorge called Wyżnia Chochołowska Brama, at Polana Trzydniówka. The route at first climbs the dry gully Krowi Żleb to reach the spur called Kulawiec, then you follow this all the way, passing out of the forest into dwarf pine then open rock, to reach Trzydniowiański Wierch at 1,758m. (1h 45m up/1h 15m down)

Here is the junction with green route 502. Red 001 continues by descending steeply for several hundred metres along a rib, then turns left to cross and recross a gully before re-entering the forest. A stream is crossed before reaching a meadow with shepherds' huts, then you follow the brook called Jarząbczy Potok all the way down to Dolina Chochołowska and the junction with green route 501. (1h 30m down/2h 00m up) at the lower end, the route shares its path with yellow route 100.

002: RACZKOWA PRZEŁĘCZ (1,959m) - STAROROBOCIAŃSKI WIERCH (2,176m) - STAROROBOCIAŃSKA PRZEŁĘCZ (1,963m) - KOŃCZYSTY WIERCH (2,003m) - JARZĄBCZA PRZEŁĘCZ (1,904m) - JARZĄBCZY WIERCH (2,137m) - NISKA PRZEŁĘCZ (1,831m) - ŁOPATA (1,957m) - DZIURAWA PRZEŁĘCZ (1,836m) - WOŁOWIEC (2,063m)

Grade: strenuous   Distance: 7.5km   Average gradient: 20%
E-W Height gain: 810m/loss 706m   Time: 3h 30m
W-E Height gain: 706m/loss 810m   Time: 3h 20m
Winter/spring: closed

This excellent ridge walk, known as Długi Upłaz (long ridge), along the border with Slovakia provides some of the finest views in the whole of the Tatras, especially from Starorobociański Wierch, one of the highest summits of the Western Tatras. It is not difficult, but being remote from roads and transport requires a long approach and descent to make a tough day. It is best approached from the east, since this involves a more gradual ascent.

Green route 503 brings you to the saddle called Raczkowa Przełęcz (1,959m). A path comes up to here from Slovakia, but you must not be tempted to go down it. Turn right to follow red 002 and start your switchbacking with a long climb along the ridge to the summit of Starorobociański Wierch (2,176m). (0h 40m E-W/0h 20m W-E)

The height of the next saddle, Starorobociańska Przełęcz, is not marked on the map, but is approximately 1,963m. At Kończysty Wierch (2,003m) is the junction with green route 502. Jarząbcza Przełęcz is at 1,904m, then comes the longest climb of the route, to Jarząbczy Wierch (2,137m). (1h 10m E-W/1h 20m W-E)

Another path from Slovakia joins here, and keeps very steep company with the Polish one to Niska Przełęcz (low saddle), which is in fact the lowest point of the route (just) at 1,831m. The summit of Łopata is inaccessible to walkers, and to bypass it you must enter Slovakia (legally) for 300 metres to reach Dziurawa Przełęcz (pockmarked saddle, 1,836m). Finally you climb to Wołowiec (2,063m). (1h 35m E-W/1h 45m W-E)

A short stretch (500 metres) of a blue route from Slovakia follows the border down to the junction with Polish green route 501. (0h 10m)

003: POLANA PISANA (1,015m) - MYLNA JASKINIA (1,300m)

Grade: moderate   **Distance: 0.5km**   **Average gradient: 20%**
S-N Height loss: 285m   **Time: 1h 20m**
Winter/spring: normally open

This short but fascinating route descends Mylna Jaskinia (wrong cave), discovered in 1887. Spending an hour negotiating the caves, you must be prepared to get wet and dirty, and each person must carry a torch with spare battery and bulb. There is one-way traffic, from south to north.

Polana Pisana can be reached from Kiry along **Dolina Kościeliska** on foot (green route 504) or by horse-drawn taxi (dorożka). The entrance is from the south end of the route, near the great cliff called Skała Pisana. Having turned right from the valley, you soon pass on your right a very short dead end route with black waymarks leading to another explorable cave called Raptawicka Jaskinia (this takes 25 minutes extra).

Then you come to the southern outlet (wylot południe) and begin your passage through the cave. The route inside is waymarked, and there are two scrambly sections, one with a fixed chain, the other with an iron railing. The floor is very rough, so you must watch your step. As you leave the northern outlet (wylot północ), there is a beautiful view along Dolina Kościeliska.

004: ZAHRADZISKA (1,000m) - CHUDA PRZEŁĄCKA (1,853m) - CIEMNIAK (2,096m)

Grade: strenuous   **Distance: 5km**   **Average gradient: 22%**
NW-SE Height gain: 1,096m   **Time: 3h 15m**
SE-NW Height loss: 1,096m   **Time: 2h 15m**
Winter/spring: normally open

A useful access route to the Czerwone Wierchy ridge. Though comparatively monotonous in itself, it is mostly in the open and has some good views. The walking is mostly very steep though without difficulty.

The route starts from black route 901B at Zahradziska and climbs steeply up a ridge (Adamica) to reach a meadow called Polana Upłaz (0h 55m up/0h 40m down).

More forest brings you to another meadow that steeply ascends a ridge to a great rock called Piec, above which you can see **Giewont** to your left. The route continues very steeply through the dwarf pine, then comes into the open below Przełącka przy Kopie (little saddle near the stacks). Skirting the summit of Chuda Turnia (thin cliff), you come to Chuda Przełącka (thin saddle) at 1,853m. (1h 30m up/1h 00m down)

Here is the junction with green route 505, which contours round to your right. Red 004 continues up Twardy Upłaz (hard slope) to the summit of Ciemniak (2,096m). (0h 45m up/0h 35m down) Here is the junction with red route 007.

005: NEDZÓWKA (960m) - PRZYSŁOP MIĘTUSI (1,187m)

Grade: moderate	Distance: 4km	Average gradient: 6%
NW-SE Height gain: 227m		Time: 1h 30m
SE-NW Height loss: 227m		Time: 1h 00m
Winter/spring: normally open		

This route starts from **Nedzówka** *on the main road running westwards out of Zakopane. It follows at first a farm track, opposite the junction with a side road, then after 300 metres turn right along a forest road. In another 300 metres you turn left up a gully (Staników Żleb) where the path is usually wet. You climb steadily, passing through a meadow, to an unnamed broad saddle at about 1,275m below the minor summit of Hruby Regiel, then follow a forested ridge before descending to Przysłop Miętusi (1,187m), a saddle which is well known for its beautiful views of the Czerwone Wierchy.*

Here is the junction with black route 901B and blue route 202.

006: TOMANOWA POLANA WYŻSZY (1,480m) - TOMANOWA PRZEŁĘCZ (1,686m)

Grade: moderate	Distance: 1.5km	Average gradient: 14%
W-E Height gain: 206m		Time: 0h 30m
E-W Height loss: 206m		Time: 0h 15m
Winter/spring: closed		

This side route leads to Tomanowa Przełęcz, one of the lowest passes in the main ridge of the Western Tatras at 1,686m. It was once much used by traders, and afflicted with robbers. The path still continues into Slovakia, but you must return the way you came.

From green route 505 at the east end of Tomanowa Polana Wyższy (upper Tomanowa meadow), the path immediately enters the forest, but soon comes into dwarf pine, and finishes on a scree slope.

007: KASPROWY WIERCH (1,987m) - PRZEŁĘCZ GORYCZKOWA NAD ZAKOSY (1,820m) - POŚREDNI GORYCZKOWY (1,873m) - PRZEŁĘCZ GORYCZKOWA ŚWINSKA (1806m) - CZUBA GORYCZKOWA (1,913m) -

SUCHE CZUBY (1,800m) - SUCHY WIERCH KONDRACKI (1,890m) - PRZEŁĘCZ POD KOPĄ KONDRACKĄ (1,863m) - KOPĄ KONDRACKĄ (2,005m) - MAŁOŁĄCKA PRZEŁĘCZ (1,929m) - MAŁOŁĄCZNIAK (2,096m) - LITWOROWA PRZEŁĘCZ (2,040m) - KRZESANICA (2,122m) - CIEMNIAK (2,096m)

Grade: moderate	**Distance: 9km**	**Average gradient: 11%**
E-W Height gain: 551m/loss 444m		**Time: 3h 00m**
W-E Height gain: 444m/loss 551m		**Time: 2h 45m**
Winter/spring: closed		

A splendid and comparatively easy ridge walk, much of it on grass, and quickly accessible via the chair-lift from Kuźnice to Kasprowy Wierch. For the whole length you have extensive panoramic views into Poland and Slovakia. The route follows the border between the two countries, marked by short white posts with red tops. As the ridge is quite broad in places you can step across from one country to another and back again without difficulty, but at present this route is only accessible from Poland.

You are strongly advised not to attempt this route in mist, since there are places where a few steps in the wrong direction could lead to a dangerous fall.

From **Kasprowy Wierch** (1,987m) the route heads west, descending to Przełęcz Goryczkowa nad Zakosy (1,820m). You then face a series of climbs up rounded summits that increase in height as you progress westwards. The first two are Pośredni Goryczkowy (1,873m) and Czuba Goryczkowa (1,913m), then you descend to the saddle of Przełęcz pod Kopą Kondracką, where green route 508 joins. (1h 20m E-W/1h 25 W-E)

The next three summits are Kopa Kondracka (2,005m), Małołączniak (2,096m) and finally Krzesanica (2,122m). A further summit remains (Ciemniak at 2,096m), but you hardly notice as the section leading to it from Małołączniak is virtually level - this is the part where you must particularly watch out for a sudden vertiginous drop at the edge of the grass. (1h 30m E-W/1h 25 W-E)

008: ZAKOPANE Strazyska (900m) - POLANA STRĄŻYSKA (1,000m) - PRZEŁĘCZ W GRZYBOWCU (1,311m) - WYŻNIA PRZEŁĘCZ KONDRACKA (1,780m)

Grade: easy to Polana Strążyska; strenuous to Wyżnia Przełęcz Kondracka.

Distance: 6.5km	**Average gradient: 6% to Polana Strążyska; 16% to Giewont**
N-S Height gain: 880m	**Time: 2h 30m**
S-N Height loss: 880m	**Time: 1h 55m**
Winter/spring: closed	

Though a much frequented route, the ascent is very steep and tiring, and it is more often used for the descent from Zakopane's "mascot" peak of Giewont. It is mostly in forest until it reaches the west end of the Giewont massif, then it is in the open all the way to the pass below the summit - there is little if any dwarf pine.

The route begins at the end of Strążyska (900m), a continuation of the street called Kasprusie, which starts opposite the Old Cemetery. It ascends the valley called **Dolina Strążyska,** frequently crossing the brook Strążyski Potok, and eventually reaches the meadow Polana Strążyska (1,000m). (0h 35m up/ 0h 25m down)

Here you join black route 901B, and share its path for the next 1.5km to Przełęcz w Grzybowcu (1,311m). (0h 35m up/0h 30m down)

The black route descends westwards, while red 008 climbs to a spur called Grzybowiec, which it follows, now with Giewont ahead. The path leaves the forest to skirt the west shoulder of the mountain (here you have a beautiful view down **Dolina Małej Łąki**) before climbing very steeply to a saddle called Wyznia Przełęcz Kondracka (1,780m) - here you may find an itinerant seller of canned drinks! (1h 15m up/1h 00m down)

Here you join blue route 206 for the final assault on **Giewont** summit.

009A: KASPROWY WIERCH (1,987m) - BESKID (2,012m) - LILIOWE (1,952m) SKRAJNA TURNIA (2,097m) - SKRAJNA PRZEŁĘCZ (2,075m) - POŚREDNIA TURNIA (2,128m) - ŚWINICKA PRZEŁĘCZ (2,050m) - ŚWINICA (2,301m)

Grade: strenuous	**Distance: 3.5km**	**Average gradient: 18%**
W-E Height gain: 474m/loss 160m		**Time: 1h 40m**
E-W Height gain: 160m/loss 474m		**Time: 1h 15m**
Winter/spring: closed		

Much used as an access route to the Eagle's Perch, this is a fine ridge walk in its own right, with little difficulty except on the final ascent to Świnica. There are splendid views in one direction over the tarns of Dolina Gąsienicowa in Poland, and in the other towards Kriváň in Slovakia.

From the cable-car station you descend south-east for a few hundred metres to Sucha Przełęcz (1,955m). Here yellow route 811 descends into Dolina Gąsienicowa, while red 009A continues up to the summit of Beskid (2,012m), the first of four summits on this route. At the next saddle, Liliowe (1,952m), green route 511 joins from the same valley. (W-E 0h 25m/E-W 0h 25m)

With little effort, two more summits (Skrajna Turnia at 2,097m and Pośrednia Turnia at 2,128m) are surmounted on the way to Świnicka Przełęcz (2,050m), where black route 908 joins by yet another route from Dolina Gąsienicowa. (W-E 0h 20m/E-W 0h 15m)

Now the going gets tougher, steeper and more exposed on the way to Świnica (2,301m). (W-E 0h 55m/E-W 0h 35m)

009B: (Orla Perć = Eagle's Perch) ŚWINICA (2,301m) - ZAWRAT (2,159m) MALI KOZI WIERCH (2,226m) - ZMARZŁA PRZEŁĘCZ (2,126m) - ZAMARŁA TURNIA (2,179m) - KOZIA PRZEŁĘCZ (2,137m) - KOZIE CZUBY (2,266m) - KOZI WIERCH (2,291m) - PRZEŁĘCZ NAD DOLINĄ BUCZYHOWĄ (2,225m) GRANATY (2,239m) - GRANACKA PRZEŁĘCZ (2,145m) - ORLA BASZTA (2,175m) - PRZEŁĘCZ NOWICKIEGO (2,105m) - WIELKA BUCZYNOWA TURNIA (2,182m) - BUCZYNOWA PRZEŁĘCZ (2,127m) - MALA BUCZYNOWA TURNIA (2,171m) - KRZYŻNE (2,113m)

Grade: strenuous	Distance: 5.5km	Average gradient: 20%
W-E Height gain: 439m/loss 627m		Time: 6h 25m
E-W Height gain: 627m/loss 439m		Time: 7h 10m
Winter/spring: closed		

At the saddle called Zawrat, a sign warns that you follow this route at your own risk! Between Zawrat and Mala Buczynowa Turnia it is very exposed and worn. There are many fixed chains and railings. You will need a cool temperament and a head for heights.

It is possible that this part of the route will be removed from the waymarked network in the near future, then it will only be accessible with a mountain guide (see above). If this happens, the routes leading up to Orla Perć (blue 207, yellow 812/813/814, and black 911) would still provide a means of reaching some of its summits.

010: TOPOROWA CYRHLA (992m) - PSIA TRAWKA (1,195m) - ROWIEŃ WAKSMUNDZKA (1,410m) - DOLINA WAKSMUNDZKA (1,250m) - NIŻNIA KOPKA (1,340m) - WODOGRZMOTY MICKIEWICZA (1,100m)

Grade: easy	Distance: 14km	Average gradient: 7%
NW-SE Height gain: 500m/loss 400m		Time: 3h 15m
SE-NW Height gain: 400m/loss 500m		Time: 3h 15m
Winter/spring: open		

A long but easy route, mostly in forest, with an occasional opening into a meadow.

The route starts in **Toporowa Cyrhla** (992m), about 100 metres back towards Zakopane from the bus stop. There is no official car park here, just space for a few cars. You climb gently into the forest, sharing the path with

The right-angled turns of Wodogrzmoty Mickiewicza

green route 512 for the first 1.5km. At a fork in the paths, while the green route bears right, red 009 bears left and continues climbing to an unnamed saddle at about 1,150m. You contour to the right above Dolina Suchej Wody, crossing the brook at a point called Psia Trawka (1,183m), where green route 513 sets out to your right up a forest road. (1h 00m NW-SE/0h 50m SE-NW)

Red 009 continues on a path opposite, still gently climbing for another 3km through forest. It levels out at a large meadow called Polana Waksmundzka, then climbs a little further to a smaller one, Rowien Waksmundzka (1,400m), where you cross green route 514. (0h 50m NW-SE/0h 40m SE-NW)

The path now descends comparatively steeply into **Dolina Waksmundzka,** and crosses its stream at about 1,250m, before climbing again, quite steeply at one point, to cross the shoulder of Niżnia Kopka (lower stack). The path descends once more, shortly crossing a meadow called Polana pod Wołoszynem (1,250m), at the far side of which is the junction with black route 914. (NW-SE 0h 35m/SE-NW 0h 50m)

The path rises a little then starts to descend, becoming steeper as it continues and crossing a stream at one point. When you reach the road, you can either turn left for 2.5km to the car park at **Palenica Białczańska**, or right to **Wodogrzmoty Mickiewicza** (1,100m), a picturesque waterfall at the junction with routes red 011 and green 517. (NW-SE 0h 50m/SE-NW 0h 55m)

If walking SE-NW, from route 011 near Wodogrzmoty Mickiewicza, you must look carefully for some narrow steps which may be overgrown and easily missed. You may more easily spot the red waymarks on the trees on the slope above.

011: PALENICA BIAŁCZAŃSKA (990m) - WODOGRZMOTY MICKIEWICZA (1,100m) - WŁOSIENICA (1,320m) - MORSKIE OKO (1,406m)

Grade: easy	Distance: 9km	Average gradient: 5%
N-S Height gain: 416m		Time: 2h 00m
S-N Height loss: 416m		Time: 1h 30m
Winter/spring: normally open only as far as Włosienica.		

The lower section of this route, from **Palenica Białczańska** *to the junction with route 009, is not coloured on the map, nor is it waymarked, but is included here for convenience. It leads to Morskie Oko, acknowledged as the most beautiful lake in Poland, and is the main approach route to Poland's highest point, Rysy. Unfortunately, the route is nearly all on hard surfaced road, though it is not without interest. There are short cut paths through some of the hairpin bends. The first 7.5km can be covered by inexpensive horse-drawn bus to Włosienica (see Gazetteer) - this takes 1 hour 20 minutes uphill, 45 minutes downhill. It used to be possible to take motorised buses and cars as far as Włosienica, but* *subsidence has resulted in closure of the road to all except service vehicles. There are no plans to re-open it to general traffic in the foreseeable future.*

After 1.5km you pass the little farm of Niżnia Polana pod Wołoszynem (Lower Meadow below Wołoszyn, 1,000m) among the meadows below to your left. Another 1km or so, passing a cascading stream on your right, brings you to the junction with red route 010 (N-S 0h 35m/S-N 0h 25m)

You come to two wooden chalets - a depot of the Nowy Targ Region Public Roads Department - after which you can soon hear the crashing waters of **Wodogrzmoty Mickiewicza** (1,100m), several hundred metres further on. (N-S 0h 10m/S-N 0h 05m)

Passing green route 517 you continue up the road, with the minor summit of Roztocka Czuba (1,428m) to your right. A long series of hairpin bends is avoided by a short cut path, then you rejoin the road as it now climbs the valley of **Dolina Rybiego Potoku,** with Rybi Potok (Fish Brook) below, to **Włosienica** (1,310m, refreshments). (N-S 0h 55m/S-N 0h 45m)

A little further up, to your right in the forest, is the **Szałasiska** campsite. The forest now starts to thin out, with more meadows, and you come to the junction with blue route 209 shortly before reaching **Morskie Oko** (1,406m, refreshments). (N-S 0h 20m/S-N 0h 15m)

012: MORSKIE OKO (1,406m) - CZARNY STAW pod Rysami (1,580m) - RYSY (2,490m)

Grade: strenuous	**Distance: 5km**	**Average gradient: 22%**
NW-SE Height gain: 1,084m		**Time: 3h 30m**
SE-NW Height loss: 1,084m		**Time: 3h 00m**
Winter/spring: closed		

This is one of the most popular and scenic routes in the Polish Tatras, liking the country's most beautiful lake and its highest summit. The summit is accessible from both sides of the border (remember that you cannot continue from Poland into Slovakia), and gets very crowded, so you are advised to make an early start to beat the "rush hour".

You can save some of your energy by taking the horse-drawn bus along most of the long approach road from Palenica Białczańska to Morskie Oko (see red route 011).

From Schronisko **Morskie Oko** (1,406m), follow the shore of the tarn round to your left. At the far end, though a path continues all the way round the tarn, the red route zigzags up the moraine to reach another "black tarn", the southern one, known as **Czarny Staw pod Rysami** (below Rysy, 1,580m). (NW-SE 0h 45m/SE-NW 0h 40m)

The shore of this tarn is also followed to the left, then the path continues climbing again, now more and more steeply to the summit of Rysy (2,490m). The final section is extremely strenuous. (NW-SE 2h 45m/SE-NW 2h 20m)

013: DOLINA ZA MNICHEM (1,785m) - WROTA CHAŁUBIŃSKIEGO (2,022m)

Grade: strenuous	**Distance: 1.5km**	**Average gradient: 16%**
NE-SW Height gain: 237m		**Time: 1h 00m**
SW-NE Height loss: 237m		**Time: 0h 45m**
Winter/spring: closed		

A side trip from yellow route 814 to a border saddle overlooking the two Temnosmrecinske (Ciemnosmreczyński) tarns in Slovakia. You are on open rock all the way, and pass between a number of very small tarns.

014: SZLAK IMIENIA POWSTANIA CHOCHOŁOWSKIEGO (Chochołów Uprising Trail): CHOCHOŁÓW (760m) - GUBAŁÓWKA (1,120m) - SUCHE (750m)

Grade: easy	**Distance: 20km**	**Average gradient: 4%**
W-E Height gain: 360m/loss 370m ●		**Time: 3h 00m**
E-W Height gain: 370m/loss 360m		**Time: 3h 00m**
Winter/spring: open		

This easy trail in the low hills to the north of Zakopane was created in the 1950s in commemoration of the Chochołów Uprising of 1840, when just six people from the village of that name, to the north-west of Zakopane, held out for two days against the Austrian army.

*If you take the chair-lift or rack railway to **Gubałówka,** you can follow the trail in two directions, generally downhill, and in each case mostly along a ridge at about 1,000m: either north-west for 13km to Chochołów, mostly through fields, passing the tops of Tominow Wierch (1,019m) and Ostrysz (1,025m); or north-east for 7km to Suche, much of it along roads or tracks coinciding with yellow route 809.*

***Chochołów** is worth visiting in its own right (see Gazetteer). From there or Suche, buses will bring you back to Zakopane.*

BLUE ROUTES

200: GRZEŚ (KONĆISTA) (1,653m) - WOŁOWIEC (2,063m)

Grade: easy to moderate	Distance: 4km	Average gradient: 10%
N-S Height gain: 410m		Time: 2h 15m
S-N Height loss: 410m		Time: 1h 45m
Winter/spring: closed		

Grassy and rounded, this is a comparatively easy ridge route along the border, with fine views. From the Polish side it is accessible near the south end via green route 501. It is also accessible from Slovakia at either end, but if you arrived from Poland you must not be tempted to descend into Slovakia.

201: STARE KOŚCIELISKA (970m) - POLANA STOŁY (1,340m)

Grade: moderate	Distance: 2km	Average gradient: 18%
NE-SW Height gain: 370m		Time: 0h 45m
SW-NE Height loss: 370m		Time: 0h 35m
Winter/spring: normally open		

A little used and peaceful route, mostly in forest but grassy at the top, from where there are good views of the Czerwone Wierchy. Polana Stoły has a collection of disused but very attractive shepherds' huts.

202: GRONIK (942m) - PRZYSŁOP MIĘTUSI (1,187m) - MAŁOŁĄCZNIAK (2,096m)

Grade: easy to Przysłop Miętusi; strenuous to Małołączniak
Distance: 8km
Average gradient: 9% to Przysłop Miętusi; 18% to Małołączniak

N-S Height gain: 1,154m	Time: 3h 15m
S-N Height loss: 1,154m	Time: 2h 30m
Winter/spring: closed	

A popular route providing a direct ascent from the outskirts of Zakopane to the **Czerwone Wierchy.** *It is in forest for two thirds of the way, though there are good views of the mountains and over Dolina Mietusia from Przysłop Miętusi. The last third is on open rock, climbing steadily to Małołączniak. There is just one difficult section, to the south of Kobylarz, which includes a fixed chain.*

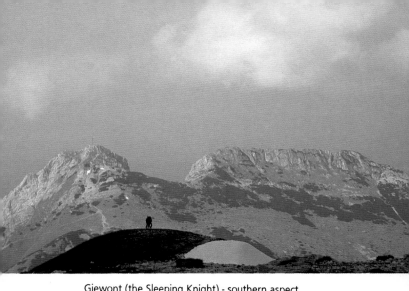

Giewont (the Sleeping Knight) - southern aspect
Koskielec

203: ZAKOPANE Hotel Kasprowy (870m) - BLACHÓWKA (1,160m) - GUBAŁÓWKA Stacja Gorna (1,120m)

Grade: easy	Distance: 5km

Average gradient: 10% to Blachówka; 2% to Gubałówka

S-N Height gain: 290m/loss 40m	Time: 0h 30m
N-S Height gain: 40m/loss 290m	Time: 0h 20m

Winter/spring: open

A gentle climb through forest and meadows to the popular ridge of **Gubałówka,** *on the ridge to the north of Zakopane, where it joins black route 906 for a level walk along the ridge. There are lovely views of the Tatras, both from the top and on the descent.*

204: ZAKOPANE Stacja Dolna Gubalówka (820m) - POLANA GUBAŁÓWKA (1,080m) - PAWELKÓWKA (860m)

Grade: easy	Distance: 5km	Average gradient: 10%
SE-NW Height gain: 260m/loss 220m		Time: 1h 15m
NW-SE Height gain: 220m/loss 220m		Time: 1h 00m

Winter/spring: open

Similar to route 203, but crossing red route 809 at the ridge summit and continuing further to the hamlet of Pawelkówka on the north side.

205: ZAKOPANE Bystre Rondo (890m) - MUROWANICA (990m) - KUŹNICE (1,000m)

Grade: easy	Distance: 2km	Average gradient: 6%
N-S Height gain: 110m		Time: 0h 30m
S-N Height loss: 110m		Time: 0h 30m

Winter/spring: open

This is actually the road up to Kuźnice, now closed to private vehicles (unless they have a reservation at the hostel). Nevertheless it is a waymarked route, and there are some points of interest along it.

From the east end of the car park, at the Rondo traffic roundabout in the **Bystre** district of Zakopane (890m), the road called Aleja Przewodników Tatrzańskich (Tatras Guide Avenue) leads south-east. Horse-drawn cabs (*dorożka*) wait for customers at the side of the road. The lower part of the road runs between sections of fenced off forest to the small settlement of **Murowanica** (990m). (10 minutes)

In Mengusovská Dolina, Slovak High Tatras (photo: Derek Goddard)

Soon afterwards to the left are the semi-open meadows of Wielka Polana Kuźnicka (Big Smithy Clearing), while the slope to the right is a practice ski area in winter. The unusual memorial on your right, to the local victims of fascism during World War II, consists of artillery and a fixed ladder; it was created by local artist Władisław Hasior. (10 minutes)

Where the road divides (there is a one-way traffic system here), take the right fork to reach **Kuźnice** (1,000m)

206: KUŹNICE (1,000m) - POLANA KALATÓWKI (1,198m) - POLANA KONDRATOWA (1,333m) - PRZEŁĘCZ KONDRACKA (1,772m) - GIEWONT (1,894m)

Grade: easy to Polana Kondratowa; strenuous to Giewont
Distance: 8km   **Average gradient: 7% to Polana Kondratowa; 19% to Giewont**
NE-SW Height gain: 909m   **Time: 3h 00m**
SW-NE Height loss: 909m   **Time: 2h 30m**
Winter/spring: normally open only as far as Polana Kondratowa

*A well used route up the valleys of **Dolina Bystrej** and **Dolina Kondratowa** to two popular refuges and to Giewont, the nearest and most distinctive mountain as seen from Zakopane. It is mostly in the forest, but there are extensive sections through the meadows and dwarf pine. The final ascent to the summit of Giewont involves some scrambling and fixed chains.*

From **Kuźnice,** take the steep, cobbled road which at first climbs parallel to the cable-car wires, then passes under them. You soon reach **Klasztor Albertynek** (1,100m). An unwaymarked path to the right climbs to Klasztor Albertynow. 50 metres further on, the blue route divides. (10 -15 minutes)

The right fork, which involves more climbing up the cobbled road but has better views, leads to the junction with black route 901C (10 -15 minutes) and **Polana Kalatówki** (1,198m, refreshments) (5 minutes). The left fork, a sort of by-pass, avoids some climbing by using a lower track. The two routes reunite a little over a kilometre further up the valley. (25-30 minutes)

After passing Jaskinia Kalacka (not accessible) on your right, the blue route turns to the right up a stone path. This then undulates for a while at about 1,350m, then climbs steeply to join a broad stone track by a picnic table. (Note: if walking SW-NE, watch out for the path which bears left off the main track 15m beyond the picnic table - the sign ahead, translated, reads "no entry".) The track leads out of the forest to Hala Kondratowa (1,333m, refreshments) and the junction with green route 508. (30-35 minutes)

Continue on the blue route which gently climbs the hill on the right side of Dolina Kondratowa, a wide, open valley with scattered clumps of dwarf pine and a profusion of red admiral butterflies. (Below, the green route passes up the middle of the valley then snakes up to Kondracka.) After a while the gradient increases, quite steeply in places, and for some metres care is needed where a stream shares the path, making it slippery. Eventually you reach Przełęc Kondracka (1,772m) and the junction with yellow route 805. A sign here uses the word "przielom", meaning a gap created by constant erosion by a stream. Away to the right is the summit of Giewont with its tall iron cross. (50-60 minutes)

The route turns right on a path which leads gently up to a ledge, passing the junction with red route 008 - you may find an itinerant seller of canned drinks here. Continue on a rocky path which gets steeper as you approach the summit, to the point where you are scrambling. You have to keep a careful eye out for the waymarks, because the path divides to provide a one-way system to and from the summit of **Giewont.** Watch for the arrow which keeps ascending walkers to the right. Do not attempt to use the left-hand route because you may cause problems for those coming down. The summit is rocky and windy, but you may have to squeeze yourself into any space you can find, as it is a popular picnic spot. (30-40 minutes)

207: KUŹNICE (1,000m) - PRZEŁĘCZ MIĘDZY KOPAMI (1,501m) - HALA GĄSIENICOWA (1,500m) - CZARNY STAW Gąsienicowy (1,620m) - ZAWRAT (2,159m)

Grade: moderate to Czarny Staw; strenuous to Zawrat
Distance: 10km Average gradient: 9% to Czarny Staw; 18% to Zawrat
NW-SE Height gain: 1,160m   **Time: 3h 30m**
SE-NW Height loss: 1,160m   **Time: 3h 00m**
Winter/spring: normally open only as far as Schronisko Murowaniec

A picturesque route leading mostly through dwarf pine and above the tree-line to the pleasantly situated refuge at Murowaniec, and on to the northernmost of three tarns called Czarny Staw (black tarn). Shortly after that it becomes very steep and difficult on the way to the high saddle of Zawrat on the Eagle's Path (red route 009B). The lower part of the route is very popular, as can be judged by its eroded condition in some parts, though refurbishment was under way in 1992.

From **Kuźnice** (1,000m), go east between the restaurant and grocery to cross a bridge over the Bystra stream, beside a tiny tarn. The blue and green routes turn left (yellow goes right) and climb together for five minutes, then the blue one turns right to climb steeply through the forest for another twenty minutes to reach a viewpoint on an eroded bluff. Here you look out over **Dolina Bystrej** towards Polana Kalatówki and its mountain hotel, beneath Giewont -

a spiked summit from this angle. You can repeat this a little further on by diverting a little to your right at Boczań (1,224m). (25-30 minutes)

Now climbing through forest and stormswept trees on the crest of the northern spur of Kasprowy Wierch, the path eventually emerges into the open on an eroded, rocky slope called Skupniów Upłaz. Here you have superb views of Nosal, Zakopane and the countryside beyond, as you climb to Przełęcz między Kopami (pass between the stacks, 1,501m) and the junction with yellow route 810. The "stacks" in question are the minor summits of Królowa (Great and Little), which, according to a notice, are inaccessible to walkers. (45-55 minutes)

The path continues on the level for a while, passing a vantage point with a picnic table, then descends through a collection of summer huts, including Betlejema (Bethlehem), a bothy belonging to the PTTK (Polish Alpine Club), and a weather station. Where the path divides, bear left to reach Schronisko **Murowaniec** (1,500m).

From the main entrance of the refuge, turn right then in 100 metres bear left, now among the dwarf pine. The path climbs gently to reach Pomnik Karlowicza (a monument to Mieczysław Karlowicz, a composer and pioneer skier who was killed by an avalanche here in 1909) then continues up the valley of Czarny Potok (Black Brook). On reaching the moraine, you climb it steeply to the big tarn called **Czarny Staw Gąsienicowy** (to distinguish it from the other two tarns of the same name) (1,620m).

Beyond Czarny Staw, the path climbs steadily, passing above Zmarzły Staw (icy tarn), as far as the rock face below Zawrat. Here the character changes dramatically - there are several fixed chains, scrambling and exposed situations, and there can be danger from falling rocks. At Zawrat you are on the famous "Eagle's Perch" (see red route 009B) - do not continue along it unless you are a very experienced and confident mountain walker.

208: ZIELONY STAW (1,672m) - KARB (1,853m)

Grade: moderate Distance: 1.5km	Average gradient: 12%
W-E Height gain: 181m	Time: 0h 40m
E-W Height loss: 181m	Time: 0h 30m
Winter/spring: closed	

A useful link route, entirely above the tree-line.

From Zielony Staw (1,672m) on black route 908, this route climbs steadily, round the south side of the tarn called Kurtkowiec which is noted for containing the highest island in Poland. The path steepens as it follows a stream, and zigzags as it approaches the saddle called Karb (1,853m), where it joins black route 909 and green route 515.

209: MORSKIE OKO (1,406m) - KĘPA (1,683m) - ŚWISTOWA CZUBA (1,763m) - PRZEDNI STAW (1,668m) - ZAWRAT (2,159m)

Grade: moderate to strenuous Distance: 10km Average gradient: 8%
SE-NW Height gain: 753m   **Time: 3h 00m**
NW-SE Height loss: 753m   **Time: 3h 00m**
Winter/spring: closed

A switchback route with great views, passing through dwarf pine and above the tree-line. It climbs over two shoulders and finally via the lovely Valley of Five Polish Tarns to Zawrat, a high saddle on the Eagle's Perch (red route 009B). It is quite tricky in places, with some scrambling and fixed chains.

From the refuge at the north end of **Morskie Oko,** walk north for 400 metres along the hard surfaced road, and as you come to the small tarns on your right, look out for the blue waymarks on your left. These indicate your path which climbs steeply through the dwarf pine - you must walk with care, as the rocks are uneven underfoot, and some low branches may catch your head. At two points you cross a landslip, the result of avalanches, requiring a scramble across loose rock, with fixed chains for support. The gradient becomes more gentle as you approach the saddle above Kępa (Nad Kępą) at about 1,720m, on the shoulder called Opalone (sun-burned), with fine views back over the Slovak Tatras. (45-55 minutes)

You now descend into a boulder-filled hanging valley (Świstówka Roztocka), once a lake bed, then climb again, now on the dip slope of Świstowa Czuba (1,763m). A side path leads to the sheer face, though just short of it one of the few signs in English in the Tatras warns "Attention: do not walk - life threat"! The view onwards, of three of the "Five Lakes", is breathtaking. (30-35 minutes)

The path down from Świstowa Czuba is quite steep - if you are coming in the opposite direction considerably steeper than it looks from the tarn. A short climb up its moraine leads to **Przedni Staw** (Front Tarn, 1,668m, refreshments) and the junction with black route 913. (40-50 minutes)

Passing to the west of Przedni Staw, on a fairly level path, you come in quick succession to Mali Staw (Little Tarn), above which is a small chalet belonging to PTTK (Polish Alpine Club), and **Wielki Staw** (Big Tarn, 1,665m). Shortly before the latter, an unwaymarked path to your right provides a short cut to green route 517 and the **Wielka Siklawa** waterfall. Close by is the junction with yellow route 812. (5 minutes)

Above Wielki Staw, the path is at first comparatively easy, climbing steadily in open terrain and passing the junction with routes 912 (black) and 814 (yellow). It then steepens considerably, with zigzags, to a spur, which you follow to the high saddle of Zawrat. (60-70 minutes)

210: ZAZADNIA POLANA (940m) - RUSINOWA POLANA (1,200m) - PALENICA BIAŁCZAŃSKA (990m)

Grade: easy to moderate   **Distance: 6km**   **Average gradient: 8%**
N-S Height gain: 260m/loss 210m   **Time: 1h 45m**
S-N Height gain: 210m/loss 260m   **Time: 1h 30m**
Winter/spring: open

This route goes mainly through the forest, passing the charming little church of Wiktorówki, and the open, grassy expanse of Rusinowa Polana. There is a small, unguarded space at the start of the route near Brzanówka, where cars can be left. Or take a bus or microbus from Zakopane to Zazadnia Polana (where buses terminate) from which you must then walk 1km south along the road.

From Brzanówka (940m), the route climbs gently at first, or undulates, crossing several streams on the lower slopes of Goły Wierch (Bare Hill). They all flow into Filipczański Potok. After a while the path starts to climb more steeply, bearing left out of the main valley (Dolina Filipka) into Dolina Złota, down which runs Złoty Potok (Golden Brook) - *złoty* being also the Polish currency. Approaching the head of this valley, and climbing ever more steeply, you come to the isolated monastery of **Wiktorówki** (1,140m). (75 minutes)

Continuing your ascent, you shortly reach **Rusinowa Polana** (1,200m) and the junction with green route 514. (5-10 minutes)

Keep ahead on a track which contours through the meadows at the foot of a steep hill, and passes between a number of shepherds' huts. You bear right, still in the meadows, to reach the junction with black route 914. The black route continues ahead, but the blue one goes left into the forest, just before the end of the meadows. It descends quite steeply, sometimes using flights of wooden steps, into **Dolina Waksmundzka,** whose brook guides you for most of the rest of the way, but finally the path bears left across a meadow to **Palenica Białczańska** (990m). (40-50 minutes)

GREEN ROUTES

Note: Be careful not to confuse the green waymarked routes on the Tatrzański Park Narodowy map with the borders of nature reserves, also marked by green dashes, but with a green arrow attached to their sides.

501: KIRY (927m) - SIWA POLANA (930m) - POLANA HUCISKA (982m) - POLANA CHOCHOŁOWSKA (1,146m) - WOŁOWIEC (2,063m)

Grade: easy to Polana Chocholowska; strenuous to Wolowiec
Distance: 16km

Average gradient: 3% to Polana Chochołowska; 18% to Wołowiec
NE-SW Height gain: 1,083m   **Time: 4h 00m**
SW-NE Height loss: 1,083m   **Time: 3h 30m**
Winter/spring: closed above Polana Chochołowska

There are two starting points on this route: either Kiry or Polana Huciska. Both have car parks and buses from Zakopane, though those to Huciska are infrequent.

From **Kiry,** you follow the road north-westwards for just under a kilometre, then where the road bends right, take a track to the left which skirts the foothills between forest and meadow. You soon pass the start of yellow route 804, and continue ahead on a forest road, now fully in forest, for another kilometre to reach more meadows at Siwa Polana. Here you turn left along a road, which can be quite busy, and follow it for 3 kilometres to **Polana Huciska,** where traffic must stop. There are no refreshment facilities here, though maps can be bought at the car park kiosk. (1h 30m)

The surfaced road continues for another 4 kilometres to **Polana Chochołowska,** but apart from an occasional service vehicle it is now traffic free. In this distance you climb just 164 metres, giving a very gentle introduction to one of the more remote areas of the Polish Tatras. Along the way you pass black routes 901A and 902, and red route 001. Running alongside (and mostly to your right) is Chochołowski Potok, one of the streams that soon join together to form the Dunajec river, a tributary of the Wisła (Vistula).

Refreshments are available at Schronisko Chochołowska. Here the surfaced road ends, and yellow route 100 starts. Green 501 continues up the main valley, now on a path, but still beside Chochołowski Potok. The going is rougher, and soon becomes increasingly steeper as you reach the head of the valley and climb out of the forest into the dwarf pine zone, which extends almost to the ridge.

At the ridge, which is also the border with Slovakia, you meet blue route 200. You can either turn left for a short but steep final climb to the summit of Wołowiec (2,063m), or right for an easy ridge walk (see blue route 200). (2h 00m/2h 30m)

502: TRZYDNIOWIANSKI WIERCH (1,758m) - CZUBIK (1,845m) - KOŃCZYSTY WIERCH (2,003m)

Grade: moderate   **Distance: 2km**   **Average gradient: 13%**
N-S Height gain: 245m   **Time: 0h 30m**
S-N Height loss: 245m   **Time: 0h 30m**
Winter/spring: closed

A grassy ridge providing a link between red routes 001 and 002 - the latter on the border with Slovakia. It is quite steep in places, but not difficult, and there are good views into the valleys on either side.

503: IWANIACKA PRZEŁĘCZ (1,459m) - ORNAK (1,853m) - ORNACZAŃSKA PRZEŁĘCZ (1,795m) - SIWE SKAŁY (1,867m) - SIWA PRZEŁĘCZ (1,812m) - RACZKOWA PRZEŁĘCZ (1,959m)

Grade: moderate	**Distance: 5km**	**Average gradient: 15%**
N-S Height gain: 613m/loss 113m		**Time: 2h 00m**
S-N Height loss: 613m/gain 113m		**Time: 1h 30m**
Winter/spring: closed		

A mostly grassy walk along the Ornak ridge, but with some rocky patches. It is nearly all in the open, with views of the main border ridge and into the valleys on either side.

From Iwaniacka Przełęcz (1,459m, junction with yellow route 802), you climb steeply to around 1,800m, then follow the ridge at about this height for most of the way. You pass two named saddles, Ornaczanska Przełęcz and Siwa Przełęcz - at the latter is the junction with black route 902.

The path now climbs steeply again, though with no difficulties, to the main border ridge at Raczkowa Przełęcz (1,959m). The path continues over the border into Slovakia, but you must not follow it. However, for a change, you can turn right, along red route 002, and then use green route 502 for your descent.

504: KIRY (927m) - DOLINA KOŚCIELISKA - POLANA PISANA (1,015m) - MAŁA POLANKA ORNACZAŃSKA (1,100m)

Grade: easy	**Distance: 6.5km**	**Average gradient: 3%**
N-S Height gain: 170m		**Time: 1h 15m**
S-N Height loss: 170m		**Time: 1h 00m**
Winter/spring: normally open		

Can extend for a further 6km north-east from Kiry to the Gubałówka ridge, mostly on roads.

*The most popular route in the Polish Tatras, being an easily accessible and gently graded stroll on a broad forest road along a pretty valley (**Dolina Kościeliska**). Furthermore, it leads to an attractively situated refuge (Schronisko Ornak), with several short side trips to caves possible along the way. Aim to start early, and avoid the weekend if possible. Horse-drawn taxis (dorożki) ply between Kiry and Polana Pisana - they may save energy but not much time.*

As you set off through the broad meadows south of **Kiry,** you see the spire of Kończysta Turnia, a minor summit at 1,248m, to your left. Roedeer graze here, and one or two may scurry away into the forest as you approach.

After 30 minutes or so, as you enter the forest, you pass the junctions with black route 901 (A and B). Shortly after the second junction is the tiny rustic Kaplica Zbojnicka - the robbers' chapel - where it seems to be the practice to throw coins.

Another five minutes brings you to the start of routes 903 (black) to the cave of Jaskinia Mroźna to your left, and 201 (blue) to Polana Stoły to your right. Also to your left is an unmarked path to Jaskinia Czynna.

In 25 minutes you reach **Polana Pisana,** the terminus for the horse-drawn taxis, and a popular picnic spot. Several side-trips are possible here: to Mylna Jaskinia (red 003), Smocza Jama (yellow 803), and Raptawicka Jaskinia (black 904).

Half an hour later you reach **Mała Polanka Ornaczańska** and its refuge, Schronisko Ornak, and the junctions with routes 505 (green), 905 (black) and 802 (yellow).

505: SMYTNIA POLANA (1,100m) - TOMANOWA POLANA (1,400m) - CHUDA PRZEŁĄCZKA (1,853m)

Grade: moderate to strenuous Distance: 6km   Average gradient: 13%
W-E Height gain: 753m   **Time: 3h 15m**
E-W Height loss: 753m   **Time: 2h 30m**
Winter/spring: normally open

This U-shaped route passes through remote terrain which is a favourite hibernation area for bears - do not come here alone in the autumn! The going is generally not difficult, but there is one very steep section.

From Smytnia Polana, near Schronisko Ornak, you climb the valley of **Dolina Tomanowa**, with its brook below to your right, in the forest. As you approach the valley head, the forest thins and you climb steeply to the junction with red route 006. Continue climbing for a while before contouring round into Czerwony Żleb (red gully). Now the path climbs very steeply, and you pass the remains of a furnace, bearing testimony to the iron ore that was mined here in the early nineteenth century.

After rounding the rocky western shoulder of Ciemniak, whose summit is to your right, you descend for a while, then contour to meet red route 004 at Chuda Przełączka (thin mini-saddle).

506: ZAKOPANE Mrażnica (870m) - DOLINA ZA BRAMKĄ (1,000m)

Grade: easy	**Distance: 2km**	**Average gradient: 7%**
NE-SW Height gain: 130m		**Time: 0h 20m**
SW-NE Height loss: 130m		**Time: 0h 15m**
Winter/spring: normally open		

A short dead-end stroll from Zakopane along Dolina za Bramką (Little Gate Valley), which is very picturesque and noted for its dolomitic rocks. Because of this, and its proximity to the town, this route can be very crowded at times.

From Stary Cmentarz (Old Cemetery) in the town centre, take the side street opposite called Kasprusie. This shortly continues ahead to become Strążyska, which you follow for 2km all the way to the edge of the town (to the point where red route 008 starts). Here turn right, to follow a lane bordering the forest. After a little over 1km, you cross a stream (which may be dry), then come to a bigger one (Potok za Bramką), where green 506 heads off to your left.

507: ZAKOPANE Szymony (800m) - ELIASZÓWKA (1,019m) - ZĄB (950m) SZAFLARY (640m)

Grade: easy	**Distance: 18km (to Szaflary)**	**Average gradient: 8%**
S-N Height gain: 219m/loss 69m		**Time: 1h 15m**
N-S Height gain: 69m/loss 219m		**Time: 1h 00m**
Winter/spring: normally open		

This is actually part of a long distance trail that leads for some 50km in total from Zakopane, mostly using tracks and lanes through quiet villages, providing a fascinating glimpse into the rural life of this part of Poland. The whole route can be traced on the 1:75,000 scale Tatry i Podhale *map.*

From the railway station in **Zakopane**, go north along Chramcówki to the junction with the main road (Jana Kasprowicza), then turn right for 500 metres into the district called Szymony. Here you turn left along a street called Szpitalna, which shortly crosses Zakopane's river, the Zakopianka, then climbs and bears right, past two large sanatoria. At the second, you go left, climbing steeply up a meadow, to a road which leads to the top of the ridge. Here your route briefly joins that of 014 (red) and 809 (yellow), and to the left you have beautiful views of the Tatras.

At the next road junction, the routes part company. Green 507 now heads northwards along an open, populated ridge for the next 10km on a quiet road through the elongated villages of Ząb, Sierockie and Skrzypne-Górne towards Nowy Targ. Before reaching this major town, it swings north-eastwards on paths and lanes to Szaflary, from where you can return by bus or train to Zakopane.

Continuing eastwards beyond Szaflary, the route crosses first the Biały Dunajec river, then another ridge at the village of Gronków-Środkowy, before descending to the small town of Nowa Biała where the Białka river is crossed. Finally it climbs into a more remote area to follow a third, forested ridge to the main Dunajec river at Niedzica.

508: POLANA KONDRATOWA (1,333m) - PRZEŁĘCZ POD KOPĄ KONDRACKĄ (1,863m)

Grade: moderate	Distance: 3km	Average gradient: 18%
NE-SW Height gain: 530m		Time: 1h 10m
SW-NE Height loss: 530m		Time: 0h 40m
Winter/spring: closed		

A pleasant, open route along the upper part of Dolina Kondratowa to the ridge that forms the border with Slovakia.

From **Polana Kondratowa** (1,333m) follow the route with green waymarks along the centre of the valley in front of the refuge. It runs level for some time, then starts to climb steeply on stepped boulders, and zigzagging as it gets higher, to reach the border ridge at Przełęcz pod Kopą Kondracką (the pass below Kondracką Stack, 1,863m). The red-topped white posts here mark the actual border.

509: ZAKOPANE Murowanica (950m) - NOSAL (1,206m) - NOSALOWA PRZEŁĘCZ (1,101m) - KUŹNICE (1,000m)

Grade: moderate	Distance: 4km	Average gradient: 12%
N-S Height gain: 256m/loss 206m		Time: 1h 10m
S-N Height gain: 206m/loss 256m		Time: 1h 10m
Winter/spring: normally open		

A scenic, semi-circular link between Zakopane and Kuźnice via Nosal, one of the minor summits that overlook the town. There is a very steep section just to the north of Nosal. Most of the route is in forest, though there are good views from the summit over Zakopane and Kuźnice. Striking a temporary gloomy note, Nosal has a reputation as a favourite spot for suicide jumps!

From the Rondo car park, south of the town centre, go east for a short distance past the roundabout, then turn right, up the road called Bulwary Słowackiego (Slovak Boulevard). After 500 metres, continue past a crossroads and past the Willa Tea, shortly after which green route 509 leads off to your left, immediately climbing very steeply.

The route climbs relentlessly to the summit of Nosal (1,206m), then descends almost as steeply to a saddle (Nosalowa Przełęcz, 1,101m, junction with black 915 and yellow 811). It contours round two gullies, and finally descends to **Kuźnice.**

510: KUŹNICE (1,000m) - KASPROWA POLANA (1,180m) - MYŚLENICKIE TURNIE (1,352m) - KASPROWY WIERCH (1,985m)

Grade: moderate	**Distance: 8km**	**Average gradient: 13%**
N-S Height gain: 985m		**Time: 2h 30m**
S-N Height loss: 985m		**Time: 2h 00m**
Winter/spring: closed		

A monotonous, twisting and rather pointless route, leading from **Kuźnice** *to the summit of Kasprowy Wierch, as does the cable-car that plies tauntingly up and down overhead. It is mostly in forest, though at the halfway stage (Myślenickie Turnie, 1,352m) there is a view down the cable-car wires towards Kuźnice. To add to the frustration, there are no refreshment or toilet facilities at the halfway station, but you can if you feel so inclined give up and take the cable-car for the rest of the way. Above the halfway point, you are mostly climbing grassy ski-slopes among the dwarf pine. You won't miss much!*

511: SUCHA DOLINA (1,700m) - LILIOWE (1,952m)

Grade: strenuous	**Distance: 1.5km**	**Average gradient: 17%**
N-S Height gain: 252m		**Time: 0h 40m**
S-N Height loss: 252m		**Time: 0h 30m**
Winter/spring: closed		

A corner-cutting route used by walkers from Schronisko **Murowaniec** *aiming for the Eagle's Perch route. Entirely on open, bare rock, it is steep but not difficult.*

512: JASZCZURÓWKA (900m) - KOPIENIEC WIELKI (1,328m) - TOPOROWA CYRHLA (1,000m)

Grade: moderate	**Distance: 7km**	**Average gradient: 11%**
W-E Height gain: 428m/loss 328		**Time: 2h 15m**

E-W Height gain: 328m/loss 428m   **Time: 1h 45m**
Winter/spring: open

A horseshoe-shaped route, mostly in forest but with some good views, linking two points on the road east of Zakopane with Hala Kopieniec. At the top you have a choice: either to tackle the minor summit of Kopieniec Wielki (very steep on its south side); or to take the low route through Polana Kopieniec with its picturesque shepherds' huts and sheep.

It is probably best to start from **Toporowa Cyrhla,** *since this involves less climbing. However, if you prefer to ascend the very steep south side of Kopieniec Wielki, you should start from Jaszczurowka.*

513: PSIA TRAWKA (1,190m) - SCHRONISKO MUROWANIEC (1,500m)

Grade: easy   **Distance: 5.5km**   **Average gradient: 6%**
NE-SW Height gain: 310m   **Time: 1h 20m**
SW-NE Height loss: 310m   **Time: 1h 00m**
Winter/spring: normally open

This is actually the service road for Schronisko **Murowaniec** *- gravel surface, always in the forest. For most of the way, it follows the brook in* **Dolina Suchej Wody** *(dry water valley), climbing out of the valley towards the top, where some hairpin bends are negotiated.*

514: WIERCH PORONIEC (1,105m) - GOŁY WIERCH (1,206m) - RUSINOWA POLANA (1,200m) - GĘSIA SZYJA (1,490m) - PRZYSŁOP WAKSMUNDZKI (1,443m) - POLANA WAKSMUNDZKA (1,395m) - SCHRONISKO MUROWANIEC (1,500m)

Grade: moderate (but with some strenuous sections)
Distance: 14km   **Average gradient: 5%**
NE-SW Height gain: 490m/loss 95m   **Time: 4h 15m**
SW-NE Height gain: 95m/loss 490m   **Time: 3h 45m**
Winter/spring: normally open

Though mainly along the foothills in the forest, this switchback route crosses open meadows and passes some fine viewpoints, including Gęsia Szyja, possibly the best outlook from any minor summit in the Tatras.

Buses from Zakopane to Lysa Polana stop at Wierch Poroniec. There is no parking here; the nearest is at Głodówka (2km north), where there is also a cafe.

From Wierch Poroniec (1,105m), the path climbs gently but steadily to G&ły Wierch (Bare Hill, 1,206m, viewpoint) then levels out to reach **Rusinowa Polana** (1,200m) and the junction with blue route 210. (1h 30m)

(A five-minute detour to the right is worth considering, along blue route 210 to the forest monastery of **Wiktorówki**.)

You now face a fearsome climb ahead up a long, very steep grassy slope, passing an icon at the bottom. At the top, the slope continues between the trees, and can be muddy and slippery after wet weather - care is needed when coming down. A broad grass track leads through the forest, and soon narrows to become an earth-and-root path, climbing to the ridge of the shoulder which leads to **Gęsia Szyja** (1,490m). (30-40 minutes)

The route now descends first to the little saddle called Przysłop Waksmundzki (1,443m), then to the clearing called Rowień Waksmundzka (1,413m) where red route 010 is crossed. You continue down, through the pastures of Polana Waksmundzka (1,390m) with its shepherds' huts, then climb and descend once more to Polana Pańszczyca (1,400m).

There is now a long section of steady climbing up **Dolina Pańszczyca,** crossing first a side stream, then the main brook (Pańszczycki Potok), after which you pass round the lower part of Zadni Upłaz, where you reach 1,560m, the highest part of this route. (Zadni Upłaz is in fact the northern shoulder of the Eagle's Perch range - see red route 009.)

Next comes a long descent into **Dolina Suchej Wody** (dry water valley), where you cross its brook (Sucha Woda) and join yellow route 812B for a final short climb to Schronisko **Murowaniec**.

515: CZARNY STAW Gąsienicowy (1,620m) - KARB (1,853m)

Grade: strenuous	**Distance: 0.75km**	**Average gradient: 31%**
NE-SW Height gain: 233m		**Time: 0h 45m**
SW-NE Height loss: 233m		**Time: 0h 30m**
Winter/spring: closed		

A route linking blue route 207 at Czarny Staw Gąsienicowy to black route 909 and Kościelec. It is a stiff, rocky climb, with a short, slightly airy section at Karb, but not difficult.

From the north-west corner of **Czarny Staw Gąsienicowy** (1,620m), climb steeply and steadily south-west, away from the lake, on a zigzag path leading to Mali Kościelec (1,863m), a minor summit. The route bears left along a ridge to the saddle called Karb (1,853m). This bit is slightly exposed at one point, but with excellent views on both sides down to the lakes.

516: KOZIA DOLINKA (1,780m) - GRANATY (2,239m)

Grade: strenuous	**Distance:** 1km	**Average gradient:** 46%
W-E Height gain: 459m		**Time:** 1h 30m
E-W Height loss: 459m		**Time:** 1h 00m
Winter/spring: closed		

*A very steep, but not difficult, access route to **Granaty,** the central peaks of the Eagle's Perch range (see red route 009B). It is all on open rock, and leads from yellow route 814 to the southernmost and highest Granaty summit at 2,239m.*

517: SCHRONISKO STARA ROZTOKA (1,031m) - WODOGRZMOTY MICKIEWICZA (1,100m) - WIELKI STAW (1,665m)

Grade: moderate	**Distance:** 6.5km	**Average gradient:** 10%
NE-SW Height gain: 634m		**Time:** 2h 15m
SW-NE Height loss: 634m		**Time:** 1h 45m
Winter/spring: open from Wodogrzmoty Mickiewicza to Stara Roztoka; the upper section is closed.		

A popular route leading through the forest to the beautiful Dolina Pięciu Stawów Polskich (Valley of Five Polish Tarns), passing on the way the impressive Wielka Siklawa waterfall.

From the east end of the former car park (furthest from the waterfall at **Wodogrzmoty Mickiewicza** (1,100m), the lower section of this route leads on a stone path down to Schronisko **Stara Roztoka** (1,031m). (15-20 minutes)

From the west end of the car park (nearest the waterfall), the route starts steeply up stone cobbles for some metres, then bears left up even steeper stone steps - these can be avoided by using a track to the right, which shortly rejoins the waymarked route. You descend a little to join Potok Roztoka, a brook which is soon crossed on a wooden bridge. An undulating path continues up the valley to reach Nowa Roztoka, a wooden shelter beside a glade frequented by jays. (35-40 minutes)

Potok Roztoka now divides into several streams, which you cross on a series of wooden bridges - if the first is flooded, use a smaller one a little way upstream. After this the waymarked path takes a sharp right fork and starts to climb steeply. In 10-15 minutes you come to the dwarf pine zone and have a view of the mountains above. To your left are the gnarled crags of Świstowa Czuba (1,763m). In another 15-20 minutes the junction with black route 913 is reached, climbing steeply up Niźnia Kopa (Lower Stack), then you pass under the wires of the lift taking goods to the chalet beside Przedni Staw. 20-25 minutes more bring the reward of the sight of **Wielka Siklawa** (1,640m), an impressive waterfall with two narrow falls at the top combining to form a wide one at the bottom. (45-60 minutes)

The path zigzags up beside the falls, and you soon reach **Wielki Staw** (1,665m). Halfway between falls and tarn, a waymarked path (not shown on the map) goes left to provide a short cut to **Przedni Staw**.

518: CZARNY STAW pod Rysami (1,580m) - PRZEŁĘCZ POD CHŁOPKIEM (2,307m)

Grade: strenuous	**Distance: 1.75km**	**Average gradient: 42%**
N-S Height gain: 743m		**Time: 1h 45m**
S-N Height loss: 743m		**Time: 1h 30m**
Winter/spring: closed		

A twisting, turning and very steep serpentine of a route, always on open rocky terrain, to one of the highest accessible saddles in the Polish Tatras.

It starts from red route 012 at **Czarny Staw pod Rysami** and first climbs south-west into Mięguszowiecki Kocioł (kettle), then south-east to the minor summit of Kazalnica (2,159m), then south-west once more to the saddle, always with much zigzagging on every section. The saddle, Przełęcz pod Chłopkiem (the saddle below Chłopek), is also known as Mięguszowiecka Przełęcz (2,307m).

Here, on the border with Slovakia, you are among the highest summits in Poland: just south-east of the saddle is Chłopek (Little Peasant) also called Mięguszowiecki Szczyt Czarny (Black Mengusovce Peak, 2,404m), the fourth highest, while beyond is Rysy, the highest at 2,499m. To the north-west is the fifth highest, Mięguszowiecki Szczyt Pośredni (Middle Mengusovce Peak, 2,393m), with the main Mięguszowiecki Szczyt (2,438m, second highest) beyond.

YELLOW/BROWN ROUTES

These routes, marked by yellow waymarks, are in some places difficult to identify on the Polish Tatrzański Park Narodowy map, especially within the green of the forested areas. They are more clearly identifiable on the Zakopane town map (in brown), or on the Slovak maps (in yellow).

801: POLANA CHOCHOŁOWSKA (1,100m) - DOLINA WYŻNIA CHOCHOŁOWSKA (1,150m)

Grade: easy	Distance: 1.5km	Average gradient: 4%
NE-SW Height gain: 50m		Time: 0h 30m
SW-NE Height loss: 50m		Time: 0h 25m
Winter/spring: may be closed due to avalanches		

*An alternative route (to green 501) giving access to the upper parts of **Dolina Chochołowska** on the east side of Chochołowski Potok, it links green 501 at Schronisko Chochołowska with red route 801. On the TPN map the route is given a title: "Szlak papieski biało żółty" (the Pope's white and yellow trail). Mostly in forest, it crosses on the way the meadow of Wyżnia Jarząbcza Polana. In 1990, this route was the scene of a very serious avalanche accident.*

802: POLANA IWANÓWKA (1,100m) - IWANIACKA PRZEŁĘCZ (1,459m) - MALA POLANKA ORNACZAŃSKA (1,100m)

Grade: moderate	Distance: 6km	Average gradient: 12%
NW-SE Height gain: 359m/loss 359m		Time: 3h 00m
SE-NW Height gain: 359m/loss 359m		Time: 3h 00m
Winter/spring: closed		

*This route links two valleys, Dolina Starorobociańska and **Dolina Kościeliska,** via a saddle at the foot of the Ornak ridge, Iwaniacka Przełęcz. It is mostly in forest, but from the saddle you should have good views of the Western Tatras peaks.*

From the top of Polana Iwanówka, the path goes behind a shepherd's hut to climb the valley of Iwaniacki Potok (usually dry in summer). Two thirds of the way up, it makes a temporary diversion into a side valley and a small meadow below the minor summit of Kominiarski Wierch (1,829m). The route is steep nearly all the way, and very steep on either side of the saddle.

East of the saddle, another usually dry valley is followed most of the way down, still steeply. Towards the bottom, at the confluence of two streams (or stream beds), the path contours to the right then descends to Mała Polana Ornaczańska.

803: POLANA PISANA (1,040m) - SMOCZA JAMA (1,120m) - SKALA PISANA (1,060m)

Grade: mostly easy, but with one strenuous and exposed section.
Distance: 2km   **Average gradient:** 7%
S-N Height gain: 60m/loss 80m   **Time:** 0h 45m
Winter/spring: closed
This route can only be followed in the S-N direction. To explore the cave you will need your own torch.

Part of this route passes through Wąwóz Kraków, a canyon which was once a cave whose roof fell in. You will see hundreds of sticks propped up at the side of the path - this is a sarcastic gesture by local people to help support the walls from further collapse! One section is steep and exposed, with a fixed chain and a 10-metre ladder to negotiate.

Smocza Jama is still a cave, and makes a worthwhile side-trip if you have your own torch. However it goes steeply down, including a fixed chain, and is very muddy in places. Then you have to come all the way up again.

804: POLANA BIAŁY POTOK (920m) - DOLINA LEJOWA - NIŻNIA POLANA KOMINIARSKA (1,110m)

Grade: easy   **Distance:** 4km   **Average gradient:** 5%
N-S Height gain: 190m   **Time:** 1h 10m
S-N Height loss: 190m   **Time:** 1h 00m
Winter/spring: normally open

A mostly gently graded route along a peaceful valley, Dolina Lejowa, beside its brook, Lejowy Potok, with alternate stretches through forest and meadow.

The route starts from green route 501 at the meadow of Polana Biały Potok, 1.5km from Kiry. Near the top, the path leaves the brook and climbs more steeply leftwards to join black route 901A at Niżnia Polana Kominiarska.

805: DOLINA MAŁEJ ŁĄKI (1,040m) - RÓWIENKI (1,160m) - PRZEŁĘCZ KONDRACKA (1,772m) - KOPA KONDRACKA (2,005m)

Grade: moderate   **Distance:** 7km   **Average gradient:** 14%
NW-SE Height gain: 965m   **Time:** 3h 00m
SE-NW Height loss: 965m   **Time:** 2h 15m
Winter/spring: normally open only as far as Rowienki

A popular access route to Giewont and the Czerwone Wierchy. It is a pleasant route, with some forest and long stretches of meadow. The start and finish are quite steep, but the long central part is gentle.

Soon after the start on blue route 202 in **Dolina Małej Łąki** (1,040m), you cross black route 901B, and at Przełęcz Kondracka saddle (1,772m), blue route 206 takes the traffic for **Giewont** off to the left. From the saddle, route 805 turns right to climb fairly steeply up the crest of a spur to Kopa Kondracka (2,005m) on the border ridge (red route 007).

806: ZAKOPANE Old Cemetery (820m) - PAŁKÓWKA (1,140m) - DZIANISZ (900m) - CHOCHOŁÓW (760m)

Grade: easy	**Distance: 15km**	**Average gradient: 5%**
SE-NW Height gain: 320m/loss 380m		**Time: 3h 30m**
NW-SE Height gain: 380m/loss 320m		**Time: 3h 30m**
Winter/spring: normally open		

This is an alternative route (to red 014) between Zakopane and Chochołów, mostly at a lower level, and using roads or tracks nearly all the way.

From Stary Cmentarz (Old Cemetery) in the town centre, turn right off the main street (Kościeliska) down a lane that passes underneath the main road flyover. 400 metres after that, you must turn left to cross a stream, then immediately turn right, just before the holiday house "Juhas".

The route now climbs quite steeply to Pałkówka at the west end of the **Gubałówka** ridge (look back for splendid views of the Tatras). Here is the meeting point of several routes (also red 014, blue 203, green 504, black 906). Yellow 806 now runs together with red 014 for 1.5km to a road junction on a broad saddle. While the red route continues ahead, the yellow turns left to descend the valley of Dzianiski Potok, through the long drawn out village of **Dzianisz,** all the way to **Chochołów,** from where buses return to Zakopane.

807: ZAKOPANE Pod Skocznią (900m) - BIAŁE (1,200m)

Grade: easy	**Distance: 4.5km**	**Average gradient: 7%**
NE-SW Height gain: 300m		**Time: 1h 00m**
SW-NE Height loss: 300m		**Time: 0h 45m**
Winter/spring: normally open		

A popular route, entirely in forest, that ascends the pretty valley called Dolina Białego. Its stream, Biały Potok (white brook), with its many small waterfalls and cascades, is aptly named since its bed is of white limestone. Though the gradient is mostly gentle, there are a couple of steep stretches near the top.

From the post office in Krupówki street in Zakopane town centre, go past the Orbis office then turn right along Galicy street. This leads into Grunwaldzka street, at the end of which you turn right then immediately left to continue in the same direction along Droga do Białego. At the end of this is the start of route 807, which goes straight ahead into **Dolina Białego.**

At the top of the route is the junction with black route 901C.

808: ZAKOPANE (850m) - UGORY (906m) - HARENDA (810m)

Grade: easy	**Distance: 4.5km**	**Average gradient: 3%**
S-N Height gain: 56m/loss 96m		**Time: 1h 15m**
N-S Height gain: 96m/loss 56m		**Time: 1h 15m**
Winter/spring: open		

An easy promenade along a ridge called Ugory above the east side of Zakopane, with outstanding views of the Tatras and over the town. The route has a name: Szlak imienia Jana Kasprowicza (Jan Kasprowicz Trail), named after the poet who is commemorated in a museum at Harenda.

From the railway station in **Zakopane,** go south along Jagiellońska street to its end by a church. Climb the waymarked path outside the fence (not the one inside the park). On reaching a minor road, turn right for 50 metres, then climb steps to the left. Where they turn sharp left, bear right up a grassy slope, beside a skilift, to the top of the hill. This is a fine viewpoint, with the Tatras to the south and the rolling hills of Podhale to the north.

Ignore the ridge track to your left and continue ahead to join a lane (Ulica Antałówka). At a major road (Droga Homolacka) turn left, past a modern chapel (note the big, covered bell at the corner of the churchyard), and follow this direction for the next 2.5km along the ridge. Here you may see a lark ascending. The distinctive yellow building with a green roof, on the outskirts of Zakopane to your left, is the Sokołówski Hospital.

Towards the end of the ridge you pass an icon encased in a concrete pillar. Here you turn sharp left to a track which descends to cross the railway line (unguarded - look both ways) and continue to the main road. (If walking in the opposite direction, look for the track to the left of the stream.)

Continue ahead along a track to the left of a stream which shortly reaches a minor road in Harenda, running parallel to the main one, where there are buses back to Zakopane town centre.

809: HARENDA (810m) - FURMANOWA (1,000m) - GUBAŁÓWKA (1,120m)

Grade: easy to moderate   **Distance: 5.5km**   **Average gradient: 6%**
E-W Height gain: 310m   **Time: 1h 30m**
W-E Height loss: 310m   **Time: 1h 15m**
Winter/spring: open

A longer and quieter route to the popular Gubałówka ridge. It can be linked with route 808 to provide an easy but satisfying half circuit above Zakopane.

From the village road in Harenda (parallel to the main road), follow the sign across the footbridge to the Jan Kasprowicz Museum. Go round to the right of the building and continue to the next road, where you turn right (to the left is a pretty wooden church with an onion spire). You pass a wooden well, then where the road bears right down to the river, take the second track on your left, which leads to a very steep path up to the ridge. It climbs a pretty, wooded combe, where brimstone butterflies abound.

At the top, you turn left to join red route 014 along a track, which soon becomes a village road with houses. After 1.5km green route 507 comes in from the left at a road junction, and the three routes run together for 400 metres to the next junction. The green goes right; the red and yellow go left, still on a minor road, which climbs steadily for just over 1km to a junction where blue route 204 crosses. Continue ahead for a further 1km to **Gubałówka.**

810: KUŹNICE (1,000m) - PRZEŁĘC MIĘDZY KOPAMI (1,501m)

Grade: easy to moderate   **Distance: 4.5km**   **Average gradient: 12%**
NW-SE Height gain: 501m   **Time: 1h 30m**
SE-NW Height loss: 501m   **Time: 1h 20m**
Winter/spring: normally open as far as Polana Jaworzynka

Of all the routes from Kuźnice, this one gets out of the forest most quickly, soon reaching the extensive and pretty meadows of Polana Jaworzynka on a gentle path. Higher up it becomes quite steep and rocky.

From **Kuźnice,** go east between the restaurant and the grocery, cross the stream beside the little tarn then turn right. You soon recross the stream and climb gently in the forest, soon to reach the meadows of Dolina Jaworzynka, with its collection of summer huts. The stream is usually dry here, as is the little reservoir which you pass at the start of the meadows - they are filled with meltwater in the spring. The valley narrows as you climb, and shortly after a point where the stream beds divide, the path turns right to climb steeply through a forested section. (30-40 minutes)

Emerging from the forest, you continue to climb steeply on a zigzag path to reach Przełęcz między Kopami (1,501m) and the junction with blue route 207.

811: NOSALOWA PRZEŁĘCZ (1,101m) - POLANA OLCZYSKO (1,080m)

Grade: easy   **Distance: 1km**   **Average gradient: 2%**
NW-SE Height loss: 21m   **Time: 0h 20m**
SE-NW Height gain: 21m   **Time: 0h 25m**
Winter/spring: normally open

No details known. Appears to be a dead end on the map.

812A: SCHRONISKO MUROWANIEC (1,500m) - SUCHA PRZEŁĘCZ (1,955m)

Grade: moderate   **Distance: 3.5km**   **Average gradient: 13%**
NE-SW Height gain: 455m   **Time: 1h 10m**
SW-NE Height loss: 455m   **Time: 0h 50m**
Winter/spring: closed

*A popular route on open rock for people taking the easy way to reach Schronisko **Murowaniec** (via cable car to Kasprowy Wierch).*

812B: SCHRONISKO MUROWANIEC (1,500m) - CZERWONY STAW (1,654m) KRZYŻNE (2,113m)

Grade: easy to Czerwony Staw; strenuous to Krzyżne   **Distance: 6.5km**
Average gradient: 5% to Czerwony Staw; 18% to Krzyżne
NW-SE Height gain: 613m   **Time: 2h 30m**
SE-NW Height loss: 613m   **Time: 2h 00m**
Winter/spring: closed

A comparatively easy access route to the east end of the Eagle's Perch route (red 009B) at the spectacularly situated saddle of Krzyżne, from where there are incredible views in all directions.

The route starts, together with green 514, from Schronisko **Murowaniec** (1,500m, routes blue 207, green 513, yellow 812A, black 908). At first it descends through forest into **Dolina Suchej Wody** (dry water valley), then parts company with green 514 to climb steadily through dwarf pine to Zadni Upłaz, the northern shoulder of the Granaty massif.

You descend into the broad **Dolina Pańszczyca** containing Czerwony

Staw (red tarn, 1,654m), then start to climb more steeply on open rock to Krzyżne (crosswise, 2,113m) - the last stretch is very steep, but not difficult.

812C: WIELKI STAW (1,665m) - KRZYŻNE (2,113m)

Grade: strenuous	Distance: 3km	Average gradient: 30%
S-N Height gain: 448m		Time: 1h 30m
N-S Height loss: 448m		Time: 1h 15m
Winter/spring: closed		

A delightful route linking one of the biggest tarns in the Tatras with one of its finest viewpoints. From **Wielki Staw** *(1,665m) you follow the fringe of the dwarf pine for most of the way, to finish with a very steep climb up to the saddle of Krzyżne (2,113m).*

813: CZARNY STAW Gąsienicowy (1,620m) - GRANATY north peak (2,226m)

Grade: strenuous	Distance: 2km	Average gradient: 30%
NW-SE Height gain: 606m		Time: 1h 45m
SE-NW Height loss: 606m		Time: 1h 30m
Winter/spring: closed		

A short and comparatively easy route to the Eagle's Perch and the **Granaty** *massif. From blue route 207 on the east shore of the northernmost* **Czarny Staw (Gąsienicowy)** *at 1,620m, you start among the dwarf pine, but soon reach the open rock. The final ascent to the summit is very steep, with a short fixed chain. This is the northernmost summit of the Granaty massif, called Skrajny (outer) Granat (2,226m) - see red route 009B.*

814: ZMARŁY STAW (1,700m) - KOZIA PRZEŁĘCZ (2,137m) - CZARNY STAW pod Kotelnicą (1,722m) - SZPIGLASOWA PRZEŁĘCZ (2,114m) - MORSKIE OKO (1,406m)

Grade: strenuous	Distance: 10km	Average gradient: 20%
N-S Height gain: 829m/loss 1,123m		Time: 4h 15m
S-N Height gain: 1,123m/loss 829m		Time: 5h 00m
Winter/spring: closed		

A long and tortuous route linking the three main tarn areas of the Polish Tatras, and almost entirely in open rock. There are two high saddles to cross, each involving very steep climbs with fixed chains.

Leaving blue route 207 above **Czarny Staw Gąsienicowy**, you pass round the small Zmarzły Staw (icy tarn), then climb steeply past the junction with green route 516 to cross the Eagle's Perch (red route 009B) at Kozia Przełęcz (goat saddle, 2,137m), with outstanding views. It lies between the summits of Kozie Czuby (goat's tuft, 2,266m) to the east and Zamarła Turnia (2,179m) to the west. There are fixed chains on either side of the saddle, and snow often lies here to hide the chains and make progress difficult - an ice-axe may be helpful. (1h 00m)

You now descend into **Dolina Pięciu Stawów Polskich** (the valley of five Polish tarns), one of the most beautiful valleys in the Tatras, first crossing blue route 209, then between two of the larger tarns, **Czarny Staw pod Kotelnicą** and **Wielki Staw Polski,** at around 1,720m.

Climbing again, there is another fixed chain to tackle just before Szpiglasowa Przełęcz (2,114m), a saddle between the peaks of Miedziane (2,233m) to the north-east, and Szpiglasowy Wierch (2,172m) to the south-west. (1h 45m)

The descent follows a serpentine route below Miedziane, passing above a small tarn called Staw Staszica. Finally you enter the dwarf pine above the great tarn, **Morskie Oko** (eye of the sea) for a gentle descent to the refuge at its north end, Schronisko Morskie Oko (1,406m). (1h 30m)

BLACK ROUTES

Ścieżka nad Reglami and Droga pod Reglami

These two parallel routes may be useful to walkers based in Zakopane wishing to reach one of the outlying valleys, or to return on foot to their starting point in a neighbouring valley. In winter and spring, all of Droga pod Reglami and most of Ścieżka nad Reglami are open, so may then provide several pleasant outings in themselves. "Regle" is the name of both the foothills and the lower stratum of vegetation of the Tatras.

Ścieżka nad Reglami (path above the regle) runs for about 16.5km from a point 750 metres south of the car park at Polana Huciska in Dolina Chochołowska, at its west end, to Polana Kalatówki, 1.5km from Kuźnice, at its east end. Its altitude varies from around 950m to 1,350m, and in places it is quite rough and steep. The route links seven main valleys (Chochołowska, Lejowa, Kościeliska, Małej Łąki, Strażyska, Białego, Bystrej) and six saddles (pod Kopą Spaleniską, Kominiarski, Miętusi, w Grzybowcu, Czerwona, Białego). It is marked as a continuous black route on the 1:30,000 Tatrzański Park Narodowy map, and we describe it below in three sections (901 A-B-C).

Droga pod Reglami (road below the regle) runs for 9km from **Kiry** (at the foot of Dolina Kościeliska) in the west, to **Murowanica** at the foot of the road to **Kuźnice** in the east. By including part of green route 501, the concept can be extended westwards for a further 4km to the foot of **Dolina Chochołowska.** The terrain is level and easy going all the way. The route is not waymarked, and we do not describe it in detail here.

901A (Ścieżka nad Reglami): POLANA POD JAWORKI (980m) - PRZEŁĘCZ POD KOPĄ SPALENISKĄ (1,307m) - NIŻNIA POLANA KOMINIARSKA (1,140m) - PRZYSŁOP KOMINIARSKI (1,110m) - STARE KOŚCIELISKA (960m)

Grade: moderate	Distance: 6km	Average gradient: 10%
W-E Height gain: 340m/loss 360m		Time: 1h 30m
E-W Height gain: 360m/loss 340m		Time: 1h 30m
Winter/spring: normally open		

From the car park/bus terminus at **Polana Huciska,** follow the road southwards along **Dolina Chochołowska** (green route 501) for 750 metres, to find the start of this route (black waymarks). It climbs quite steeply through forest to Polana Jamy (pits clearing), and continues up to go round a gully, past the crags of Kobyle Głowy (mares' heads) to the forested saddle called Kominiarska Przełęcz pod Kopą Spaleniską (1,307m) - it is unnamed on the map, though not in fact due to lack of space! It lies a little to the south of the minor summit shown as Wierch Spalenisko (smoky hill, 1,327m).

You now descend into the upper part of Dolina Lejowa, emerging at the shepherds' huts of Niżnia Polana Kominiarska (1,140m), at the far end of which is the junction with yellow route 804. The route contours a little north of eastwards to the next saddle, Przysłop Kominiarski (1,110m), then descends steadily into **Dolina Kościeliska,** joining green route 504 near the Kaplica Zbojnicka (robbers' chapel) at Stare Kościeliska (960m).

901B: (Ścieżka nad Reglami): CUDAKOWA POLANA (950m) - PRZYSLOP MIETUSI (1,187m) - PRZEŁĘCZ W GRZYBOWCU (1,311m) - POLANA STRĄŻYSKA (1,020m)

Grade: moderate	Distance: 6km	Average gradient: 10%
W-E Height gain: 361m/loss 291m		Time: 1h 30m
E-W Height gain: 291m/loss 361m		Time: 1h 30m
Winter/spring: normally open		

Ścieżka nad Reglami continues eastwards after a short break from section 901A. From Stare Kościeliska, go northwards for a few hundred metres along green route 504 to the south end of Cudakowa Polana (950m), to find the black waymarks leading off to the right (left if coming from **Kiry**).

The route starts on the level through a meadow called Zahradziska, beside Miętusi Potok (mint stream). On entering the forest, where red route 004 turns off to the right, the path starts to climb, increasing steeply, still beside the stream. On reaching a clearing, it turns left away from the stream to climb a meadow to the popular saddle called Przysłop Miętusi (1,187m), from where there are good views. Here is the junction with routes 005 (red) and 202 (blue).

The black route contours through forest round the head of **Dolina Małej Łąki** to a clearing called Rówienki (1,160m), where yellow route 805 is crossed. It starts to climb again, skirting another clearing (Mała Polanka) on the way to the next saddle, Przełęcz w Grzybowcu (1,311m), which lies between the forested hills of Grzybowiec (1,417m) and Łysanki (1,447m).

Here you join red route 008, with which a steep drop below the saddle is tackled on a series of zigzags, then a stream is followed quite steeply down to Polana Strążyska in **Dolina Strążyska** (1,020m). Here you have the choice of making a speedy return along red 008 to Zakopane, or continuing further along Ścieżka nad Reglami (see 901C below).

901C (Ścieżka nad Reglami): POLANA STRĄŻYSKA (1,020m) - CZERWONA PRZEŁĘCZ (1,303m) - BIAŁE (1,200m) - (SARNIA SKAŁA 1,377m) - PRZEŁĘCZ BIAŁEGO (1,320m) - POLANA KALATÓWKI (1,180m)

Grade: moderate   **Distance: 4.5km**   **Average gradient: 10%**
W-E Height gain: 357m/loss 197m   **Time: 1h 10m**
E-W Height gain: 197m/loss 357m   **Time: 1h 10m**
Winter/spring: normally open only as far as Biale

From Polana Strążyska in **Dolina Strążyska** (1,020m) (access from Zakopane via red route 008), the black route continues up beside the left-hand stream, through the meadow and into the forest. Here a short diversion with yellow waymarks leads up to the waterfall of Wodospad Siklawica.

The black route now climbs very steeply, using zigzags at first, to Czerwona Przełęcz (red saddle, 1,303m). Another diversion, adding some 30 minutes, is possible here to **Sarnia Skała** (1,377m), a rocky outcrop with fine views over Zakopane and up to Giewont. This may be open in winter.

From the saddle, the route descends to Białe, where yellow route 807 goes off to the left. The black route climbs round the head of **Dolina Białego,** becoming more rocky and a little more exposed than is usual for Ścieżka nad Reglami, as it curves and contours in and out of several gullies. This is in fact the long eastern shoulder of the Giewont massif.

You descend a spur called Upłaz Kalacki to a saddle called Przełęcz Białego, then a snaking path with zigzags takes you steeply down to the cobbled road called Droga Brata Alberta (blue route 206). A short distance to the right, refreshments can be obtained at Schronisko Kalatówki, while just 1.5km down to the left is Kuźnice.

902: WYŻNIA CHOCHOŁOWSKA BRAMA (1,040m) - SIWA PRZEŁĘCZ (1,812m)

Grade: moderate	**Distance: 6km**	**Average gradient: 13%**
N-S Height gain: 772m		**Time: 3h 00m**
S-N Height loss: 772m		**Time: 2h 30m**
Winter/spring: closed		

A comparatively easy access route to the main ridge of the Western Tatras. The ascent is gradual, though it steepens towards the top.

From green route 501, a little way south of Wyżnia Chochołowska Brama, black 902 climbs Dolina Starorobociańska, beside its stream, to a clearing called Polana Iwanówka, where yellow route 802 goes off to the left. Climbing further through another clearing. Starorobociańska Polana, the stream is left some way below, and several dry gullies are crossed. Eventually the forest is left behind and you continue up among dwarf pine and meadows, with the path steepening considerably as you reach Siwa Przełęcz (grey saddle, 1,812m). Here, green route 503 takes over for the short distance to the main ridge.

903: STARE KOŚCIELISKA (960m) - JASKINIA MROŹNA (1,100m)

Grade: moderate	**Distance: 1.5km**	**Average gradient: 15%**
N-S Height gain: 220m		**Time: 1h 30m**
Winter/spring: normally open to the spring (cave closed)		
This route can only be followed from north to south.		

350 metres past Kaplica Zbojnicka (highwaymen's chapel) on green route 504 at Stare Kościeliska, a bridge crosses Kościeliski Potok. Immediately to the right is a level path leading to the small Jaskinia Czynna (active cave). Ahead, a steep path leads up to the main cave. You shortly pass Lodowe Zródło (icy spring), the source of three streams. Its water, at a constant temperature of about 5 degrees Celsius, flows at between 245 to 620 litres per second.

Jaskinia Mroźna (frosty cave) is a level, lit cave for which there is a small admission charge. It is 500 metres long, and there is one-way traffic - you emerge from a different opening - then a steep, zigzag path takes you quickly back down to the valley and green route 504.

904: DOLINA KOŚCIELISKA - JASKINIA RAPTAWICKA

Grade: strenuous   **Distance: 1.5km round trip**
Winter/spring: normally open

A short diversion from red route 003. The cave is unlit, so you must have your own torch. A ladder and fixed chains take you down to the bottom of the cave, which is a dead end, so you have to climb up again.

905: SMYTNIA POLANA (1,100m) - SMRECZYŃSKI STAW (1,226m)

Grade: easy	**Distance: 1.5km**	**Average gradient: 8%**
NW-SE Height gain: 126m		**Time: 0h 30m**
SE-NW Height loss: 126m		**Time: 0h 20m**
Winter/spring: normally open		

Shortly before Schronisko Ornak on green route 504, this route climbs up to the left through the forest. It leads to a muddy tarn called Smreczyński Staw (1,226m), where there are many flies. It may be of interest to naturalists.

906: ZAKOPANE (820m) - GUBAŁÓWKA Stacja Gorna (1,120m) - PALENICA KOSCIELISKA (1,185m) - PLAZÓWKA (940m) - WITÓW (800m)

Grade: easy	**Distance: 14km**	**Average gradient: 6%**
SE-NW Height gain: 365m/loss 385m		**Time: 3h 00m**
NW-SE Height gain: 385m/loss 365m		**Time: 3h 00m**
Winter/spring: open		

Apart from the start (which can be avoided by using the chair-lift), this is a gentle route through the low hills on the north side of Zakopane to the straggling village of Witów.

The route is actually waymarked from the post office in Zakopane, twisting through back lanes to the main street called Kościeliska. Cross over and go left past the old cemetery (Stary Cmentarz), then turn right down a lane to pass under the main road flyover. Here the route is shared with yellow 806, which shortly goes left across a stream.

Black 906 continues steeply up the hill, eventually leaving the road to climb the ski-slope. When you reach the bridge over the rack railway line, you can either continue up to the left of the line, or cross the bridge and follow the right-hand side. Either way brings you to the **Gubałówka** ridge.

Turn left along the ridge and follow the road for 1.75km, together with routes red 014, blue 203, and yellow 809. At the crossroads, continue ahead (with green 504 for the first 300 metres) to the next road junction, where you bear left. At the second T-junction, continue ahead on a path climbing through forest to another road, on which you turn right for 2km.

A few hundred metres after the next junction, you take a track to the right which descends, eventually quite steeply, to a road, where you turn right and follow it for 4km into Witów.

907: ZAKOPANE Strążyska (880m) - DZIURA (1,010m)

Grade: easy	**Distance: 1.5km**	**Average gradient: 11%**
N-S Height gain: 130m		**Time: 0h 30m**
S-N Height loss: 130m		**Time: 0h 25m**
Winter/spring: open		

A suitable route for an evening stroll, or a pre-breakfast appetizer.

From the old cemetery (Stary Cmentarz), take the side street opposite and a little to the left (southwards) called Kasprusie. This leads on into Strążyska. A little over 1km from the cemetery, take the second of two side turnings close together, called Droga do Daniela, then bear right after crossing a stream. Keep ahead along a track which leads out of town to the forested slopes. Ahead is the short valley called **Dolina ku Dziurze.**

Near the head of the valley, the path turns left to climb the hillside more steeply. It leads to a cave called Dziura (hole), which is accessible and not too deep, though a torch may prove useful.

908: SCHRONISKO MUROWANIEC (1,500m) - ZIELONY STAW (1,672m) - ŚWINICKA PRZEŁĘCZ (2,050m)

Grade: moderate to strenuous	**Distance: 4.5km**	**Average gradient: 13%**
N-S Height gain: 550m		**Time: 1h 30m**
S-N Height loss: 550m		**Time: 1h 00m**
Winter/spring: closed		

A rocky path up the western branch of **Dolina Gąsienicowa,** through the dwarf pine at first then above the tree-line, leading to a saddle with fine views into Slovakia.

From Schronisko **Murowaniec** (1,500m), follow blue route 207 for 100m until it turns left, then continue ahead on the route with black and yellow waymarks. A little further on is a path junction, unmarked, but actually an extension of green route 514 - on the way down it provides a bypass to blue route 207 if you wish to avoid descending to the refuge. Climb steadily to the point where the black and yellow routes part. (15 minutes)

The black route continues to climb steadily up the valley, passing Litworowy Staw, and with a good view of the summit of Kościelec ahead and to your left. At Zielony Staw you come to the junction with blue route 208. The path now steepens considerably and zigzags as it approaches Świnicka Przełęcz (2,050m).

909: KARB (1,853m) - KOŚCIELEC (2,158m)

Grade: strenuous	Distance: 1km	Average gradient: 35%
N-S Height gain: 305m		Time: 0h 45m
S-N Height loss: 305m		Time: 0h 45m
Winter/spring: closed		

An airy climb to an outlying summit in the Świnica range, providing a challenge for more experienced and confident walkers. There is one fixed chain, a couple of scrambles without the help of a chain, and a few exposed places which require a good head for heights. The summit of Kościelec is a mass of boulders, likely to be crowded, and you may have to settle for an outlying vantage point.

From the saddle of Karb (1,853m), the route starts fairly moderately but soon begins to steepen, on a zigzag route. About halfway up, you come to a fixed chain providing support in a cleft which you climb. The zigzags continue, in some places over bare, convex rock - on the descent this increases the sense of exposure. The final route to the summit of **Kościelec** is comparatively easy.

910: DOLINA PAŃSZCZYCA (1,520m-1,620m)

Grade: easy	Distance: 1.5km	Average gradient: 7%
N-S Height gain: 100m		Time: 0h 20m
S-N Height loss: 100m		Time: 0h 15m
Winter/spring: closed		

A short link path through the dwarf pine between routes green 514 and yellow 812B. It is very little used, and therefore tends to be overgrown.

911: KOZIA DOLINKA (1,936m) - PRZEŁĘCZ NAD DOLINĄ BUCZYHOWĄ (2,225m)

Grade: strenuous	Distance: 1km	Average gradient: 37%
NW-SE Height gain: 365m		Time: 1h 00m

SE-NW Height loss: 365m   **Time: 1h 00m**
Winter/spring: closed

A short route on open rock providing a different means of access from the north to the Eagle's Perch (red route 009B), leading off green route 516. It is quite difficult at the bottom, being steep, slippery and exposed, with chains, scrambling and exposed situations. The route levels out towards the top and the final approach to the saddle of Przełęcz nad Doliną Buczyhową (2,225m) is comparatively easy.

912: WIELKI STAW (1,705m) - KOZI WIERCH (2,291m)

Grade: strenuous   **Distance: 2km**   **Average gradient: 30%**
SE-NW Height gain: 586m   **Time: 1h 20m**
NW-SE Height loss: 586m   **Time: 1h 00m**
Winter/spring: closed

A comparatively easy access route on open rock to the Eagle's Perch (red route 009B), this time from the south, leading off blue route 209 a little way above **Wielki Staw.** *It is steep but not difficult, with a gradual climb on zigzags up the dip slope to the summit of Kozi Wierch (2,291m).*

913: DOLINA ROZTOKI (1,400m) - PRZEDNI STAW (1,668m)

Grade: moderate   **Distance: 1.5km**   **Average gradient: 18%**
N-S Height gain: 268m   **Time: 0h 30m**
S-N Height loss: 268m   **Time: 0h 20m**
Winter/spring: closed

A steep but not difficult short cut from green route 517 in **Dolina Roztoki** *to* **Przedni Staw** *and its refuge on blue route 209. (see p136)*
    The path starts with a long series of short zigzags on the lower slope of Niźnia Kopa. Towards the top, it levels out a little to traverse below the cliff face.

914: RUSINOWA POLANA (1,220m) - WAKSMUNDZKI POTOK (1,200m)
POLANA POD WOŁOSZYNEM (1,260m)

Grade: easy   **Distance: 3km**   **Average gradient: 3%**
N-S Height loss: 20m/gain 60m   **Time: 0h 30m**
S-N Height loss: 60m/gain 20m   **Time: 0h 30m**
Winter/spring: normally open

A link route between blue 210 and red 010.

From the south end of **Rusinowa Polana** (1,220m), at the junction with blue route 210, where a large black spot and arrow are painted on top of a flat boulder, the route goes at first along a broad track, then into the forest, contouring at about 1,200 metres for a while before descending into **Dolina Waksmundzka.** After crossing the brook (Waksmundzki Potok), it climbs round the shoulder of Niżnia Kopka (Low Heap) to reach Polana pod Wołoszynem and the junction with red route 010 (1,260m)

915: NOSALOWA PRZEŁĘCZ (1,101m) - POLANA OLCZYSKO (1,040m)

Grade: easy	**Distance: 1km**	**Average gradient: 12%**
W-E Height loss: 61m		**Time: 0h 15m**
E-W Height gain: 61m		**Time: 0h 20m**
Winter/spring: normally open		

A recently opened route (shown on the most recent Zakopane town map but not on the 1:30,000 TNP map) providing a descent from Nosalowa Przełęcz eatwards into Dolina Olczyska at Polana Olczysko.

SELECTED TIMINGS

This section provides a quick-reference guide to selected walking times. Taken from a variety of sources, they are approximate, and intended to provide a rough guide only - always allow extra time for your journey, in case of unforeseen difficulties. By adding together the various sections, these tables can be used to compute the total times for your own routes.

Of course, people walk at differing speeds. On your first day of walking, you can compare your own times with those shown to get an idea of whether you are faster or slower. This is only for your information; there is no point in racing the signposts!

Remember that: routes beginning with
"0" = red, "2" = blue, "5" = green, "8" = yellow, "9" = black.

FROM/to	Time	Via routes
BUNDÓWKI to:		
Giewont	3h 00m	008
Polana Strążyska	0h 35m	008
Przełęcz w Grzybowcu	1h 10m	008
Sarnia Skała	1h 10m	008/901C
BYSTRE Rondo to:		
Kuźnice	0h 30m	205 (by 509 = 1h 10)
Murowaniec	2h 00m	205/207
Nosal	0h 50m	205/509
Nosalowa Przełęcz	1h 00m	205/509
Polana Olczysko	1h 20m	205/509/811
CZARNY STAW Gąsienicowej to:		
Granaty	1h 45m	207/813
Kościelec	1h 30m	515/909
Przełęcz Karb	0h 45m	515
Zawrat	1h 45m	207
GRONIK to:		
Przysłop Miętusi	0h 45m	202
Małołączniak	3h 15m	202
KASPROWY WIERCH to:		
Ciemniak	3h 00m	007
Kuźnice	2h 00m	510
Schronisko Murowaniec	0h 55m	812A
Świnica	1h 40m	009A
KIRY to:		
Ciemniak	3h 30m	504/004
Gubałówka	1h 45m	504
Mała Polanka Ornaczańska	1h 00m	504
Polana Pisana	1h 00m	504
Stare Kościeliska	0h 30m	504
Tomanowa Przełęcz	2h 30m	504/505/006
KUŹNICE to:		
Dol. Kościeliska (Zahradziska)	5h 00m	901C/901B
Giewont	2h 30m	206
Kalatówki Schronisko	0h 30m	206
Kasprowy Wierch	2h 45m	510
Kondratowa Schronisko	1h 00m	206
Murowaniec Schronisko	1h 45m	207 or 810/207
Nosal	1h 00m	509
Sarnia Skała	2h 00m	206/901C
MORSKIE OKO to:		
Przedni Staw	2h 00m	209

FROM/to	Time	Via routes
Mieguszowiecka Przelecz	4h 00m	012/518
Szpiglasowa Przelecz	2h 30m	814
NEDZÓWKA to:		
Małołączniak	4h 00m	005/202
Przysłop Miętusi	1h 30m	005
PALENICA BIAŁCZAŃSKA to:		
Morskie Oko	2h 00m	011
Przedni Staw	2h 35m	011/517/913
Rusinowa Polana	0h 45m	210
Rysy	5h 30m	011/012
Wodogrzmoty Mickiewicza	0h 35m	011
Zazadnia Polana	2h 00m	210
POLANA BIAŁY POTOK to:		
Niżnia Polana Kominiarska	1h 10m	804
POLANA HUCISKA to:		
Polana Chochołowska	1h 00m	501
Raczkowa Przełęcz	3h 00m	501/902/503
Trzydniowiański Wierch	3h 00m	501/801/001
Wołowiec	3h 45m	501/200
Wyżnia Chochołowska Brama	0h 25m	501
POLANA KALATÓWKI to:		
Dolina Kościeliska	4h 30m	901C/901B
Dolina Małej Łąki	3h 30m	901C/901B
Dolina Strążyska	2h 15m	901C
Giewont	2h 00m	206
Kondratowa Schronisko	0h 45m	206
PRZEDNI STAW to:		
Kozi Wierch	2h 00m	209/912
Kozia Przełęcz	1h 45m	209/814
Krzyżne	2h 30m	209/812C
Morskie Oko	1h 45m	209
Szpiglasowa Przełęcz	2h 30m	209/814
Zawrat	2h 00m	209
RUSINOWA POLANA to:		
Murowaniec Schronisko	3h 30m	514
Palenica Białczańska	0h 35m	210
Stara Roztoka	1h 30m	914/010/517
Wierch Poroniec	1h 00m	514
Zazadnia Polana	1h 25m	210
SCHRONISKO HALA KONDRATOWA to:		
Giewont	2h 00m	206
Kopa Kondracka	2h 00m	206/805

FROM/to	Time	Via routes
Kuźnice	1h 00m	206
Przełęcz pod Kopą Kondracką	1h 30m	508
SCHRONISKO MUROWANIEC to:		
Granaty	2h 15m	207/813
Kasprowy Wierch	1h 30m	812A
Kościelec	2h 00m	207/515/909
Kozia Przełęcz	2h 30m	207/814
Krzyżne	3h 30m	812B
Kuźnice	1h 15m	207
Przełęcz Liliowe	1h 15m	812A/511
Świnica	3h 00m	908/009A
Wierch Poroniec	3h 45m	514
Zawrat	2h 15m	207
SPADOWIEC to:		
Białe	1h 00m	807
Sarnia Skała	1h 30m	807/901C
TOPOROWA CYRHLA to:		
Nosalowa Przełęcz	1h 10m	512/915
Wodogrzmoty Mickiewicza	3h 00m	010
WIERCH PORONIEC to:		
Gęsia Szyja	1h 30m	514
Murowaniec Schronisko	4h 15m	514
Rusinowa Polana	1h 30m	514
Wodogrzmoty Mickiewicza	1h 45m	514/210/914/010
WODOGRZMOTY MICKIEWICZA to:		
Morskie Oko	1h 25m	011
Przedni Staw	2h 00m	517/913
Stara Roztoka	0h 12m	517
ZAZADNIA POLANA to:		
Rusinowa Polana	1h 15m	210
Wodogrzmoty Mickiewicza	2h 30m	210/914/010

HIGHEST SUMMITS
(2,000m and above)

* = shared with Slovakia
+ = accessible to walkers

Many of these names are untranslatable, but where possible we show an approximate translation in an attempt to facilitate identification where pronunciation may be difficult.

Summit	Translation	Height
Rysy *+	Scars	2,490m
Mięguszowiecki Szczyt *	Mengusovce Peak	2,438m
Niżnie Rysy *	Lower Scars	2,430m
Chłopek *	Little Peasant	2,404m
(also called Mięguszowiecki Szczyt Czarny)		
Mięguszowiecki Szczyt Pośredni *	Middle Mengus.Peak	2,393m
Cubryna *	-	2,376m
Wołowa Turnia *	Ox Crag	2,373m
Hinczowa Turnia *	Hincova Crag	2,372m
Żabia Turnia *	Frog Crag	2,335m
Świnica *+	The Pig	2,301m
Kozi Wierch +	Goat Peak	2,291m
Gąsienicowa Turnia	Caterpillar Crag	2,280m
Kozie Czuby +	Goats' Tufts	2,266m
Niebieska Turnia	Heavenly Crag	2,262m
Wyżni Żabi Szczyt *	Higher Frog Peak	2,259m
Spadowa Kopa *	Drop Stack	2,250m
Zawratowa Turnia	Zawrat Crag	2,245m
Granaty +	Grenades or Pomegranates	2,239m
Miedziane	Copper	2,233m
Mali Kozi Wierch +	Little Goat Hill	2,226m
Wielka Koszysta	Great Koszysta	2,193m
Waksmundzki Wierch	Waksmund Peak	2,186m
Wielka Buczynowa Turnia	Great Beech Crag	2,182m
Zamarła Turnia +	Petrified Crag	2,179m
Starorobociańsky Wierch *	Old Works Peak	2,176m
Orla Baszta +	Eagle Tower	2,175m
Szpiglasowy Wierch *	Spiglas Peak	2,172m
Zadni Mnich *	Hinder Monk	2,172m
Mała Buczynowa Turnia +	Little Beech Crag	2,171m
Błyszcz *	Sparkle	2,158m
Kościelec +	Church or Bones	2,158m
Walentkowy Wierch *	Valentine Peak	2,156m

Summit	Translation	Height
Wielki Wołoszyn	Great Wołoszyn	2,155m
Żabi Mnich *	Frog Monk	2,146m
Mały Wołoszyn	Little Wołoszyn	2,144m
Ciemnosmreczyńska Turnia *	Dark Spruce Crag	2,142m
Wierch pod Fajki	Peak below Pipes	2,135m
Pośrednia Turnia *	Middle Crag	2,128m
Opalony Wierch	Burnt Peak	2,124m
Krzesanica *+	Craggy	2,122m
Pośredni Wołoszyn	Middle Wołoszyn	2,117m
Niżni Żabi Szczyt	Lower Frog Peak	2,098m
Skrajna Turnia *+	Furthest Crag	2,097m
Ciemniak *+	-	2,096m
Małołączniak *+	Little Meadow	2,096m
Skrajny Wołoszyn	Furthest Wołoszyn	2,090m
Żółta Turnia	Yellow Crag	2,087m
Wyżni Koštur *	Higher Stave	2,083m
Żabia Czuba *	Frog Tuft	2,080m
Mała Koszysta	Little Koszysta	2,071m
Gładky Wierch *	Smooth Peak	2,065m
Wołowiec *	The Ox	2,063m
Niżni Koštur *	Lower Stave	2,055m
Wierch nad Żleb Zagonnym	Peak above Clump Gully	2,039m
Beskid *+	-	2,012m
Kopa Kondracka *+	Kondracka Stack	2,005m
Konczysty Wierch *	End Peak	2,003m

TRAVEL

To and From the Polish Tatras

The nearest airport to Zakopane is at Kraków, about 100 kilometres north-east, from where there are trains and buses to Zakopane. Kraków is served by LOT Polish Airlines with direct flights from London. Many international airlines fly to Warsaw, from where there are connecting flights to Kraków.

Several direct train services go daily from Warsaw to Zakopane via Kraków, including a sleeper.

Long distance buses serve Zakopane from Warsaw and Kraków.

Within the Polish Tatras

Frequent buses link Zakopane with the outlying villages, including Lysa Polana on the border with Slovakia. There are also "przevoz osoba" (people's transport). These are minibuses which can be hired like taxis, though since you have to pay

Horse-drawn taxis (dorožki) in Zakopane

for a minimum of eight passengers in practice people club together or wait until the minibus fills up. Some are allowed to cross into Slovakia.

Zakopane has a large fleet of horse-drawn taxis (dorożki), as well as motorised ones. They operate from several stands, including one near the post office in the main street called Krupówki, one at the railway station, and another at the foot of the road leading to Kuźnice.

A horse-drawn bus runs up the long Dolina Białki valley towards Morskie Oko, where all private vehicles and motor buses are banned. Horse-drawn taxis ply for hire along Dolina Kościeliska between Kiry and Polana Pisana.

A cable-car climbs from Kuźnice to the summit of Kasprowy Wierch.

By Car
You should approach via Kraków, then take highway number 95 south-east to Nowy Targ, beyond which it continues to Zakopane.

Self-drive cars can be rented in Kraków, but not in Zakopane.

Private vehicles are banned at all times from side roads leading up into the mountains. They may only be parked in the official car parks, shown on the maps, where a small charge is made.

The ban applies to the tarmac road leading from Zakopane to Kuźnice, and also the ones which lead up the long Dolina Białki to Morskie Oko, and Dolina Chochołowska. Vehicles must be left at the large car parks at the foot of these roads, then you can either walk or take a horse-drawn bus or taxi.

Passports and Visas
The following requirements are those that applied in March 1993. You are advised to check the latest position with your travel agent, airline or a consulate of Poland.

All visitors to Poland need a valid full passport. Short-term passports and identity cards are not accepted. Nationals of European Union and Scandinavian countries, the USA and Canada do not need visas for Poland. Visitors from other countries will probably need a visa, obtainable in advance from a Polish consulate in your country of residence (see Appendix 3).

DIVERSIONS

If you need a break from walking, or if the weather is bad, or you have enough energy left to do something in the evening, Zakopane offers the following:

Sightseeing Excursions
The following can be booked through travel agencies in Zakopane:
Kraków: historic city centre; Wawel (royal castle, where most Polish kings were crowned and are buried); Wieliczka (thirteenth-century salt mine).

Auschwitz (Oswieńcim): former military barracks converted during World War II into a notorious concentration camp; now a museum and memorial to those who perished there.

Wadowice (birthplace of Pope John Paul II).

Rafting trip on Dunajec river, including a tour of the Pieniny mountains (a limestone range considerably different from the Tatras).

Debno: town with a unique wooden church and a castle.

Tour into Slovakia.

The following facilities are in or near Zakopane, and can be visited on foot or by bus or taxi.

Museums and Art Galleries

Muzeum Tatrzańskie, Krupówki 10: a reconstructed wooden cottage containing folk costumes, features on shepherding, geology, fauna and flora.

Muzeum Tatrzańske Parko Narodowego (TPN), at Bystre Rondo, behind the guides association building: fauna and flora of the Tatras.

Muzeum Jana Kasprowicza, Harenda: memorabilia of the poet Jan Kasprowicz.

Szymanowsky Collection, in a house called "Atma": museum about the composer Karol Szymanowski.

There are also six art galleries in Zakopane, including one dedicated to Władisław Hasior, whose monumental sculpture can be seen on the road to Kuźnice.

In Kuźnice/Murowanica:

Willa "Tea", Bulwary Słowackiego 39, Murowanica (just off the road to Kuźnice). A typical house of the Goral people.

Sports

Swimming pools: Olympic size pool at the COS Stadium near Bystre Rondo; Hotel Kasprowy (outdoor, open to the public); Antałówka (indoor, east side of Zakopane, fed by a thermal sulphuric spring).

Tennis: Sports Centre (COS Centralny Ośrodek Sportu) near Bystre Rondo (south side of Zakopane); Hotel Kasprowy (open to the public)

Dining with entertainment

Hotel Morskie Oko (cabaret); Obrochtówka restaurant (old style Zakopane folk music); Redykolka (folklore evenings).

Nightclubs etc.

Many restaurants offer discos and striptease, particularly: Hotel Kasprowy (disco); Hotel Giewont (disco); Watra (striptease).

Theatres and Cinemas

Teatr in St Ignacego Witkiewicza, Chramcówki 15.
Miejski Ośrodek Kultury (Municipal Culture Centre), Kościuszki 4.
Sokół Kina (Cinema), Orkana 2

SHOPPING AND LOCAL SERVICES

Zakopane has a wide range of shops and other facilities. Shops generally open from 10am to 6pm, but food shops usually open at 7am. There are a few "convenience" shops which are open for 24 hours.

Little English or German is spoken - you are advised to take a Polish phrasebook or dictionary with you.

The following is a summary of the services available. For more details enquire at the tourist information centre.

Tourist Information Centre
Tadeusza Kościuszki 7, 34500 Zakopane (phone 0165-12211 or 66051); on the ground floor of Pension Kolejarz, near the rail and bus stations. Open 24 hours in season.

Supermarkets/Foodshops (sklep żywnościowe)
The main food supermarket is on the ground floor of the department store "Granit" which lies just off the main shopping street (Krupówki), near Hotel Giewont. There are also many small food shops around the town.

Post Offices (poczta)
The central post office is in Krupówki, the main shopping street, opposite Hotel Giewont. There are several sub post offices in the outlying districts.

Travel Agencies (biuro podrózy)
The main agencies are: Trip Travel, Ulica Zamoyskiego 1 (phone 0165-5947/4577); Orbis, Krupówki 22 (phone 0165-5051/4812)

Currency Exchange (kantor)
Many hotels and all banks and travel agencies offer currency exchange facilities (see also under "Other Useful Information").

Department Stores
Granit (see under Supermarkets).

Bookshops (księgarnia)
There are two bookshops in Krupówki street; they sell walking maps and dictionaries.

Pharmacies (apteka)

There are two in the main street (Krupówki), also in the streets called Chramcówki (near the railway station), Kościeliska, Witkiewicza, and Droga do Olczy (Bystre).

Souvenirs (pamiątka)

Several shops in the town centre sell a variety of souvenirs.

Camera Film (błona)

Can be bought at pharmacies and a variety of other shops.

Sport Shops (sklep sport)

Walking equipment can be bought at Alpin Sport in the street called Jozefa Piłsudskiego.

National Park Office

At the Muzeum TPN, near Bystre Rondo.

Mountain Guides

PTTK/BORT, Ulica Krupkówki 12, 34500 Zakopane (phone 0165-5848). At the time of writing the guide booking system was in process of reorganisation. In case of difficulty contact one of the local travel agencies.

Taxis

Taxi-ranks (postóje taksówek) at several locations. There are also ranks (postóje dorożek) for horse-drawn taxis (dorożki) at several locations, but these are much more expensive.

Car Hire

There are as yet no self drive car hire/rental facilities in Zakopane. The nearest are in Kraków or Nowy Targ.

Filling stations (stacje benzynowe)

There are three in or near Zakopane: in the town centre (Piłsudskiego); Bystre Rondo (south-east side); and at Ustup (3 kilometres north-east, open 24 hours).

Car Service Stations (stacje obsługi samochódov)

There are several in or near Zakopane - for details enquire at the tourist information centre.

OTHER USEFUL INFORMATION

Here are some more useful bits of information:

Currency

The Polish currency unit is the złoty, pronounced "zwotty", which means "golden", though regrettably one such unit is nowadays worthless. There is very high inflation (40% in 1993), and a single unit of most overseas hard currencies converts into thousands of złoty. You can only obtain złoty inside Poland, and it is unconvertible outside. You must therefore transact all your currency exchange inside Poland, and it is advisable not to change too much at once.

You can exchange your currency at all travel agencies and banks, at many hotels, and at Warsaw and Kraków airports.

If you are travelling between Poland and Slovakia or vice versa, there is a currency exchange office at the Łysa Polana frontier station. Do not try to buy Slovak currency anywhere else in Poland, as it may be "pre-divorce" Czechoslovak currency which is not accepted in Slovakia.

Meals

There is a wide choice of restaurants (restauracje) and cafes (kawiarnie) in Zakopane, as well as street kiosks. Food and drink in cafes, mountain chalets and restaurants are very inexpensive. Meat tends to be quite spicy. Vegetarians may struggle to find much other than pizzas, cheese and egg dishes.

Specialities include trout (pstrąg), lamb (czaczlyk), goat cheese (oścypek). There is also a powerful brew called "herbata z pradem" (electric tea) - a hot, sweet tea with very alcoholic spirit added.

Electricity

220 volts.

Phoning Home from Poland

Calls are most easily made from the central telephone and telegraph office, at the rear of the main post office in Kruptówki street. On hearing the dialling tone, you first dial an "0" and wait for a second tone; then another "0" followed by the appropriate national prefix (UK 44, Australia 61, New Zealand 64; South Africa 27; USA/Canada 1); followed by the area code (for the UK omit the initial "0"), then the personal number.

Tipping

Generally 10%.

Cost of Living

Public transport and food are inexpensive. Hotel accommodation is quite moderately priced. Woollen sweaters are good value, but other clothing and luxury goods are expensive.

GAZETTEER

Beskid (2,113m). The first of the Polish High Tatras peaks, as viewed from Zakopane. Because of its proximity to the cable-car at Kasprowy Wierch, it is usually crowded.

Brzegi (800-1,000m). A straggling village, one of the highest in the Podhale region, occupying a ridge in the hills to the north-west of Zakopane and north of Łysa Polana, at the extreme top right of the TPN map. It is traffic-free (though served by bus from Zakopane), and has a pretty wooden church.

Bukowina Tatrzańska (800-1,000m). Close to Brzegi, this village climbs the northern slope of Wysoki Wierch, and is also one of the highest in the Podhale region. It is served by bus from Zakopane.

Bystre (Swift, 920m). The southern part of Zakopane, with a hotel, a trade union holiday centre, a few shops and bars. The Galeria Sztuki im. W.J. Kulczyckich (Kulczyckich Art Gallery) displays tapestries by local artists. Near the Rondo traffic roundabout are the stadia of the COS (Centralny Ośrodek Sportu, Central Sport Centre) and the TPN (Tatrzański Park Narodowy, Tatras National Park) Museum, while a little way towards the centre of Zakopane lies the memorial to Tytus Chałubiński, the founder of Zakopane. The large building on the eastern outskirts is an orthopaedic rehabilitation centre for children.

Czarny Staw (Black Tarn). The name of three large tarns in the Polish High Tatras, all so called because they spend much of the time in the shadow of high mountains. They are referred to as (in order from north-west to south-east): *Czarny Staw Gąsienicowy* (1,620m): lies in the shadow of the "Eagle's Perch" range. It covers nearly 18 hectares and is 51 metres deep. *Czarny Staw pod Kotelniçą* (1,722m): lies below the group of summits called Kotelnica in the Liptowskie Mury range. It covers a little over 12.5 hectares and is 50.4 metres deep. *Czarny Staw pod Rysami* (1,580m): the largest and deepest of the three, at 20.64 hectares and 76.4 metres. It obviously lies in the shadow of Rysy, Poland's highest summit.

Czerwone Wierchy (Red Peaks). The name of a range of rounded, grass-topped mountains in the Western Tatras, to the south-west of Zakopane, so called because the grass turns a reddish-brown in the autumn. The range has four peaks (from east to west): Ciemniak (2,096m), Krzesanica (2,122m), Małołączniak (2,096m) and Kopa Kondracka (2,005m).

Dolina Białego. The pretty valley that runs due south from Zakopane town centre.

Dolina Białki. The valley of the river Białka, which forms part of the border with Slovakia, and runs through Łysa Polana. Towards its head, it divides into three branches: Dolina Roztoki, Dolina Rybiego Potoki (both in Poland) and Dolina

Białej Wody (or Bielovodska Dolina) in Slovakia. The Białka is one of the main tributaries of the Dunajec, itself one of the major rivers of southern Poland, flowing into the Wisła (Vistula) and thus to the Baltic.

Dolina Bystrej, also known as Dolina Bystrej Wody (Swift Water Valley). The main valley from Zakopane, running at first south-east, taking in the Rondo at Bystre, to Kuźnice, then south towards Kasprowy Wierch.

Dolina Chochołowska. The remotest valley (from Zakopane) in the Polish part of the Western Tatras, taking its name from the village of Chochołów. Together with Dolina Kościeliska, its streams flow into the Czarny (Black) Dunajec river, while those of the valleys further east flow into the Biały (White) Dunajec.

Dolina Gąsienicowa (Caterpillar Valley). One of the most visited valleys in the Polish Tatras, actually the upper part of Dolina Suchej Wody, to the south-east of Zakopane. It is divided into two by the Kościelec ridge: the western part, Sucha Dolina (Dry Valley), has Kasprowy Wierch at its head; the eastern part, Kozia Dolina (Goat Valley), has the Granaty peaks at its head.

Dolina Goryczkowa. This valley is not accessible to walkers, being off the waymarked routes, though it is traversed by ski routes in winter. It can be best seen from the cable-car to Kasprowy Wierch.

Dolina Kościeliska. A popular, pretty valley running south from Kiry. The chalet called Schronisko Ornak lies at the point where it divides into several branches. It takes its name from the Kościeliska ridge, the watershed between the Czarny (Black) Dunajec and Biały (White) Dunajec river basins.

Dolina ku Dziurze. A short valley close to Zakopane on its south-western side. It has the cave called Dziura (Hole) at its head.

Dolina Małej Łąki (Little Meadows Valley). The shortest of the main valleys leading directly off the Zakopane basin.

Dolina Olczyska. A valley immediately to the east of Zakopane, taking its name from a community called Olcza.

Dolina Pańszczyca. A side valley of Dolina Suchej Wody, to the east of Schronisko Murowaniec. It is very quiet, with a rather dejected atmosphere - it is said that no birds will sing here.

Dolina Pięciu Stawów Polskich (Valley of Five Polish Tarns). One of the prettiest valleys in the Polish Tatras, with the Eagle's Perch range at its head. It is one of the heads of Dolina Białki, which runs south through Łysa Polana. There are actually six tarns; the four main ones are Przedni (Front), Wielki (Big), Czarny (Black) and Zadni (Black), plus two tiny ones called Mali Staw (Little Tarn) and Wole Oko.

Dolina Roztoki. The valley that connects Dolina Białki with Dolina Pięciu Stawów Polskich. It has the refuge called Schronisko Stara Roztoka at its foot, by the border with Slovakia.

Dolina Rybiego Potoku (Fish Brook Valley). One of the most popular valleys in the Polish Tatras, despite its remoteness from Zakopane, since it contains the beautiful tarn called Morskie Oko, and has at its head the country's highest mountain, Rysy. It is the central branch at the head of Dolina Białki.

Dolina Strążyska. A short but much visited valley leading south-westwards directly out of the centre of Zakopane. At its head is a beautiful waterfall called Wodospad Siklawica.

Dolina Suchej Wody (Dry Water Valley), so called because its stream disappears into the limestone bedrock for about 1 kilometre of its length. It is one of the main valleys of the Polish High Tatras, to the south-east of Zakopane. It contains the busy refuge called Schronisko Murowaniec, above which the valley is known as Dolina Gąsienicowa.

Dolina Tomanowa. A side valley of Dolina Kościeliska, leading eastwards from Schronisko Ornak. It is very quiet, and much frequented by bears.

Dolina Waksmundzka. The upper part of this quiet side valley of Dolina Białki, to the south-east of Zakopane, is a strict nature reserve with no marked paths - it is a haunt of bears - though two routes cross the lower part.

Dzianisz (850-1,000m). A village in the hills to the north-west of Zakopane, beyond the Gubałówka ridge. It has many old houses and a pretty wooden church.

Gęsia Szyja (Goose Neck, 1,490m). A high knoll in the foothills of the High Tatras, south-east of Zakopane. It makes a marvellous picnic spot and viewpoint, from where you can see the High, White and Western Tatras. The grassy east end has a fine panorama, overlooking (eastwards) Rusinowa Polana, the slate-roofed border post of Łysa Polana, the Białka valley, the town of Nowy Targ, and the White Tatras in Slovakia; and (westwards) Zakopane, Giewont and the rounded summits of the Western Tatras, with the cable-car station on Kasprowy Wierch visible. The craggy west end of Gęsia Szyja overlooks the High Tatras.

Giewont (1,894m). The twin humped peaks of this mountain, the nearest to and most visible from Zakopane, gave rise to the legend that it is in fact a sleeping giant, who will rise when Poland needs his help. Unfortunately he was in such deep sleep during World War II that he could not be woken. Only the higher, eastern summit is accessible to walkers, and this is surmounted by a huge, iron frame cross - the altitude is sometimes shown as 1,909m, which is in fact that of the top of the cross.

Głodówka (1,130m). A popular viewpoint on the road from Łysa Polana to Nowy Targ, on the TNP map to the east of Zakopane, and within walking distance (2 kilometres by road) of the waymarked route at Wierch Poroniec. There is a small car park and a cafe, and a fine view of the High Tatras.

Granaty. A mountain on the Eagle's Perch with twin peaks: Skrajny (Outer)

Granat (2,225m) and Zadni (Inner) Granat (2,240m) - these are shown on the TPN map as 2,226m and 2,239m respectively. The meaning of the name is a matter of some doubt - it could be either "grenades", "pomegranates" or even "navy blue"! Both summits are comparatively easily accessible, though with some use of fixed chains.

Gubałówka (1,120m). A very popular ridge in the hills to the north-west of Zakopane, bearing some resemblance to Brighton's Esplanade! There are cafes, pizzerias, bars, kiosks, a restaurant and pay-telescopes (Tatras for the viewing of). It can be reached from Zakopane either by rack railway or chair-lift, as well as several waymarked walking routes - all quite steep in places.

Jaszczurówka (900m). A village at the foot of Nosal and Dolina Olczyska to the south-east of Zakopane. A little to the east along the main road is Kaplica Witkiewicza, a beautiful wooden chapel set on a rise above the road, and well worth a visit. Also of interest to walkers are the refreshments obtainable at Bar Gawra and Hotel pod Piorem.

Kasprowy Wierch (1,985m). The easternmost of the Western Tatras summits, and the top station of the cable-car from Kuźnice.

Kiry (927m). A hamlet 7 kilometres west of Zakopane at the foot of Dolina Kościeliska. It is a popular starting point for walks, with a bar and a refreshment kiosk. It is served by bus from Zakopane, and there is a large car park. From here, horse-drawn taxis ply along Dolina Kościeliska as far as Polana Pisana.

Klasztor Albertynek (Albertina Convent, 1,100m). A small convent in the forest above Kuźnice, based on the hut in which lived Brother Albert, canonised in 1989. Opposite the entrance, a track climbs for 1 kilometre to Klasztor Albertynow (1,180m), the monastery. Both are open to visitors.

Kościelec (2,158m). One of the more accessible minor peaks in the Polish Tatras, though reaching its summit is quite hard work with some exposure and a length of fixed chain. Looking north from the top you have an excellent view down to Zakopane, while behind to the left is the frontier ridge with Slovakia, and to the right the Orla Perć (Eagle's Perch) ridge.

Kościelisko. A sprawling community occupying the low hills and ridge at around 900-1,000m to the west of Zakopane. The ridge forms the watershed between the basins of the Czarny (Black) and Bialy (White) Dunajec rivers. The community consists of a large number of separate hamlets, the chief one being Wojdylówka which has shops, several bars and restaurants. Neighbouring Szeligówka has a bar, Myśliwsky (Hunting), a food kiosk, a grocery and a pretty wooden church.

Kozi Wierch (Goat Peak, 2,291m). One of the Eagle's Perch summits, this is the highest mountain that is totally within Poland - the higher ones being shared with Slovakia.

Krzeptówki. A community on the south-western outskirts of Zakopane. At Krzeptówki Potok is a military establishment, Wojskowy Ośrodek Szkoleniowo Kondycyjny w Zakopanem (Zakopane Military Training Centre).

Krzyżne (2,113m). A high saddle at the east end of the Eagle's Perch route. It has comparatively easy access and some of the finest views in the Polish Tatras.

Kuźnice (Smithy, 1,010m). The main starting point for walks in the Polish Tatras. As the name suggests, it was once the centre of the local iron-smelting industry; a huge waterwheel remains as evidence. Now it is the main starting point for walks in the Polish Tatras, with a hostel, a restaurant, several refreshment facilities, a grocery, a souvenir shop, and a cable-car to Kasprowy Wierch - the latter is extremely busy and you need to arrive with plenty of time in hand.

Private vehicles are banned (unless you have a reservation at the hostel). You can easily walk here from Zakopane along the 1.5 kilometres, gently graded road (see blue route 205), but there are plenty of buses, minibuses and taxis - both motorised and horse-drawn. If you return here at the end of the day, you will find a large fleet of minibuses waiting, and you just pile into the first in line.

Łysa Polana (971m). The only legal border crossing in the Tatras between Poland and Slovakia. Note that, in Polish, the pronunciation is "Weesa" (in Slovakia it is "Leesa"). There are a buffet and a small shop on the Polish side.

Mała Polanka Ornaczanska (1,100m). An idyllic meadow at the head of Dolina Kościeliska, the meeting point of several routes. Here is situated Schronisko Ornak, a large refuge with a dining-room where you order and pay for your food at the bar, then collect it at the kitchen counter.

Miedziane (Made of Copper, 2,233m). A summit in the High Tatras, wholly within Poland, to the south-west of Zakopane. It lies on a spur of the Liptowskie Mury leading up to Rysy. The name comes from the discovery during the eighteenth century of veins of copper, though these turned out to be unviable. Though the summit is inaccessible to walkers, you traverse its foot on yellow route 814 between Morskie Oko and Szpiglasowa Przełęcz.

Morskie Oko (Eye of the Sea, 1,393m). Considered to be the most beautiful tarn in Poland and the whole of the Tatras, this is also reckoned to be the largest - though it is being infilled by scree and may now be smaller than Wielki Staw. It was formerly measured as occupying 34.93 hectares and is 50.8 metres deep. The name refers to the improbable legend of an underground connection to the Adriatic Sea.

At the north end of the tarn is Schronisko Morskie Oko, officially Schronisko w Dolinie Rybiego Potoku (Refuge at Fish Brook Valley, phone 0165-900), set above the tarn at 1,406m. It was built in 1908, and received a complete refurbishment in 1992.

Murowanica (Bricks, 1,040m). A locality on the road to Kuźnice, not to be confused with Murowaniec.

Murowaniec Schronisko (1,505m). Officially Schronisko Murowaniec na Hala Gąsienicowej (Brick Refuge in Caterpillar Pasture, phone 0165-2633). Built in 1923 for the Warsaw Section of the Polish Tatras Society, it is a substantial and picturesque refuge of brick and stone in the traditional local style. It is very popular, being at the junction of several routes and easily accessible from Kuźnice and the cable-car at Kasprowy Wierch. There is a large dining hall, where you order and pay for your main meal at the bar, then collect it from a nearby serving hatch. Outside is a large terrace with picnic tables.

Murzasichle (920-1,050m). A village draped along a ridge to the east of Zakopane, with a pretty wooden church.

Myślenickie Turnie (l,352m). A minor summit to the south of Kuźnice, that serves as the middle station for the cable-car to Kasprowy Wierch. It is not of much use to walkers, with no facilities, though you can alight here, but in winter this is the starting point of one of the ski-pistes.

Nedzówka (957m). A village 6 kilometres south-west of Zakopane, served by bus. It lies at the foot of red route 005, and has two cafes, a grocery and a bank.

Orla Perć (literally Eagle's Perch) - see red route 009B.

Palenica Białczańska (990m). The closest point of access for motor vehicles to Morskie Oko and Rysy, served by bus and minibus from Zakopane. Subsidence has resulted in the closure of the road to Morskie Oko, and only service vehicles and horse-drawn buses are now allowed to use it. The horse-drawn buses are inexpensive, but wrap up well - they are open to the elements, the journey lasts 45-60 minutes, and you may get cold. Strangely, despite the large number of visitors, there are no refreshment facilities here - the nearest are at the Łysa Polana border post (1.5 kilometres).

Polana Chochołowska (1,146m). A large collection of shepherds' hut at the head of Dolina Chochołowska, served by horse-drawn taxi from Polana Huciska. Schronisko Chochołowskie was built for the Warsaw Ski Club in 1933, and in 1983 was visited by Pope John Paul II.

Polana Huciska (980m). The highest point in Dolina Chochołowska which is accessible to vehicles, also served by bus and minibus from Zakopane. The kiosk at the car park sells maps and books, but alas no refreshments! (There is a large, covered picnic table.) Horse-drawn taxis run along the valley from here to Polana Chochołowska.

Polana Kalatówki (1,198m). A sloping summer pasture above Dolina Bystrej near Kuźnice, which in winter forms a ski-piste. The dry valley above it (Suchy Żleb) leads up to Wrótka (1,592m), the easternmost crag of the Giewont range. Meals and refreshments can be obtained at Schronisko Kalatówki (officially

Hotel Górski na Polanie Kalatówki, Polana Kalatówki Mountain Hotel, phone 0165-2827/3644), a large, imposing stone building, opened in 1938 - it is open all year.

Polana Kondratowa (1,333m). A summer pasture in Dolina Kondratowa, below Giewont. The refuge here, Schronisko Kondratowa (officially Schronisko na Hali Kondratowej, Kondratowa Pasture Refuge, phone 0165-5214) is small and friendly, with an outside, south-facing terrace, and was built in 1948. It is owned by the TPN (Tatras National Park), and is open all year.

Polana Pisana (1,015m). A meadow in Dolina Kościeliska, where the horse-drawn taxis turn round. Here can be found the remains of a furnace used for smelting iron ore during the eighteenth and nineteenth centuries.

Przedni Staw (Front Tarn, 1,668m). The first and lowest of the "Five Polish Tarns" in Dolina Pięciu Stawów Polskich. At its north end, slightly above the tarn at 1,672m, lies Schronisko w Doline Pięciu Stawów Polskich (Five Lakes Refuge, no phone). Its name is shown on some maps as Schronisko imienia Leopolda Mieczysława Swierzow, but this has fallen out of use since the communist era.

Rusinowa Polana (1,200m). A summer pasture with a scattering of shepherds huts - and this is one of the few places in the Tatras where sheep still graze. One of the huts, by the junction of the blue and green routes, has an exhibition of shepherding, and you can buy sheep and goat cheese here (sadly, no refreshments).

Sarnia Skała (1,377m). A rocky outcrop lying a little way off Ścieżka nad Reglami (black route 901C) to the south of Zakopane. From here you can get a grandstand view of the town, and looking back you have a close-up view of the north wall of Giewont.

Schronisko. This means "refuge" in Polish. The list below shows the common names of all the refuges in the Polish Tatras, followed by the alternative names that appear on some maps, and an indication of where to find more information in this gazetteer. Some of the alternative names were given during the former communist era, and are little used in practice; they include the words "schronisko imienia ..." which means "the refuge called ..." followed by the name of some local dignitary. The common names, which are more descriptive of their locations, are not yet shown on maps currently published.

Schronisko Chochołowskie (Schronisko na Chochołowskiej Polanie) - see Polana Chochołowska.

Schronisko Kalatówka or Schronisko na Polanie Kalatówki (Hotel Kalatówki or Hotel Górski na Polanie Kalatówki) - see Polana Kalatówka.

Schronisko Kondratowa (Schronisko na Hali Kondratowej) - see Polana Kondratowa.

Schronisko Morskie Oko, Schronisko w Dolinie Rybiego Potoku or Schronisko

Sanctuary of Our Lady Fatima, Skibówki (Zakopane)

imienia Stanisława Staszica - see Morskie Oko.

Schronisko Murowaniec or Schronisko na Hali Gąsienowicej - see Murowaniec.

Schronisko Ornak, Schronisko przy Małej Polance Ornaczańskiej or Schronisko imienia Walerego Goetela - see Mała Polanka Ornaczańska.

Schronisko Pięciu Stawów, Schronisko w Dolinie Pięciu Stawów Polskich or Schronisko imienia Leopolda i Mieczysława Swierzow - see Przedni Staw.

Schronisko Roztoka, Schronisko w Starej Roztoce or Schronisko imienia Wincentego Pola - see Stara Roztoka.

Skibówki. A district on the west side of Zakopane on the road to Kiry. It is noted for its handsome, modern church - Sanktuarium Matki Bozej Fatimskiej (Sanctuary of Our Lady Fatima) - which was opened in 1981 and visited in 1983 by Pope John Paul II.

Stara Roztoka (1,031m). A small clearing in Dolina Białki at the foot of Dolina Roztoki, close to the border with Slovakia. Here is situated Schronisko Roztoka, on a dead-end path (green route 517), 10-15 minutes' walk from Wodogrzmoty Mickiewicza. The track that approaches from the north via Niżnia Polana pod Wołoszynem is not currently accessible to walkers.

Sucha Przelecz (Dry Saddle, 1,955m). Considered in Poland to be the dividing point between the High and Western Tatras, though in Slovakia Ľaliové Sedlo (Liliowe in Polish) to the south-west is the official break. This means that the intervening peak Beskid/Beskyd, may be in the High or Western Tatras, depending on which authority you follow.

Szałasiska (1,380m). A campsite on the road to Morskie Oko, which is reserved for members of mountaineering clubs. It serves as a base camp for climbing expeditions into the High Tatras.

Toporowa Cyrhla (Axe Clearing, 950-1,040m). A small resort on the road to Łysa Polana, east of Zakopane from which it is served by bus. There is a beautiful church (under reconstruction in 1993), as well as the Restaurant Siedem Kotów (Seven Cats) and a grocery. Accommodation can be obtained in a number of pensions and private houses.

Wielka Koszysta (2,193m). An unremarkable minor summit to the south-west of Zakopane, frustratingly blocking what would otherwise be a splendid view of the High Tatras from the town.

Wielka Siklawa (1,600m). A huge waterfall in Dolina Roztoki, a little below Wielki Staw. With a fall of 70 metres it is the biggest in the Tatras.

Wielki Staw (Big Tarn, 1,665m), properly Wielki Staw Polski. Though Morskie Oko has been measured to be the biggest tarn in the Tatras, Wielki Staw is now thought to be larger, at 34.35 hectares, since the other is being naturally infilled with scree. It is one of the "Five Polish Tarns" (Pięciu Polskich Stawów). At the north end of the tarn, a high rocky islet, like a miniature sugar-loaf, provides a

THE POLISH TATRAS

popular photo-opportunity for the agile.

Wiktorówki (1,140m). A charming, lonely monastery in the forest. Visitors are welcomed, and cups of tea can be obtained. Inside is a statue of Our Lady the Queen of the Tatras (Witamy na Wiktorówkach Matka Boza Jaworzynska). The monastery is also a mountain rescue point. On his visit in 1983, Pope John Paul II described this to be one of his favourite places in the Tatras.

Witów (835m). A straggling village to the north-west of Zakopane on the way to Chochołow. It consists almost entirely of wooden buildings in traditional Podhale style. There is a bar (Hanka) in the village centre, and at its north end a grocery kiosk.

Włosienica (1,300m). A huge, former car park on the road to Morskie Oko, now usually deserted, except for the horse-drawn buses from Palenica Białczanska, which turn round here. Nearby is the big, barn-like Pawilion Turystyczny na Włosienicy (Włosienica Tourist Pavilion) where refreshments can be obtained.

Wodogrzmoty Mickiewicza (1,100m). A picturesque waterfall which performs a couple of right-angled bends during its descent, before cascading beneath the road from Palenica Białczańska to Morskie Oko. Wodogrzmoty means water thunderclap; Mickiewicz was a famous Polish nineteenth-century romantic poet. The large, former car park, now deserted, is a popular picnic site.

Zakopane (830m). The only holiday resort of any size in the Polish Tatras, and the largest in the whole Tatras region on either side of the border, with a resident population of 30,000. Its economy is largely dependent on tourism, although it is also the main market town for the Podhale region of Poland. It offers a good choice of accommodation in hotels, pensions and private houses. The main shopping street (Krupówki) is pedestrianised (there is a small charge at official car parks) and there are good shopping and currency exchange facilities. The pleasant, relaxed atmosphere is enhanced by attractive wooden buildings in the distinctive, steep-roofed Podhale style, and others in the Góral style.

Some modern buildings are being refurbished or extended in the old style. Church architecture is an intriguing mixture of traditional and modern - the latter often being highly original in design. Public transport within the town and to outlying villages is provided by frequent buses, backed up by minibuses (see above). For something more unusual, try the horse-drawn taxis (dorożka) - they are to be found principally at the north end of Krupówki street (near the post office), by the Rondo roundabout on the road to Kuźnice, and at the railway station.

For the history of the Zakopane area, see the introduction to the Polish Tatras section.

*　　*　　*

Supplementary Information

APPENDIX 1: GLOSSARY

See the chapter on languages in Section 1 for a general introduction to the Slav languages. There follows a guide to pronunciation in both Slovak and Polish. Letters are pronounced as in English, except as shown below. Some sounds in both languages have no exact equivalent in English; there are distinctions between similar sounds that an "English-speaking ear" would be incapable of detecting, and are impossible to explain in a book such as this. Consequently the explanations that appear below can only be a rough guide.

SLOVAK

Vowels. A as in "map"; Á as in "father"; Ä like "ai" in "hair"; AJ like "ie" in "tie"; E as in "bed"; É like "a" in "cat"; Ě like "e" in "yes"; EJ like "ai" in "rain"; I and Y like "i" in "pit"; Í and Ý like "i" in "police"; O as in "dog"; Ô like "aw" in "paw"; OU like "oa" in "boat"; U as in "bull"; Ú as in "rule".

Consonants. C like ts "tsar"; CH like ch Scottish "loch"; J like y in "yes". H is always aspirated, even before another consonant. Some are subtly changed by the addition of an accent or stroke: Č like "ch" in "char"); Ď like "d" in "due"; Ľ like "li" in "lieu"; Ň like "ni" in "onion"; Š like "sh" in "cash"; Ť like "t" in "picture"; Ž like "s" in "leisure".

"R" and "L" are used both as consonants and vowels. As consonants, "L" is as in English, "R" is rolled as in Scotland. As vowels, a short preceding "e" as in "meringue" or "model" is implied.

Note that, in the Slovak alphabet, "č" comes after "c", "ch" after "h", "š" after "s" and "ž" after "z".

Here are some examples using places you will find on the maps: Štrbské Pleso = shturrbska plesso; Starý Smokovec = starree smockovets; Tatranská Lomnica = tatranskah lomnitsa; Ľaliové Sedlo = lialiova sedlo; Jahňací Štít = jahh-niatsi shteet; Zdiar = zhdee-arr.

Here is a translation of some of the words you are likely to come across in the Tatras. Note that most of these have varying endings, depending on the gender and case - see above. Where some help with pronunciation is needed, this is shown in brackets (xh = ch as in Scottish "loch"; do not forget to roll your Rs). In both Polish and Slovak, the accent tends to go on the first syllable.

biely (byellee)	white
červený (chervenee)	red
chata (xhata)	mountain hut, refuge or chalet
čierny (chernee)	black
dobrý deň	good morning, hello
dolina	valley
dolinka	little valley
hnedý	brown
hora, horský	mountain
hrebeň	ridge
jaskyňa (yaskinya)	cave
juh (yooh)	south
južný (yoozhnee)	southern
kabínová lanovka	gondola (mountain lift)
kopa	stack (bulky summit)
koruna	crown (Slovak currency)
kotlina	basin (geographical)
malý (mahlee)	little, small
modrý	blue
na	by, at
nad	above
nebezpečenstvo	danger
nízky	low
nižný (nizhnee)	lower
nový	new
obchod (obxhod)	shop
pleso	tarn
pod	below
poľana	meadow
poľský	Polish
pošta	post, post office
potok	brook, stream
potraviny	grocery
prameň	spring, source
predný	front, foremost, outer
prostredný	middle
sedačková (sedatchkova) lanovka	chair-lift
sedielko	little saddle, pass
sedlo	saddle, pass
šedý (shedee)	grey
sever	north
severný	northern
skala	cliff

slovenská	Slovak
starý	old
štít (shteet)	peak, summit
suchý (sooxhee)	dry
úplaz	slope (steep, narrow)
vchod (vxhod)	entrance
veľký	big, large, great
veža (vayzha)	tower
voda	water
vodopád	waterfall
vrch (verxh)	hill
východ (veexhod)	exit, east
východný	eastern
vyhliadka	viewpoint
vysoký	high
vyšný (veeshnee)	upper
zadný	back, hindmost, inner
západ	west
západný	western
zastávka	bus stop
zelený (zhelenee)	green
žľab (zhlyab)	flood stream (usually dry in summer)
žltý (zhultee)	yellow

POLISH

Vowels: A as in "rather"; Ą like "on" in French "bon"; E as in "bed"; Ę like "ien" in French "chien"; I as in "police"; IE like "ye" in "yes"; O as in "dog"; Ó as in "shoe"; U as in "rule"; Y as in "cryptic".

Consonants: C like ts "tsar"; Ć like j in "jug"; CH like ch Scottish "loch"; CI is like "ci" in cigar"; CZ like "ch" in "chat"; J like y in "yes"; Ł like w in "water"; Ś, SI and SZ like "sh" in "ship"; W like "v" in "vat". Some are subtly changed by the addition of an accent or stroke: Ń like "ni" in "onion". Ż, Ź and RZ are all like "s" in "leisure".

A soft consonant at the end of the word becomes hard, eg. a W is pronounced as "f".

Note that, in the Polish alphabet, ą comes after a, ć after c, ę after e, ł after l, ń after n, ó after o, ś after s, ż after ź after z.

Here are some examples using places you will find on the maps: Kuźnice = koozhnits-e; Świstowa Czuba = shvistova chooba"; Łysa Polana = Weesa Polana (but note that in Slovak the "L" in Lysa is pronounced as in English).

biały	white
brązowy	brown
czarny (charnee)	black
czerwony (chervonee)	red
czuba (chooba)	tuft
dolina	valley
dolinka	little valley
dzień dobry (jean dobree)	goodday, hello
góra (noun), górsky (adjective)	mountain
grzbiet (gurzbyet)	ridge
hala	mountain pasture (alp)
hruby (hroobee)	thick
jaskinia (yaskinya)	cave
kolejka linowa (kolika linova)	cable-car
kopa	stack (bulky summit)
kopka	little stack
łąka (waka)	meadow
mali (mawee)	little, small
na	on, by, at
nad	above
niebezpieczeństwo	danger
niebieski (nyebyeskee)	blue
niski	low
niźnia (nizhnya)	lower
nowy (novee)	new
poczta (potchta)	post, post office
pod	below
polana	clearing
polanka	little clearing
północ (pouwnots)	north
polski	Polish
południe (pouwoodniye)	south
pośredni (poshredni)	middle
potok	brook, stream
przedni (pshednyi)	front, foremost
przełacka (pshewangchka)	little pass
przełęcz (pshewengch)	pass, saddle
przysłop (psheeswop)	a kind of saddle
przystanek (psheestanek)	bus stop
schronisko (sxhronisko)	mountain chalet or refuge
siwy (sivvee)	grey
skała (skahwa)	cliff
sklep	shop

slowak (swovak)	Slovak
spożywczy (spozheevchee)	grocery
stary (starree)	old
staw (stav)	tarn
suchy (sooxhee)	dry
szczyt (shcheet)	peak, summit
turnia (toornya)	crag
upłaz (oopwaz)	slope (dialect)
widzenie (vidzenye)	viewpoint
wielki (vyelky)	large, big, great
wierch (veerxh)	hill
wjazd (vyazd)	entrance
woda (voda)	water
wodospad (vodospad)	waterfall
wschod (vsxhod)	east
wyjscie (veechtche)	exit
wysoki (veesoki)	high
wyżnia (veezhnya)	upper
zachod (zaxhod)	west
zadni	back, hindmost, inner
zielony (zhelonee)	green
żleb (zhleb)	gully
złoty (zwotee)	gold, Polish currencey
żólty (zhouwtee)	yellow
źródlo (zhrodwo)	spring, source

USEFUL WORDS AND PHRASES

English	Polish	Slovak
FOOD	ŻYWNOŚĆ	POTRAVINY
MEAL	POSIŁEK	JEDLO
breakfast	sniadanie	raňajky
lunch	lunch	obed
dinner	obiad	večera
beer	piwo	pivo
coffee	kawa	káva
juice	sok	džús
milk	mleko	mlieko
tea	herbata	čaj
water	woda	voda
bread	chleb	chlieb
butter	masło	maslo
jam	dżem	džem

English	Polish	Slovak
honey	miód	med
soup	zupa	polievka
omelette	omlet	omleta
bacon	boczek	slanina
beefsteak	befsztyk	biftek
chicken	kurczę	kurča
egg	jajko	vajce
ham	szynka	šunka
kidney	nerka	oblička
lamb	jagnię	jahňacie mäso
liver	wątroba	pečeň
pork	wieprzowina	bravčové mäso
sausage	kiełbasa	klobása
veal	cielęcina	teľacie mäso
bean	fasola	fazuľa
cabbage	kapusta	kapusta
carrot	marchewka	mrkva
cauliflower	kalafior	karfiol
pea	groch	hrach
potato	ziemniak	zemiak
salt	sól	soľ
pepper	pieprz	čierne korenie
vinegar	ocet	ocot
apple	jabłko	jablko
cake	placek	koláč
fruit	owoc	ovocie
orange	pomarańcza	pomaranč
pudding	budyń	puding
cream	śmietana	smotana
ice cream	lody	zmrzlina
bill please	proszę płacić	platím prosím

DAYS OF THE WEEK, TIMES OF DAY

Monday	poniedziałek	pondelok
Tuesday	wtorek	utorok
Wednesday	środa	streda
Thursday	czwartek	štvrtok
Friday	piatek	piatok
Saturday	sobota	sobota
Sunday	niedziela	nedeľa
morning	rano	ráno

English	Polish	Slovak
midday	południe	poludnie
afternoon	popołudnie	popoludnie
evening	wieczór	večer
midnight	północ	polnoc
night	noc	noc
o'clock	godzina	hodina

NUMBERS

one	jeden	jeden
two	dwa	dva
three	trzy	tri
four	cztery	štyri
five	pięć	päť
six	sześć	šest
seven	siedem	sedem
eight	osiem	osem
nine	dzewięć	deväť
ten	dzesięć	desať

GREETINGS etc

hi	cześć	ahoj, servus
hallo	dzień dobry	dobrý deň
good morning	dzień dobry	dobrý deň
good afternoon	dzień dobry	dobrý deň
good evening	dobry wieczór	dobrý večer
goodnight	dobranoc	dobrú noc
goodbye	do widzenia	dovidenia
cheers!	sto lat!	na zdravie!
good appetite!	smacznego!	dobrú chuť!
please	proszę	prosím
thank you	dziękuję	ďakujem

OTHERS

ladies	kobieti	ženy
gents	człowieki	muži

APPENDIX 2: ACCOMMODATION

See also the chapter on Accommodation in Section 2.

This section lists accommodation available for visitors from other countries. Inclusion does not imply a recommendation, and before booking you are advised to obtain further information about places which interest you. You can approach these establishments direct, but it is a good idea to contact instead a local travel agency in the Tatras (see the Shopping and Local Services chapter for the country you are visiting), since they hold allocations at most of them and can offer alternatives if your first choice is full. Some tour operators in your home country may offer holidays to the Tatras that include accommodation.

All details are subject to change. Please note especially that, following the overthrow of communist regimes, establishments which were owned by state concerns are being sold to private enterprise, and categories or even names may have changed as a result. Some trade union establishments, formerly for the use of their members only, are now being made available to tourists, and may not be included in our list.

Postcodes (zip codes) shown below should be placed before the place name on your envelopes, on the same line, eg. 06201 Starý Smokovec.

The telephone dialling code (phonecode) is also given for each place. Note that if dialling from outside Slovakia or Poland, you will usually need to omit the initial zero after dialling the country code.

The categories are indicated as follows:

**** first class hotel; *** superior hotel; ** medium grade hotel
P pension; YH youth hostel

There are as yet no hotels of international luxury class in the Tatras. Places with (R) have a restaurant.

In some villages (as indicated), inexpensive accommodation is also available in private houses and trade union establishments - these can only be booked through the travel agencies shown in Appendix 3. Note that meals (including breakfast) are not usually served in these places. You can either eat at nearby hotels or restaurants, or at some places there is a kitchen available for the use of guests.

Accommodation is also offered at mountain hotels and chalets. At the mountain hotels it is generally of a lower standard than at those in the villages, usually in bedrooms with just a washbasin or dormitories. At the chalets, washing and toilet facilities may be quite basic, in some cases in an outhouse; accommodation is usually in dormitories, though bedrooms are available at some. Mountain hotels have a restaurant; chalets can provide basic meals in the dining room. There is always a heavy demand for beds at these places, especially during August, and you are strongly advised to book as early as possible through a local travel agency. The altitudes are shown after the names.

Self-catering. At the time of writing, there was very little in the way of villas or apartments in the Tatras, though there are self-catering bungalows at the Eurocamp near Tatranská Lomnica, small apartments at Štrbské Pleso, and summer houses at Štrbske Pleso and Stará Lesná.

ACCOMMODATION LIST

Slovakia (international code 42)

Place/establishment	Phone	Fax	Category	Rooms
Štrbské Pleso				
(postcode 05985; phonecode 0969)				
FIS Hotel (R)	92221	92422	***	60
Hotel Panoráma (R)	92111	92810	***	96
Hotel Patria (R)	92591	92590	***	152
Hotel Baník (R)	92549	92124	**	101
Tatranská Štrba				
(postcode 05941; phonecode 0969)				
Hotel Junior (R)	92691	92296	***	48
Hotel Stavbár (R)	92456	-	**	60
Batizovce				
Private houses				
Gerlachov				
Private houses				
Tatranská Polianka				
(postcode 06201; phonecode 0969)				
Cafe Restaurant HB (R)			P	
Tatranské Zruby				
(postcode 06201; phonecode 0969)				
Hotel VZ (R)	2752	2753	**	86
Nový Smokovec				
(postcode 06201; phonecode 0969)				
Park Hotel (R)	2345	2304	***	96
Villa Dr. Szontag (R)	2061	2062	***	16
Hotel MS-70 (R)	2972	-	**	24
Pension Jedla	2196	-	P	8
Private houses				
Starý Smokovec				
(postcode 06201; phonecode 0969)				
Grand Hotel (R)	2154	2157	***	81

Place/establishment	Phone	Fax	Category	Rooms
Hotel Bystrina	2618	-	★★	44
Hotel Krokus	2741	-	★	39
Horný Smokovec				
(postcode 06201; phonecode 0969)				
Hotel Bellevue (R)	2941	2719	★★★	112
Hotel Šport (R)	2361	-	★	63
Juniorhotel CKM	2661	-	YH	
Pension Marta	3296		P	
Poprad				
(postcode 05901; phonecode 092)				
Hotel Gerlach (R)	33759	35664	★★★	70
Hotel Satel (R)	471111	62075	★★★	76
Hotel Europa (R)	32744	-	★★	45
Private houses				
Nová Lesná				
Private houses				
Stará Lesná				
(postcode 05960; phonecode 0969)				
Hotel Horizont (R)	967881	967287	★★★	42
Hotel Kontakt (R)	967915	967494	★★★	40
Pension Tatrania Gym	967969	-	P	16
Private houses				
Tatranská Lomnica				
(postcode 05960; phonecode 0969)				
Grandhotel Praha (R)	967941	967891	★★★	91
Hotel Odborár (R)	967351	967581	★★★	85
Hotel Slovakia (R)	967961	967975	★★★	35
Hotel Slovan (R)	967851	967627	★★★	85
Hotel Horec (R)	967261	-	★★	40
Hotel Lomnica (R)	967251	-	★★	16
Private houses				
Tatranská Lomnica (Eurocamp)				
(postcode 05960; phonecode 0969)				
Hotel Eurocamp FICC (R)	967741	967346	★★	
Self-catering bungalows				
Tatranská Kotlina				
(postcode 05954; phonecode 0969)				
Pension Limba (R)	967470	-	P	7

Ždiar
(postcode 05955; phonecode 0969)

Hotel Magura (R)	98121	-	**	45
Pension Slovakia (R)	98127		P	12
Private houses				

Javorina
(postcode 05956; phonecode 0969)

Hotel Polana (R)	99102	99107	***	17

Mountain hotels
Horský Hotel Kpt.Morávku (1,500m) (R), Popradské Pleso (phone 0969-92177)
Sliezsky Dom (1,750m) (R), Velické Pleso (phone 092-25590)

Chalets:
Chata pod Rysmi (2,250m), below Rysy (no phone)
Bilíkova Chata (1,238m), near Hrebienok (phone 0969- 2439)
Zbojnícka Chata (1,960m), Veľká Studená Dolina (no phone)
Zamkovského Chata (1,475m), Malá Studená Dolina (phone 0969- 2636)
Téryho Chata (2,015m), Malá Studená Dolina (phone 092-24900)
Chata pri Zelenom Plese (1,551m), Zelené Pleso (phone 0969-967420)

Tentcamps (tents provided - see above):
ATK Sokolovo, Tatranská Štrba (phone 0969-92166)
Ternocamp, Dolný Smokovec (phone 0969-2406)
Eurocamp FICC, Tatranská Lomnica (phone 0969-967741)
Tatranec, Tatranská Lomnica (phone 0969-967704)

Poland (international code 48)

Place/establishment	Phone	Fax	Category	Rooms
Zakopane				
(postcode 34500; phonecode 0165)				
Hotel Kasprowy (R)	14011	15272	****	552
Hotel Gazda (R)	15011	15330	***	102
Hotel Giewont (R)	12011	-	***	82
Hotel Morskie Oko	5076 (under reconstruction)			
Hotel Biały Potok (R)	14380	-	**	77
Hotel Boruta (R)	66589	-	**	60
Hotel Juventur	6253	-	**	135
Hotel Pan Tadeusz	12228	-	**	30
Hotel Tatry	66041	-	**	115
Hotel Telimena	12228	-	**	48
Hotel Jastrzebianka	63856	-		

Also a wide choice of pensions and private houses. Dom Turysty, near the main post office in the town centre, provides inexpensive dormitory accommodation.

Place/establishment	Phone	Fax	Category	Rooms
Bystre (south/south-east side of Zakopane)				
(postcode 34500; phonecode 0165)				
Hotel Imperial	14021	-	**	170
Hotel Sport Zakopane	15021	-	**	160
Kościelisko (west side of Zakopane)				
(postcode 34500; phone code 0165)				
Hotel Siwarna (Siwarne)	14683	15031	**	220
Pension Karolina (Nedzówka)	70434	70467	**	44
Hotel Sablik (Nedzówka)	70787	-	*	34
Pension Malwa (Hołarz)	70789	-		22

Also private house accommodation in Wojdyłówka, Siwarne and Kiry

Olcza Remiza (4km east of Zakopane)				
(postcode 34500; phonecode 0165)				
Hotel Olczanka	61140	-	**	30

In the Mountains
Hotel Kalatówki, near Kuźnice   63644
And at the chalets:
Schronisko Chochołowskiej (1,150m), Polana Chochołowska
Schronisko Ornak (1,100m), Polana Ornaczańska
Schronisko Kondratowej (1,333m), Polana Kondratowa
Schronisko Murowaniec (1,500m), Hala Gąsienicowa
Schronisko w Dolinie Pięciu Stawów Polskich (1,672m), Przedni Staw
Schronisko Roztoka (1,031m), Stara Roztoka
Schronisko Morskie Oko (1,406m), Morskie Oko

Camping. There are three campsites in or near Zakopane. At each of these you must provide your own tent (there are no "tent-camps", where tents are provided, in the Polish Tatras). They are "Tatry Pod Krokwia" - the largest - in Żeromskiego Stefana near the Bystre Rondo (1.5 kilometres south-east); "Tatry" at Harenda (3 kilometres north-east); and in Za Strugiem (1 kilometre south-west).

APPENDIX 3: USEFUL ADDRESSES & PHONE NUMBERS

AIRLINES
British Airways: London 081-897-4000; New York 718-335-3030; Toronto 416-250-0880; Sydney 02-258-3300.

CSA Czechoslovak Airlines: London 071-255-1898; New York 212-682-5833; Poprad 092-62587.

LOT Polish Airlines: London 071-580-5037; New York 212-869-1074; Kraków 012-225076.

Tatra Air: Bratislava 07-292306.

EMBASSIES
Slovak Republic
UK: 28 Kensington Palace Gardens, London, W8 4QY (phone 071-243-0803; fax 071-727-5824).

USA: 3-900 Spring of Freedom Street, Washington DC, 20008 (phone 202-363-6315; fax 202-224-4139).

Canada: 50 Rideau Terrace, Ottawa, K1M 2A1 (phone 613-749-4442; fax 613-749-4989).

Australia: 47 Culgoa Circuit, O'Malley, Canberra ACT, 2606 (phone 06-290-1516; fax 06-290-1755).

New Zealand: No representation at time of writing - contact office in Australia.

South Africa: PO Box 95855, Waterkloof, Pretoria 0145 (phone 012-346-3612; fax 012-346-0226).

Polish Republic
UK: 73 New Cavendish Street, London, W1M 7RB (phone 071-580-0476; fax 071-323-2320).

USA: 2640-16th Street NW, Washington DC, 20009 (phone 202-234-3800; fax 202-228-6271).

Canada: 443 Daly Street, Ottawa, K1N 6H3 (phone 613-789-0468; fax 613-232-3463).

Australia: 7 Turrana Street, Yarralumla, Canberra ACT, 2600 (phone 06-273-1208; fax 06-273-3184).

New Zealand: 17 Upland Road, Talburn, Wellington (phone 04-712456; fax 04-712455).

South Africa: 14 Arnos Street, Colbyn, Pretoria 0083 (phone 012-346-3140; fax 012-346-1366).

TOURIST INFORMATION
At the time of writing, neither Slovakia nor Poland has an official organisation responsible for providing information to tourists, either within those countries

or abroad. However there are plans to open such offices, and you could check with directory enquiries whether this has taken place.

In the UK, you could try the following travel agencies which specialise in travel to these countries, though you should not expect the wide range of literature that is usually obtainable from a national tourist office. Remember that these companies can also organise travel tickets and hotel accommodation for you.

Čedok London Ltd, 49 Southwark Street, London, SE1 1RU (phone 071-378-6009; fax 071-403-2321).

Polorbis, 74 Beresford Avenue, London, W7 3AP (phone 081-578-8113; fax 081-578-9802).

APPENDIX 4: SUGGESTED KIT LIST

(see also Clothing and Equipment section above)

Essential items for walking in the mountains:

Rucksack	Walking boots
Windproof jacket	
Waterproof clothing (jacket, overtrousers, gaiters)	
Walking trousers or breeches	Shirts with long sleeves
Pullovers or fibre-pile jacket	Socks
Underwear	Handkerchiefs
Maps	Compass
First aid kit (including a blister kit)	Emergency food rations
Water bottle	Whistle

Torch, spare batteries and bulb (especially if you intend to explore the caves in the Polish Tatras)

Optional items for walking:
Shorts or skirt

Suggested items for the evenings:

Trousers or skirts etc.	Shirts or blouses
Socks	Jacket or pullover
Footwear	Nightwear
Toilet gear	

Miscellaneous:

Washing powder	Insect repellent
Sunglasses	Camera
Food container	Knife (for cutting food)
Thermos flask	

APPENDIX 5: THE TATRAS MOUNTAIN CODE

Before you set out:
- Check the weather forecast and state of the paths.
- Tell your hotel reception or accommodation manager where you will be going; or write it in the "walks book".
- Never go into the mountain alone.
- Don't plan a difficult walk above 2,000 metres until you have had time to adjust to the altitude (2-3 days).

In the mountains:
- Make an early start.
- Always keep a steady pace - don't push yourself too far or go too fast.
- Keep in close touch with your map - always know where you are.
- Go down if the weather turns bad.
- Keep to the waymarked paths.
- Don't take short cuts.
- Don't cause rocks to roll down the mountain.
- Avoid steep snowfields.
- Avoid difficult terrain with inexperienced walkers or children.
- Always help those in distress.
- Don't disturb plants or wildlife.
- Don't drop litter.

APPENDIX 6: HELP!

Here are some addresses and telephone numbers which may be useful in an emergency.

HOSPITALS AND CLINICS
Štrbské Pleso: Policlinic, at east end of main car park, near Hotel Baník (phone 0969-92355; open Mon-Fri mornings)
Starý Smokovec: Policlinic, on Cesta Slobody highway, opposite Slovakia holiday centre (phone 0969-2444; open daily 24 hours)
Tatranská Lomnica: Policlinic opposite TANAP museum (phone 0969-967349; open Mon-Fri mornings)
Zakopane: Szpital Miejski (Municipal Hospital), Ulica Kamieniec 10 (in Stary Kamieniec on the north side of the town centre).

MOUNTAIN RESCUE

Mountain rescue centres can be found in many places throughout the High Tatras, including all the chalets or refuges. If someone in your party is unlucky enough to suffer an accident, or if you are in a position to help someone else, go to the nearest mountain rescue station.

If you can telephone (though you may not get an English speaker) call (Slovakia) 0969-2820 or 0969-2855; (Poland) 63444.

In Slovakia, there are mountain rescue posts at all the chalets (chaty) and mountain hotels, plus:

TANAP offices at Podbanské, Tri Studničky, Tatranská Kotlina, Javorina;
At or near the chair-lift/cable-car/rack railway stations (also at Štart middle station);
Dom Horskej Služby (Mountain Rescue Office) in Starý Smokovec;
Sanatórium Helios, Štrbské Pleso;
Tichá forest house, near Podbanské;
Pod Muráňom forest house, near Javorina.

On the Slovak maps, they are indicated by a red cross within a square.

In Poland, there are mountain rescue posts at all the refuges (schroniski) and Hotel Kalatówki, plus:

Wiktorówki monastery;
Cable-car stations.

The posts are not marked on the Polish map.

CONSULATES AND EMBASSIES

If you need advice in an emergency while in Slovakia or Poland, contact the nearest consulate or embassy for the country:

UK. Slovakia: British Embassy, Panská 17, PO Box 68, 81499 Bratislava (phone 07-335922; fax 07-330369). Poland: British Embassy, Aleje Roz 1, 00556 Warszawa/Warsaw (phone 02-628-1001; fax 02-221-7161).

USA. American Embassy, Hviezdoslavovo Námestie 4, PO Box 5630, 81102 Bratislava (phone 07-330861; fax 07-335439). Poland: American Consul-General, Ulica Stolarska 9, 31043 Kraków (phone 012-229674; fax 012-218292).

Canada. No representation in Slovakia at time of writing; contact: Canadian Embassy, Mickiewiczowa 6, 12533 Praha/Prague, Czech Republic (phone 02-312-0251; fax 02-311-2791). Poland: Canadian Embassy, Ulica Matejki 1, 00481 Warszawa/Warsaw (phone 02-229-8051; fax 02-229-6451).

Australia. No representation in Slovakia at time of writing; contact: Australian Embassy, Mattiellistrasse 2, 1040 Wien/Vienna, Austria (phone 01-512-8580; fax 01-513-2908). Poland: Australian Embassy, Estońska 3, Saska Kepa, Warszawa/Warsaw (phone 02-176081; no fax).

New Zealand. No representation in Slovakia or Poland at time of writing; contact: New Zealand Embassy, Bundeskanzlerplatz 2, 53113 Bonn, Germany (phone 0228-228070; fax 0228-221687).

South Africa. Slovakia: South African Embassy, Jančova 8/B1-5, 81102 Bratislava (phone 07-315643; fax 07-312581). Poland: South African Embassy, IPC Business Centre (6th Floor), Ulica Koszykowa 54, 00675 Warszawa/ Warsaw (phone 02-625-6228; fax 02-625-7223).

*   *   *

NOTES

NOTES

NOTES

CICERONE GUIDES

Cicerone publish a wide range of reliable guides to walking and climbing in Britain, and other general interest books.

LAKE DISTRICT - General Books
A DREAM OF EDEN
LAKELAND VILLAGES
LAKELAND TOWNS
REFLECTIONS ON THE LAKES
OUR CUMBRIA
THE HIGH FELLS OF LAKELAND
CONISTON COPPER A History
LAKELAND - A taste to remember (Recipes)
THE LOST RESORT? (Morecambe)
CHRONICLES OF MILNTHORPE
LOST LANCASHIRE (Furness area)
THE PRIORY OF CARTMEL

LAKE DISTRICT - Guide Books
CASTLES IN CUMBRIA
THE CUMBRIA CYCLE WAY
WESTMORLAND HERITAGE WALK
IN SEARCH OF WESTMORLAND
CONISTON COPPER MINES Field Guide
SCRAMBLES IN THE LAKE DISTRICT
MORE SCRAMBLES IN THE LAKE DISTRICT
SHORT WALKS - SOUTH LAKELAND
WINTER CLIMBS IN THE LAKE DISTRICT
WALKS IN SILVERDALE/ARNSIDE
BIRDS OF MORECAMBE BAY
THE EDEN WAY
WALKING ROUND THE LAKES

NORTHERN ENGLAND (outside the Lakes
BIRDWATCHING ON MERSEYSIDE
CANAL WALKS Vol 1 North
CANOEISTS GUIDE TO THE NORTH EAST
THE CLEVELAND WAY & MISSING LINK
THE DALES WAY
DOUGLAS VALLEY WAY
HADRIANS WALL Vol 1 The Wall Walk
HERITAGE TRAILS IN NW ENGLAND
THE ISLE OF MAN COASTAL PATH
IVORY TOWERS & DRESSED STONES (Follies)
THE LANCASTER CANAL
LANCASTER CANAL WALKS
LAUGHS ALONG THE PENNINE WAY
A NORTHERN COAST-TO-COAST
NORTH YORK MOORS Walks
THE REIVERS WAY (Northumberland)
THE RIBBLE WAY
ROCK CLIMBS LANCASHIRE & NW
THE YORKSHIRE DALES A walker's guide
WALKING IN THE SOUTH PENNINES
WALKING IN THE NORTH PENNINES
WALKS IN THE YORKSHIRE DALES (3 VOL)
WALKS IN LANCASHIRE WITCH COUNTRY
WALKS IN THE NORTH YORK MOORS
WALKS TO YORKSHIRE WATERFALLS (2 vol)
WALKS ON THE WEST PENNINE MOORS
WALKING NORTHERN RAILWAYS (2 vol)
WALKING IN THE WOLDS

DERBYSHIRE & EAST MIDLANDS
WHITE PEAK WALKS - 2 Vols
HIGH PEAK WALKS
WHITE PEAK WAY
KINDER LOG
THE VIKING WAY
THE DEVIL'S MILL / WHISTLING CLOUGH (Novels)

WALES & WEST MIDLANDS
THE RIDGES OF SNOWDONIA
HILLWALKING IN SNOWDONIA
HILL WALKING IN WALES (2 Vols)
ASCENT OF SNOWDON
WELSH WINTER CLIMBS
SNOWDONIA WHITE WATER SEA & SURF
SCRAMBLES IN SNOWDONIA
SARN HELEN Walking Roman Road
ROCK CLIMBS IN WEST MIDLANDS
THE SHROPSHIRE HILLS A Walker's Guide
HEREFORD & THE WYE VALLEY A Walker's Guide
THE WYE VALLEY WALK

SOUTH & SOUTH WEST ENGLAND
COTSWOLD WAY
EXMOOR & THE QUANTOCKS
THE KENNET & AVON WALK
THE SOUTHERN-COAST-TO-COAST
SOUTH DOWNS WAY & DOWNS LINK
SOUTH WEST WAY - 2 Vol
WALKING IN THE CHILTERNS
WALKING ON DARTMOOR
WALKERS GUIDE TO DARTMOOR PUBS
WALKS IN KENT
THE WEALDWAY & VANGUARD WAY

SCOTLAND
THE BORDER COUNTRY - WALKERS GUIDE
SCRAMBLES IN LOCHABER
SCRAMBLES IN SKYE
THE ISLAND OF RHUM
CAIRNGORMS WINTER CLIMBS
THE CAIRNGORM GLENS (Mountainbike Guide)
THE ATHOLL GLENS (Mountainbike Guide)
WINTER CLIMBS BEN NEVIS & GLENCOE
SCOTTISH RAILWAY WALKS
TORRIDON A Walker's Guide
SKI TOURING IN SCOTLAND

REGIONAL BOOKS UK & IRELAND
THE MOUNTAINS OF ENGLAND & WALES
     VOL 1 WALES VOL 2 ENGLAND
THE MOUNTAINS OF IRELAND
THE ALTERNATIVE PENNINE WAY
THE PACKHORSE BRIDGES OF ENGLAND
THE RELATIVE HILLS OF BRITAIN
LIMESTONE - 100 BEST CLIMBS

Also a full range of EUROPEAN and OVERSEAS guidebooks - walking, long distance trails, scrambling, ice-climbing, rock climbing.

Other guides are constantly being added to the Cicerone List.
Available from bookshops, outdoor equipment shops or direct (send s.a.e. for price list) from
CICERONE, 2 POLICE SQUARE, MILNTHORPE, CUMBRIA, LA7 7PY

232

Printed by CARNMOR PRINT & DESIGN
95-97 LONDON ROAD, PRESTON, LANCASHIRE, UK.

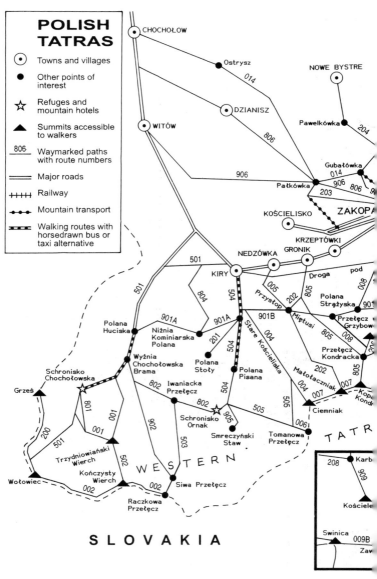

POLISH TATRAS

- ⊙ Towns and villages
- ● Other points of interest
- ☆ Refuges and mountain hotels
- ▲ Summits accessible to walkers
- 806 Waymarked paths with route numbers
- === Major roads
- ++++ Railway
- ••• Mountain transport
- ■■■ Walking routes with horsedrawn bus or taxi alternative

CHOCHOŁOW

Ostrysz
014

NOWE BYSTRE

DZIANISZ

WITÓW

Pawelkówka
204

806

906

Gubałówka
014

906 806

Pałkówka
203

KOŚCIELISKO

ZAKOPA

KRZEPTÓWKI

NEDZÓWKA GRONIK

501

KIRY

Droga pod
005 008

202 805

Polana
Strążyska
901

804

504 Przystop

901A

901B Miętusi

Przełęcz
Grzybow

Polana
Huciska

901A

Niżnia
Kominiarska
Polana

201

Stare Kościeliska

805 008

004

Przełęcz
Kondracka

Wyżnia
Chochołowska
Brama

Polana
Stoły

Polana
Pisana

Małołączniak

202 805

Schronisko
Chochołowska

Grześ

801 001

Iwaniacka
Przełęcz
802

504

505 004 007

Ciemniak 007

Kopa
Kond

Schronisko
Ornak

905

Smreczyński
Staw

Tomanowa
Przełęcz

505 0061

T A T R

902

503

200

501

Trzydniowiański
Wierch

W E S T E R N

Wołowiec

Kończysty
Wierch

502

002

Siwa Przełęcz

Karb
208 909

Kościele

Raczkowa
Przełęcz

Swinica
009B

Zaw

SLOVAKIA

234